D0884375

658.001
H68
2013
C.1

P0920382g-13
2014

Firm Commitment

Why the corporation is failing us
and how to restore trust in it

Colin Mayer

OXFORD
UNIVERSITY PRESS

SAIT - Library

OXFORD

UNIVERSITY PRESS

Great Clarendon Street, Oxford, OX2 6DP,
United Kingdom

Oxford University Press is a department of the University of Oxford.
It furthers the University's objective of excellence in research, scholarship,
and education by publishing worldwide. Oxford is a registered trade mark of
Oxford University Press in the UK and in certain other countries

© Colin Mayer 2013

The moral rights of the author have been asserted

First Edition published in 2013

Impression: 1

All rights reserved. No part of this publication may be reproduced, stored in
a retrieval system, or transmitted, in any form or by any means, without the
prior permission in writing of Oxford University Press, or as expressly permitted
by law, by licence or under terms agreed with the appropriate reprographics
rights organization. Enquiries concerning reproduction outside the scope of the
above should be sent to the Rights Department, Oxford University Press, at the
address above

You must not circulate this work in any other form
and you must impose this same condition on any acquirer

British Library Cataloguing in Publication Data

Data available

ISBN 978–0–19–966993–6

Printed in Great Britain by
Clays Ltd, St Ives plc

Links to third party websites are provided by Oxford in good faith and
for information only. Oxford disclaims any responsibility for the materials
contained in any third party website referenced in this work.

Children get,
Parents give,
But spouses go on
Unknowing

To Annette

Preface

This book draws on work that I have done with many people over three decades. At the beginning of the 1980s, when I was starting my academic career, taxation was the dominant influence on corporate finance. It took six years of interesting research at the Institute for Fiscal Studies under the directorship of John Kay, much with Jeremy Edwards in the Faculty of Economics and Politics at Cambridge University, and Michael Keen, now at the International Monetary Fund, to convince us that, while taxation was important, there were many aspects of corporate finance which it could not adequately explain. There were other institutional factors at work.

Around this time, the Centre for Economic Policy Research in London was starting under the direction of Richard Portes, and the idea of undertaking an international study of the financing of industry emerged. The directors of the project were Margaret Bray of the London School of Economics; Elisabetta Bertero, now at the London School of Economics; Jenny Corbett, now at the Crawford School of Economics and Government at the Australian National University and St Antony's College Oxford; Jeremy Edwards; and Tim Jenkinson, now at the Saïd Business School, Oxford University. The research assistants working on the project were Ian Alexander and Klaus Fischer.

The project collected a large amount of information on financial systems and the financing of industry (in particular the electronics sector) in different countries. It formed the basis of international comparisons of corporate finance and financial systems that were subsequently performed in many countries around the world. It was during this period that the notion of commitment which underpins this book was first presented.[1] Its significance, however, extended beyond corporate finance to the control of corporations and the way in which they were governed.

At the beginning of the 1990s, I started what became the third line of research with Julian Franks at the London Business School. This was still internationally comparative in nature, but focused on corporate ownership and control. The differences in corporate ownership and control across countries which we found were much more striking and robust than those in corporate finance and financial systems. There clearly were important variations that needed an explanation, and the next six years were devoted to investigating this. Some of the research was done as part of a project funded by the Economic and Social Research Council, with the assistance of several people including Luis Correia da Silva, Marc Goergen, and Myriam Soria.

Along the way, I undertook several other collaborative projects and supervised numerous doctoral students' research on related topics, for example, on business angels and venture capitalists with Mark von Osnabrugge, then a doctoral student at Oxford; on corporate restructuring with Luc Renneboog, now at Tilburg University; on the financing of investment and cash flow shocks with Oren Sussman at the Saïd Business School and Zhangkai Huang, a former doctoral student and now at Tsinghua University in Beijing; on the Eurobond markets and syndicated bank lending with Philip Davis, then at the Bank of England; on venture capital with Koen Schoors and Yishay Yafeh when they were visiting Oxford, now at Ghent University and the Hebrew University in Jerusalem, respectively; and with Damien Neven at the Graduate Institute, Geneva on the regulation of financial services.

I undertook a number of studies on transition economies and the performance of different financial systems around the world with Wendy Carlin of University College, London, assisted by Peter Richthofen and Esra Erdem, and then a study on multi-national corporations in collaboration with Andrew Charlton, now at the London School of Economics. One of the main collaborative projects was with Marco Becht at Université Libre de Bruxelles. Based on the work with Julian Franks, we started an international network of researchers undertaking comparative studies of ownership and control in several different countries. This was known as the European Corporate Governance Network and has now become the European Corporate Governance Institute, located in Brussels.

As my knowledge of financial systems and corporate sectors in different countries expanded, I became increasingly aware of the importance of the origins of these differences. At that point in 1998, at the kind invitation of Masa Aoki, I took a sabbatical at the Economics Department at Stanford University and I used the opportunity to research corporate, legal, and financial institutional history. This initially involved secondary sources, but I then began a project with Julian Franks and Stefano Rossi, now at Imperial College, London, on the evolution of ownership and control in Britain. We collected data for a hundred-year period as part of a National Bureau of Economic Research project on family firms, organized by Randall Morck at the University of Alberta. We discovered that corporate and financial history was as virgin a field of study as we had found international comparisons of corporate finance, ownership, and control some twelve years earlier. Since then I have done work on Germany with Hannes Wagner at Bocconi University, and on Japan with Hideaki Miyajima in the Faculty of Commerce at Waseda University.

My final moves have been into law and development. I have worked with Zsuzsanna Fluck at the Eli Broad Graduate School of Management, Michigan State University; John Armour in the Law Faculty in Oxford; Jeff Gordon in the Law School at Columbia University; and Andrea Polo, a doctoral student at the Saïd Business School. At the invitation of the Gates Foundation, I went on a trip to Kenya to research mobile money and since then have done joint research with Ignacio Mas, previously at the Gates Foundation, and Michael Klein at the Frankfurt School of Finance and Management.

My greatest debt of intellectual gratitude is to my teachers and supervisors, in particular to Derek Morris then and now again at Oriel College, Oxford, who first interested me in economics; John Kay at St John's College, Oxford, one of the greatest economics writers of our age, who taught me how to think; and Richard Caves in the Department of Economics at Harvard University and John Lintner, then at Harvard Business School, who introduced me, while I was studying at Harvard University as a Harkness Fellow, to the mysteries of regulation and finance at the end of the 1970s before they had become fashionable on this side of the Atlantic.

This book is a distillation of material from the research projects that have appeared in more technical forms in numerous books and articles. The results of the research have been presented at more than a hundred conferences and seminars around the world. Some of these have been to academic audiences, some to practitioners, and some to government and international agency officials. References to the research and other relevant literature are described in an appendix and endnotes to the book.

During all of this period I was running a second life, as an entrepreneur and economic consultant. In 1986, in conjunction with Dieter Helm, now at New College, Oxford, I helped develop OXERA Ltd., an Oxford-based consultancy that specializes in the provision of microeconomic advice to companies, regulators, and governments. The focus of the company was on the interface between business and government. Under the direction of Luis Correia da Silva and Helen Jenkins, OXERA has now become one of the most successful economic consultancies in Europe, and the process of creating the organization has given me first-hand experience of entrepreneurship.

This has not been my only insight into the practice of running organizations. In 1994 I returned to Oxford University as the first professor in the newly created School of Management Studies with the task of helping to establish a business school in the university, and in 2006 I became Dean of what by then had become the Saïd Business School. It was the year that I was due to deliver the manuscript of this book to Oxford University Press (OUP). While this delayed completion for five years, my period as Dean gave me exposure to leaders in business, finance, and government around the world who confirmed the practical relevance as well as academic significance of the issues discussed in the book. I also gained insights into the merits and deficiencies of existing forms of business education. Most recently, as a member of the UK Competition Appeal Tribunal, I have had the opportunity of observing the law in action from the perspective of a judge.

I am grateful to the economics commissioning editors of OUP for their patience in waiting for delivery of the manuscript and for their assistance in bringing the book to fruition. Two under-graduates at Wadham College, Oxford, Sarah Inman and Gaurav Kankanhalli, provided research assistance on the book, as did a former doctoral student, Adeel Malik, now at the Oxford Centre for Islamic Studies. I am grateful to Faber & Faber and Grove/Atlantic, Inc. for permission to use the quote in Chapter 10 from Samuel Beckett's *Endgame*.

I have received comments on the manuscript from Christopher Allsopp, Gerry Bacon, Marco Becht, Amar Bhidé, Patrick Bolton, Francesca Campbell, Paul Collier, Luis Correia, Paul Davies, Stephen Davis, Jeremy Edwards, Andrew Ellul, Guido Ferrarini, Clare Fisher, Merritt Fox, Marc Goergen, Leo Goldschmidt, Jeffrey Gordon, Hamid Hakimzadeh, Henry Hansmann, Gay Haskins, Donald Hay, Dieter Helm, Philip Henderson, Gerard Hertig, John Hicklin, Laura Hoyano, Zhang-kai Huang, Lalit Johri, Howard Jones, Kate Judge, John Kay, David Kershaw, Michael Klein, David Levy, Andrew Lodge, Adeel Malik, Christine Mallin, Roger Martin, Jose Martinez, Ignacio Mas, Annette Mayer, Hannah Mayer, Ruth Mayer, Derek Morris, Alan Morrison, David Musson, Geoffrey Owen, Andrea Polo, Thomas Powell, Luc Renneboog, Georg Ringe, Stefano Rossi, Edward Rock, Mark Roe, Philip Sadler, Andrew Schuller, Laura Spira, André Stern, Adam Swallow, Ira Unell, Terry Vaughn, Theo Vermaelen, Hannes Wagner, Stephen Wilks, and Yishay Yafeh.

Finally, the people to whom I obviously owe the most are my family, who have had to endure a continuous stream of conferences, international travel, co-authors, and worst of all the computers. To the academic, the computer is the bread of thought; to his or her family, it is the source of sin.

Fortunately I have just been able to complete this book in time for the reflections of that great literary figure Mario Vargas Llosa on 'the man in his fifties' to be still relevant: 'the age at which his intellectual powers and his sensuality are at their peak, the age at which he has assimilated all his experiences. That age at which one is most desired by women and most feared by men'. I hope that I have thereby been able to avoid 'the increasing difficulty of adaptation to new thoughts which always confronts the man past fifty' of which Albert Einstein wrote, but if by any chance I have failed to acknowledge someone here then they can take comfort from what Sam Goldwyn said: 'the only reason that so many people turned up at Mayer's funeral was to make sure that he was dead'. Fortunately it was Louis' not mine, not yet anyway.

Colin Mayer

Oxford
4 August 2012

Contents

Introduction

The 'dismal science' is how Thomas Carlyle described economics in 1849. Never mind that he was doing so in the context of advocating the reintroduction of slavery. By eulogizing the merits of markets, the laws of economics apparently condemn us to control by forces that are both anonymous and beyond our reach, and restrict our attempts to pursue a better life. The world is, according to economics, what the markets make it and none of us, not even for the most part governments, has the power to dispute their will.

Nowhere is this more in evidence than in the central instrument of economics—the corporation. Like the market, it is controlled by unknown and unreachable forces which dictate every part of our lives. This book is both a tribute to and a condemnation of this remarkable institution that has created more prosperity and misery than could have ever been imagined. As time goes by, the balance is moving increasingly in the latter direction—the corporation is becoming a creature that threatens to consume us in its own avaricious ambitions.

We need to address the corporation's failings as a matter of urgency, not only to avert its damaging effects on our prosperity, social cohesion, and the environment, but also because it offers the lifeline out of the dismal science's constrictions. It has the potential to convert our lives into something of far more significance than the narrow considerations that currently dictate them. It offers the opportunity to provide a means of extracting ourselves out of poverty, inequality, and environmental destruction.

The corporation's capacity to do this derives from its ability to complement what we as individuals are capable of realizing and to restrain us where our failings contribute to our economic impoverishment. Its potential to do this involves undertaking a journey of first appreciating mankind's remarkable achievement in creating the corporation as a legal fiction in its own image. In essence, we have conjured up something that is both of ourselves and distinct from us. By being distinct, the corporation has been able to undertake remarkable feats that have transformed our own lives, as if it were a faithful servant supplementing what we ourselves are capable of achieving and constraining us where we seek to be restrained.

The journey will then show us the limitations as well as contributions of the corporation. It will demonstrate how it has morphed into a creature that has acquired characteristics which were not part of its original design or ever intended—a faithful servant no more. Indeed we will see that the corporation has evolved substantially over the past hundred years, but the very evolutionary processes that might have been expected to make it better suited to the world in which we live have done exactly the opposite.

One cause of this is our own misconception about the nature and role of the company. It is variously characterized as a 'production function' converting inputs of capital and labour into outputs of goods and services; a device for diminishing the 'transaction costs' of undertaking certain activities; and 'a nexus of contracts' between different parties, such as employees, suppliers, and purchasers. It exists for the benefit of its owners—its shareholders—and those charged with running it—its directors—have a fundamental duty to further the interests of its owners. This promotes economic efficiency and, through the reputation of the company, the broader interests of society, including the company's employees, communities, and customers. Where conflicts arise, then these are corrected through private litigation and public regulation. Where there are broader social considerations that private companies are unable to address, then the state enters to fill the gap left by the private sector.

This combination of shareholder interests, contracts, reputation, regulation, and state engagement underpins the structure of economies around the world and is the subject of the first part of the book. It is the basis of national and international policies of domestic and global public institutions. When and where markets fail, there is a need for more regulation and state engagement; where state organizations malfunction, then privatization and more liberal markets are required. This economic and political consensus emerged progressively towards the end of the 20th century and is now widely accepted. However, it has serious defects.

Equally misconceived is the alternative, unconventional paradigm that advocates a private sector approach to the problem—'corporate social responsibility', 'social entrepreneurship', and 'stakeholder values'. These see the fundamental problem as lying with companies and markets, and a need to reposition both to broader social agenda. They seek to realign them by altering the objectives of companies and markets. Where they fail is in establishing credible criteria by which these objectives can be delivered and in ensuring an alignment of the interests of socially conscious people with the priorities of their wider communities.

The failure of the conventional and unconventional paradigms is in providing a compelling description of the corporation. The nature of the corporation does not derive from a simple relation of inputs to outputs, or lower costs of transacting within than outside the corporation, or from acting as a legal device for contracting with other parties. Its first and foremost objective is not to its shareholders, or to its stakeholders. It is to make, develop, and deliver things and to service people, communities, and nations. It does this through engaging investors—creditors as well as shareholders—and stakeholders—employees, suppliers, and communities. In the process, it balances the commitments it makes and the control it exerts over them, and it assumes a variety of forms to achieve this, of which the traditional model of the company—the shareholder oriented corporation—is one, but only one manifestation. It is neither universally right nor universally wrong, and in presuming that it is either one or the other, public policy has made serious errors.

The second part of the book explains why this has happened and what has contributed to the recent unleashing of the corporation's darker features. Behind this lie important changes in the nature of the corporation and the way in which it is owned and governed. These have altered the balance of authority between those running the organization and the other stakeholders in the corporation to a point where we are trying to control the whale by tickling its tail.

The importance of these changes in the balance of power derives from a fundamental conflict which we as individuals face between our ability to exercise control and our need to demonstrate commitment to those whose cooperation we seek. Economics has correctly emphasized the importance of control that markets have conferred on us as consumers. However, as owners, managers, and investors, the ability to demonstrate commitment—restraint on control that is to the detriment of others—is at least as important for the operation of the corporation. The notion of the corporation as a mechanism for providing commitments to others is the focus of this book and the way in which recent changes are undermining this is the subject of the second part.

The third part of the book describes how the commitment function of corporations can be re-established and how, by doing this, the corporation can address conflicts that have arisen to date, and which regulation and state intervention have sought, but failed, to resolve. There are two instruments that are available for realizing this—one concerns the governance of corporations and the exercise of authority by their officers, and the other the ownership and control of their shareholders. These should work in tandem to balance the degree of commitment and exposure of corporations to their stakeholders and they should vary across corporations depending on the nature of their activities. Diversity in corporate form across industries, countries, and time is to be welcomed and should not be constrained by pre-conceived notions about the merits of alternative arrangements, including shareholder value.

The emphasis of legal theories of the corporation is on contracts, property, and agency: the design and enforcement of contracts; the rights that derive from the holding of property; and relations of agents to their principals, the shareholders. Likewise, the focus of economics and finance has been on contracts, incentives, and control. Neither legal theory nor economics has devoted the same attention to the corresponding problems of non-contracted parties, relations, and commitment. The focus of this book is on this mirror image: limitations on contractual claims; restraints on the exercise of property rights; and the fiduciary responsibilities of corporations to third parties, the stakeholders. Put another way, the conventional concerns are with incentives, ownership, and control; those of this book are with obligations, responsibilities, and commitment.

The three parts of the book address these issues in turn. Part 1 relates to the limitations of contracts and the problems of upholding obligations to stakeholders with restricted or no contractual protection. Part 2 concerns the effects of conferring excessive property rights on shareholders and the restraints on ownership that derive from the responsibilities associated with it. Part 3 considers commitment to third parties and the mechanisms by which it can be made credible.

What I describe later as 'the miracle of the corporation' derives from its ability to combine and balance the traditional perspective on incentives, ownership, and control with the alternative view presented here of obligations, responsibilities, and commitment. It can do this on account of its distinguishing feature and that is the bifurcation between ownership and control. From a conventional perspective, that separation is a problem exacerbating deficiencies of contracts, property, and agency, and accentuating the need for incentives, ownership, and control. In this context, it is an attribute facilitating the recognition and provision of obligations, responsibilities, and commitment. The owners and directors of the corporation can in this regard be likened to the two halves of the human brain and its personality as deriving, not from its legal form per se, but from the balance and relationship between the two parties.

The corporation achieves this balance by three means: the definition of the values of the corporation; the degree of independence of the board of directors from its owners; and restrictions on the transfer of property. The values define the obligations of the corporation beyond those determined by contract. The independence of the board establishes the ability of the corporation to uphold its responsibilities to third parties when they conflict with the interests of shareholders. Restrictions on the transfer of property commit owners to their third parties.

The complexity of the corporation derives from the need to find the right balance between precise and encompassing values, autonomy, and accountability of the board, and engagement with and exposure to third parties. The balance will depend on the nature of the corporation and its activities, and will vary over time and location. The structure of the corporation allows it to identify the appropriate balance, and an advantage of the corporation over other organizational arrangements, for example public enterprise, is its ability to do this.

The financial structure of the corporation is of critical importance in this context. While in conventional theories, finance is irrelevant or made relevant by assumption, here it is intrinsic to the nature of the corporation. The commitment of owners derives from the capital that is employed in the corporation. What is held within it is fundamentally different from what remains outside as the private property of its owners. What is distributed to owners as dividends is no longer available as protection against adverse financial conditions and what is provided in the form of debt from banks and bondholders as against equity from shareholders is secure only as long as the corporation has the means with which to service it.

The book bears not only on the positive aspects of corporate conduct—what it could do—but also on the normative ones—what it should do. While principles of morality are well developed in relation to individuals, they are not in respect of corporations. Indeed, the idea of a moral corporation would generally be regarded as an oxymoron. What gives it substance and significance is the 'volume of committed capital'—a product of the amount of capital invested in the corporation, the breadth of commitment to different parties, and the length of time for which it is committed. The volume of committed capital makes credible the values that the corporation espouses to uphold. In turn, it leads naturally to the form of corporate governance and ownership which is proposed in Part 3—the 'trust firm'—and an alignment of its positive properties of promoting corporate efficiency with its normative ones of upholding corporate values.

The trust firm defines the period and the scope of the corporation's credible commitment. It delineates for how long and over what activities the corporation can credibly commit and the boundaries beyond which it cannot do so. It does this through committing its controlling shareholders to retain their share ownership for pre-determined periods of time and by conferring powers on a board of trustees to prevent the corporation from abusing parties who would otherwise be exposed to its activities. It combines responsibility with power and denies power without responsibility. It therefore defines the notion of a moral corporation and determines the form of its practical implementation. In so doing, it imbues the corporation with a degree of morality which exceeds that of the individual.

The trust firm's power to do this derives from its ability to identify precisely its values, the period of commitment of its shareholders, and the constraints on its activities which are imposed by its board of trustees. As a separate legal entity, the corporation can offer a richer array of commitments and controls than we as individuals are capable of realizing. This dual function allows us to achieve outcomes which are to our own advantage, but in its absence would be beyond our reach. The trust firm's morality is therefore a reflection of its ability to contribute to prosperity, to restrain itself from wrongdoings, and to rectify them when they nevertheless transpire. It is a degree of ethical conduct to which we as individuals may aspire, but in general fail to attain.

The corporation also provides the means by which we can internalize the welfare and interests of others as well as ourselves. There has been a steady convergence between public and corporate affairs with an increasing proportion of government activity being concerned with the delivery of public and social goods and services, and corporations becoming more concerned with their public and social profile. This is reflected in many countries in privatizations of public enterprises and the contracting out of public services to the corporate sector in the form of public–private initiatives. However, there have been serious deficiencies in both the efficient delivery of public goods and services, and the effective adherence of corporations to responsible conduct. The proposals in the third part of the book address both sets of issues and represent a natural conclusion of the process of convergence.

Through public policy instruments such as corporate taxation, the contribution of the corporation can be extended beyond its own stakeholders to society at large. In seeking to rectify the deficiencies of the corporation, regulation and state intervention have imposed a high degree of uniformity on the conduct of firms. In so doing, they have limited choice, assumed homogeneity where diversity is required, and exposed their citizens unduly to the influence of particular interest groups. In contrast, what trust firms offer is a plurality of forms in which social objectives can be delivered while avoiding the abuses to which existing public–private relationships have been subject. Together with appropriately structured public policy instruments, the interests of different parties can be placed in alignment rather than in opposition. The corporation can then assume many of the functions, including the protection of our heritage and environment, that to date we have had to rely on other institutions, such as the state, to perform. It can thereby re-establish the degree of trust that we have sought, but have thus far been denied by the corporation.

The financial crisis of 2008 and recent revelations of the manipulation of the London Bank Interbank Offered Rate (Libor) have come to exemplify the defects of the modern corporation. In both cases, the origins of two of the banks most closely associated with these events, Lehman Brothers and Barclays respectively, were families with strong ethical principles. Mayer Lehman instructed his children in the Jewish tradition of *tzedakah* (charity) by taking them regularly every Sunday to the wards of the Mount Sinai hospital in New York to see the plight of less fortunate members of society.[1] The founder of Barclays, John Freame, published *Scripture Instruction*, a textbook of morals that was used in Quaker schools for over a century.[2] The first part of the book describes how the breadth of principles of the founders came to be reduced to the single value of maximizing the earnings of the now dispersed shareholders and professional executives. The second part describes why this happened and why there is a reluctance to see a return to the sometimes privileged, autocratic, and undemocratic world of the family firm. Instead, the adoption of the long-term committed values of the founding families by more transparent and inclusive stock corporations is the preferred solution, and the third part describes how this can be credibly achieved by the trust firm.

Infusing ethics in enterprise, establishing firm commitment, and restoring trust in corporations without relying on regulators or the state to supply them are some of the most pressing needs of our age. They are critical to economic efficiency as well as social welfare because the moral corporation is an economically efficient corporation. Since most aspects of relationships cannot be specified contractually, they rely on trust. Trust depends on commitments between the parties concerned. Where there is commitment and trust, then values which reflect the interests of stakeholders and the community at large can be credibly sustained. There is therefore a coincidence between positive determinants of economic efficiency and normative ones of social welfare, and the competitive advantage of nations depends on the moral fibre of its corporations.

The book will draw in part on anthropology, law, philosophy, politics, and sociology, but its fundamental underpinnings are none other than the dismal science itself. It will set out a reconsideration of the economic concept of the corporation, which has far-reaching implications for the way in which business is conducted and public policy is formulated. It will conclude with a specific set of proposals for practitioners and policymakers. In the process, the book will demonstrate that economics can once again become the 'gay science' as the Victorians described the dismal science's counterpart—'life enhancing knowledge'. That is what the corporation can be—life enhancing—and what economics can provide—the knowledge that is required to make it so. Hopefully this book will take you a little way on that journey.

I

HOW THE CORPORATION IS FAILING US

Chapter 1: In the Beginning

How the Galapagos and the Amazon illustrate the consequences of abusing trust and how this results in intrusive regulation; how the corporation has produced remarkable benefits and prosperity for the human race; how it has also been a source of immense suffering and failures; and how both are increasing

Chapter 2: Morals and Markets

The principle of shareholder value and its significance for economic efficiency; its ethical underpinnings and the rights of shareholders; the scale and significance of stakeholders, and their exposure to shareholder interests; the limited protection that contracts provide to stakeholders; the legal framework for the protection of stakeholders; how corporate laws differ across countries; and their limitations

Chapter 3: Reputation

How reputation is reflected in the market value of corporations; how it penalizes conduct that adversely affects corporations' own customers, employees, and investors, and fails to deter conduct that adversely affects other parties; the gains to financial investment and how they can come at the expense of future generations; how this can lead to a misallocation of resources in an economy

Chapter 4: Regulation

The role of regulation in protecting the public interest; how it promotes instrumental and immoral conduct; how strengthening corporate governance has unintended consequences and contributed to the financial crisis; how companies are encouraged to promote shareholder interests at the expense of taxpayers; the failure of the current system of shareholder value, contracts, incentives, reputation, and regulation

Chapter 1

In the Beginning

An economist, a psychologist, and a sociologist are standing in front of a painting by Lucas Cranach in the museum in Berlin. The picture is of Adam and Eve. The economist says, 'I see Adam with an apple and Eve with a leaf. The economic paradigm is simple. Adam is offering to trade in his apple for a leaf.' 'No, no,' says the psychologist, 'they are about to make love.' 'No, no,' says the sociologist, 'they have nothing to eat, nothing to wear, and they think that they are in paradise.'

In Paradise

As Charles Darwin observed, there are many remarkable things about the Galapagos, but one of the most striking is the fearlessness of the animals. One can sit next to an iguana, ride on a turtle, and play with a sea lion. Even the birds sit calmly on the rocks and branches as one comes up beside them. Why don't they fly away at the slightest sound or sight as they do back home? Do they not realize that I am the same homo-sapiens as I was a few days or hours ago when I was in Britain?

Of course they could be tied to their perches as they are in some parks on the neighbouring mainland. Or they could have been put into cages like most animals on display. But these are not. They are as free to wander off as you or me. But remarkably they do not. In fact, unlike some of their human equivalent, they actually seem to like my company. What's wrong with them?

If we took a biologist to the islands, they would talk about the absence of predators. If we took a sociologist they would see contented communities of humans and animals living side by side. If we took a lawyer they would refer to the laws which prohibit interfering with the natural habitat. If we took an economist there, they would see the commercial value in all of this.

Who is right? In a sense the answer is everyone. It is a natural defence for animals to run away from humans in environments in which humans are perceived to be predators and equally natural for them not to in environments in which they are not threatened. As a consequence, the Galapagos are islands in which humans and animals have learnt to live in harmony with each other. This has been in part achieved through laws of the islands that control not just the predatory instincts of humans, but also their inclination to exploit or interfere with the environment in which animals live. And the underlying motivation for the laws is the commercial benefits that the islanders and government derive from the thriving tourist industry that the wildlife has attracted.

So biology, sociology, law, and economics have all played their part. But equally well this harmonious picture is all rubbish. For actually the history of the Galapagos is one of rape and pillage of the natural habitat over several centuries by mankind and the more familiar domestic and farm animals. Whalers came in search of whale oil, giant tortoises were exported to the US and elsewhere, and iguana was regarded as a delicacy. Where animals were not consumed by humans they fell victims to dogs, goats, and donkeys brought to the islands by humans. Even the scientists who came after Darwin compounded the misery by taking vulnerable species to museums and private collections abroad. The destruction caused the extinction of species on many islands and decimation on others.

So, far from being a haven of harmony between humans and animals, the Galapagos was a hunting ground of its indigenous species. Only over the last few years have conservation and preservation risen up the agenda as the potential for developing a tourist industry has been appreciated. What was once a barren hell for pirates, buccaneers, prisoners, and naïve adventurers is now promoted as a Pacific island paradise for up-market tourists.

How do the animals know that these tourists are not the same humans that only a few years ago came to eat them? I might be able to read the notice that tells me that it is an offence to desecrate or mistreat the environment, but as far as I am aware the frigate bird cannot, and it would take an intelligent giant tortoise to appreciate that the growth of the tourist industry meant that they were now admired for their beauty rather than their taste.

The answer is that the islands have afforded them a degree of protection that has not been available to most of the creatures of the world. While two or three hundred years of pillage is long relative to the recorded history of the islands, it is very short in relation to the life of the islands and their indigenous species. No doubt, the animals that have survived today are a little less relaxed than those that greeted Darwin. However, given the relatively short period in the evolutionary cycle, the behaviour that we observe today is possibly not that different from what it was in the benign environment that prevailed several centuries ago and the diversity of species remains high across the islands and in relation to other parts of the world. That is what captivated Darwin and continues to make the Galapagos so very special today.

On the other side of Ecuador there is another battle in progress, this time in the Amazon jungle. In contrast to the Galapagos, here the animals live in trepidation of each other. One has to crawl silently through the jungle if one wants to see anything and peer intensely through binoculars to see birds perched on distant trees. Far from riding on the dolphins, one waits for them briefly to pop their head up for air before disappearing again below the muddy waters. Here animals have not had the protection afforded by islands and their reactions have had time to adapt.

But the creatures now adapting their behaviour fastest are not animals but humans. Again, oil lies at the heart of the fear, not the sort produced by whales which brought hunters to the Galapagos, but the type that comes out of the ground. The consequent destruction of the rainforest comes at the expense of the native Indians as well as the native animals.

We can argue, as many do, that this is the march of progress. We need oil, oil exists in the Amazon, and, provided that those who are displaced as a consequence are duly compensated, it should be extracted. If we value bio- or ethnic diversity then we will have to pay for it. If there is a potential tourist industry, as it is now appreciated that there is on the Galapagos, then it should be developed. Indeed 'ecotourism' is appearing in a myriad of different guises in the Amazon, some with more 'tourism' than 'eco' associated with it. To preserve ethnic cultures, ecotourism will have to develop similar relations between humans and nature to those that I have described as necessary for the conservation of the Galapagos.

What is interesting about these three cases of the Galapagos, creatures in the Amazon, and humans in the Amazon is that they capture the different elements and consequences of trust relations. Birds and animals are relatively slow to respond to changing behaviour, whereas humans respond rapidly. Humans condition their behaviour on those of others so that, while in the case of the creatures of the Galapagos we can continue to observe similar behaviour to that encountered several centuries ago, relationships of trust amongst humans would have broken down under equivalent conditions a long time ago. It does not in general take us several centuries to flee from mass destruction by our fellow humans. So it is hard to observe how humans would have behaved if relations of trust were maintained over a long timescale, whereas in the case of animals and birds we can observe behaviour by looking at different stages in the evolutionary cycle—the end in the case of the Amazon and closer to the beginning in the case of the Galapagos.

Contrast the Galapagos Islands with a zoo. In the zoo, the animals are locked behind bars and I can walk freely and without fear. On the Galapagos, I am told exactly where I can walk, instructed not to deviate off the path, not allowed to smoke or drop litter, and asked to creep past the sleeping iguana. As a consequence, I can see animals and birds in their natural environment at close quarters. In contrast, in the zoo, while the animals are not in their natural environment, I am. So the apes looking out of their cages at humans at the zoo could be undertaking very interesting observations on humans in their natural habitat.

Furthermore, while I see a good cross-section of animals, birds, and reptiles on the Galapagos, it takes me the best part of a day and costs me a fortune to get there. So the population of visitors to the Galapagos is quite unrepresentative of the human race—it is predominantly white and well-off. On the other hand, it is easier for some people from around the world to reach London Zoo. As a consequence, not only can the apes observe humans in their natural environment, but they also see a more representative and varied sample of the world population than the Darwin finches at the Galapagos.

Having lost the trust of animals and birds by seeing them as primarily sources of food and furs, we had to put them into captivity to view them in any other way. Safari parks provide a somewhat more natural environment than zoos, but there the problem was finding the animals—at least it was until technology came to the rescue, allowing them to be tagged and tourists to be delighted to have experienced a 'rare' sighting of a leopard.

Where we have shown self-restraint, then species, forests, and communities have survived. Where we have not, they have disappeared. This is the observable and measurable contrast between the Galapagos and the Amazon. The intangible impact is even more significant. Our conduct conditions responses in others that in turn affect our own well-being. Where we have demonstrated self-restraint, then we are trusted. Where we have not, we are feared not welcomed. The process is irreversible. Just as entropy increases, there is a law of growing mistrust. Once lost, trust cannot be restored. We would like to wind the clock back and ask to be trusted again, but we cannot eradicate the word or action. They hang like a judgment against which there is no appeal.

We want to be able to demonstrate more self-restraint and we benefit where there are natural impediments that allow us to do so, such as islands. We would like to have more islands and this book will describe how we can populate our world with islands that allow us to do exactly that—corporate islands that assist us in showing a greater degree of self-restraint than we can without them. In the absence of islands, we look to others to restrain us. This interaction of trust and regulation is a familiar one. Regulation is introduced (the metal cages of the zoos) in an attempt to discourage the abuse that occurs as trust is destroyed, but regulation is in turn found to have undesirable and costly features (the unnatural environment of the zoos) and alternative, less intrusive forms of regulation based more on information and reputation than restrictions are sought (tagging animals in the wild) until these in turn are abused by those who are willing to sacrifice their reputations for riches (poachers in the game parks), and regulation has to be strengthened (like the fences round the animals).

We are currently at a nadir—a collapse of trust prompting extensive, intrusive regulation—in the institution which is potentially our island of trust of the future.

Keeping Good Company

Our lives are dominated by it—we eat from it, travel in it, are entertained by it, talk to it, are born with it, and buried by it. Much of our working life is spent in it and most of our leisure life relies on it because, as John Micklethwait and Adrian Wooldridge say, 'the most important organization in the world is the company'.[1]

The modern corporation[2] is a miracle and one of the most ingenious concepts ever devised. Imagine being able to go to your lawyer and say to him that you would like to construct a legal fiction that is you, has many of the rights and obligations that you have, and potentially enjoys eternity. Imagine that it only costs you a few hundred dollars to construct another you, and you can give it whatever name you like and launch it with great fanfare as the world's salvation. It sounds like a mixture of Alice in Wonderland and Frankenstein, and that is exactly what the modern corporation is—a parallel world to our own, inhabited by creatures that look like us but are not us.

The corporation is a legal entity that has an existence in law that is not dissimilar to you or me.[3] It is a legal personality that is distinct from the people who own it, and those who run it. It can undertake activities, raise finance, open bank accounts, and pay others under its own name. It can sue and be sued, employ and be employed.[4] It can be dormant at some times and active at others. It has been the source of some of the most important inventions and innovations in the world, brought modern technology to people's homes, created communities, and built cities. It is the producer of power and life-saving medicines.

These legal entities have been created in large numbers: there are around 6 million firms in the US (28 million if one includes sole enterprises) employing 120 million people (around two-fifths of the total US population) and holding some $30 trillion of assets.[5] And the number is growing rapidly—since 1992 the number of firms in the US has increased by about one-third. Elsewhere in the world, they are mushrooming even faster: the number of private enterprises increased by approximately 80 per cent in China between the first and second economic censuses in 2004 and 2008, and by approximately 40 per cent in India between their economic censuses in 1998 and 2005.[6] Approximately 3 million new companies are being registered each year around the world.[7]

Over the coming years, this process will accelerate still further. There are several reasons for this—the growth of entrepreneurial activity, the shift from the public to the private sector, and the emergence of global enterprises. Far from being on its last legs, the corporation is seen as being a form of commercial creativity, a solution to the inefficiency of the public sector, and a way of delivering goods and services around the world. It is remarkable that a single economic organization can be viewed as solving everything from the needs of the lone inventor working in their garden shed to those of countries and continents, but that is exactly what the corporation has done.

The corporation also has a darker side. At the same time as it is feeding, housing, educating, and transporting us, it is also exploiting, polluting, poisoning, and impoverishing us. The environmental disasters from Love Canal to Bhopal to the Gulf of Mexico to Fukushima do not need to be retold. Nor do the financial catastrophes surrounding Barings, Enron, and World-Com. Equally well known are the accounting scandals involving such companies as Polly Peck, Xerox, Royal Ahold, and Satyam.

But what has happened recently is of a different order of magnitude. Over the last few decades, corporate mistakes have caused environmental catastrophes which have destroyed towns, oceans, and animal species. It is only over the last few years that the activities of corporations have brought financial systems to a point of collapse and national governments to a state of bankruptcy. According to the International Monetary Fund (IMF), bank losses from the financial crisis amounted to over $2 trillion and nearly $1 trillion in the US alone.[8] Fiscal balances of G-20 advanced countries weakened by 8 percentage points of GDP on average and government debt rose by 20 percentage points of GDP in 2008–9.[9] The cumulative loss in GDP in the UK in 2011 was at least 25 per cent of annual GDP, and the eventual loss could be a multiple of this.[10]

The change which is occurring is that whereas previously the actions of companies could have devastating consequences for their customers, suppliers, and investors, now they can destroy economies, communities, and species. It is not an exaggeration to say that through their negligence, incompetence, greed, or fraud, corporations are a threat to our livelihood and the world we live in. And the benefits and costs of the corporation will increase in the future.

On the benefit side, as a bearer of the fruits of technical and scientific advances, the corporation is delivering riches that were unimaginable years let alone decades ago. To be able to source knowledge from around the world, communicate across continents visually as well as orally, and develop medical treatments from the sequencing of the human genome is a remarkable combination of scientific discovery and commercial implementation. And such opportunities are only going to accelerate as the pace of scientific discovery intensifies—but on the costs side, so too are the risks. The risks are not just technological—of the production of pollution as well as power, of the transmission of disease as well as its eradication, of the collapse of global security as well as its enhancement. If the problems were purely random, arising from mistakes and the unforeseen, then the chances are that we could contain and correct them.

What is more worrying is that we as the human race are being systematically encouraged to exploit these developments to the detriment of our fellow humans, animals, and environments. The means of our prosperity are increasingly becoming a weapon of our self-destruction and the legal concept that we created in our own image is turning out to be not our Alice in Wonderland, but our Frankenstein. To understand why, we need to understand how current conceptions of the corporation are contributing to its failings. Once these misconceptions are corrected, the potential for the corporation to contribute to our well-being rather than destruction far exceeds anything that has been imagined to date.

Chapter 2
Morals and Markets

There's no i in trust,
Just u and us

Incense at Insead

Theo Vermaelen is a professor of finance at Insead, the internationally renowned business school in France. He is an exceptionally gifted and entertaining academic, and is greatly admired by his students and colleagues. But in 2009, in the wake of the financial crisis, he was getting fed up. He was becoming irritated by the smug jibes that he and his finance colleagues were receiving about the failure of their discipline and its contribution to the global financial crisis. He was particularly incensed at the suggestion that it was the emphasis of finance on shareholder value which was the root cause of the problem and that, by proselytizing this evil doctrine, he and his colleagues were instructing their students in the ways of the devil.

As a consequence, Professor Vermaelen was moved to do something that he never thought he would do and that is to write an article on ethics—the ethics of the corporation.[1] It is a brilliant statement not just of why we benefit materially from the pursuit of shareholder value, but of how there is an ethical imperative, in a Kantian sense, for business people to abide by it.

The reason why this issue was touching such a raw nerve, not just in Professor Vermaelen but in many other academics, is that the principle of shareholder value that he was defending lies at the heart of economics and the teachings of business schools around the world. It is the justification of most business activity and the basis on which business policy has been formulated by governments for many generations. To attack it was therefore an onslaught against the most cherished beliefs of the corporation, governments, and business schools around the world.

The concept of shareholder value is a simple one—shareholders own their corporations and, not unreasonably, they therefore expect their employees to run the corporation in their interest. The extent to which the employees do that is reflected in the value of their shares—so shareholder value is nothing more than the result of doing one's best for those whose property one is managing. It sounds eminently reasonable, but to many it is the source of greed, of exploitative capitalism, of oppression of the workers, of the callous destruction of communities, of degradation of the environment, indeed of everything or nearly everything that is wrong in our world.[2] For example, a survey of thirty-four directors of US Fortune 200 companies reported that thirty-one of them would cut down a mature forest or release a dangerous unregulated toxin into the environment to increase corporate earnings.[3]

It is not therefore surprising that Professor Vermaelen and his colleagues have felt duty bound to defend their position, but what makes Professor Vermaelen's defence particularly interesting is that he was willing to tackle the opponents on their home turf of moral philosophy and not just resort to the normal defence of economic necessity. So let me set out his argument before I describe why, even on its own terms, I believe it to be seriously flawed.

The Shareholder Imperative

As Professor Vermaelen explains, shareholders are not just owners of companies—they have a relation with their corporations that is fundamentally different from anyone else's. If you work for a corporation, you are employed by it and have a contract that specifies how much you will be paid and what you are expected to do for it in return. If you are lending it money, then you will have a contract that will specify how much you will be repaid and when. If you are a shareholder, you have no such contract. There is nothing promised to you and you might indeed lose all your money without being able to do anything about it. If the corporation does well, you, the shareholder, will do well; if the corporation does badly, you will do badly and in the extreme your investment will be wiped out altogether.

It is that distinction which lies at the heart of what Professor Vermaelen and others argue is the central significance of shareholder value. Shareholders are vulnerable to the performance of the corporation to a greater degree than any other party. They are exposed to being exploited by those who do not have their interest at heart. Since they do not have the law to protect them through contracts as others do, then, unless they can rely on someone to take care of their interests and look after their property, they will not invest in the first place. The financing of corporations therefore requires companies to be run in the interests of the shareholders who have provided the finance.

In addition to this commercial aspect, there is an ethical dimension. To avoid exploiting the vulnerable, directors of companies must uphold the interests of their shareholders who are the weaker, more exposed party. This turns the normal ethical argument on its head. It is not, as commonly asserted, the workers or the customers who are the exploited party; it is the shareholders. They are the people who commit their capital: once it is subscribed, it is permanent and cannot be withdrawn. The moral obligation to uphold the interests of shareholders therefore derives from their unusual degree of exposure to the corporation.

This is not to say that directors of corporations will entirely ignore the welfare of others. If, by going beyond their contractual obligations, corporations can earn higher profits for their shareholders, then that is what they should do. For example, it may be in the interests of corporations to provide their customers with products of higher quality and reliability than contracts specify if by so doing they can charge their customers a premium which more than covers the additional costs incurred. Likewise, if customers prefer environmentally sound and ethically sourced products, then that is what they should be sold—not because it is inherently good to do so, but because it benefits shareholders.

Similarly, corporations should look after their employees, train them well, and offer them good working facilities if by so doing they can reduce the cost of employing them or enhance their productivity to the benefit of the corporation's profitability. They should look after local communities and support worthy causes if that is what their shareholders want them to do or if they can thereby enhance the corporation's reputation and profits. They should abstain from activities that are deemed to be socially irresponsible if these diminish the corporation's reputation to the detriment of shareholders.

Far from being unconcerned about others, the corporation will uphold the interests of many parties in addition to those of shareholders. But unlike those of shareholders, the rights of these other parties are derivative not fundamental. Directors have a duty to uphold shareholder interests. They do not have a duty to uphold other parties' interests, except in so far as they thereby enhance the interests of shareholders.

Furthermore, the directors have a duty not to go beyond what is in the interests of their shareholders. They should not source ethical products or improve employee conditions, except in so far as their customers and employees are willing to pay for them in higher prices and lower wages. Any more would be at the expense of shareholder interests. If shareholders know before they subscribe their capital that it will be spent on activities which will not yield them financial returns, then that is fine. But without their explicit consent, directors have no right to waste their money in this way. The corporation is a form of property that should be employed to the benefit of its shareholders; to do otherwise would be to suggest that there are other owners who have committed capital to the same extent as shareholders.

The justification of shareholder value is both elegant and persuasive. But it is not just of conceptual significance, it is also of profound practical importance. It is embedded in the laws that govern the conduct of our corporations. Under Section 172 of the UK Companies Act 2006, it is the directors' duty to promote the success of the company for the benefit of its members (i.e. its shareholders). In so doing, it should have regard to 'the interests of the company's employees, the company's relationships with its suppliers and customers, the impact of the company's operations on the community and the environment, and the desirability of the company maintaining a reputation of high standards'—what is sometimes termed 'enlightened shareholder value'.[4] In other words, the fundamental duty of the company is to its shareholders and the interests of other parties derive from that primary duty.

To illustrate the implication of that principle, consider the obligation of the corporation under UK company law to uphold human rights beyond those enshrined in relevant human rights legislation. The Companies Act requires directors to 'have regard to' certain issues which affect non-shareholders, including those that have an impact on the community and the environment. This could encompass human rights issues where they are relevant to the business. So directors have an obligation to abide by relevant human rights legislation and can go beyond that to the extent that it is in the interests of the company to do so, but they are not required to do more than that. Indeed, if they did so to a degree that was detrimental to the interests of their shareholders, then they would be acting beyond their authority.

The concept of shareholder rights and the obligations of the corporation to its shareholders are therefore deeply embedded in UK company law. But UK law is not unusual in this regard. In the US, directors are fiduciaries and owe duties of care and loyalty to the corporation and its shareholders. The duty of care requires directors to exercise prudence in the conduct of their business and the duty of loyalty requires directors to act in good faith in the best interests of the corporation and its shareholders. Directors are permitted to consider the corporation's impact on other parties, but only in so far as these are consistent with the interests of shareholders. In other words, once again beyond legal requirements, the interests of others, including human rights, derive from those of the corporation's shareholders.

So the argument for shareholder value has been profoundly influential in shaping the laws and conventions that govern the conduct of our corporations. So elegant is the argument, that I will employ it in coming to exactly the opposite conclusion.

The Stakeholder Obligation

The principle that justified shareholder value and the fiduciary and moral obligation of directors to shareholders is that shareholders are owners who have invested irrecoverable capital over which they have no contractual rights of return. Applying this compelling logic means that directors of corporations should have a fiduciary responsibility and a moral obligation to any party who commits irrecoverable capital over which they have no contractual rights of return. The interests of these other parties should at least rank alongside those of shareholders and, depending on the degree and extent of their commitment, potentially ahead of shareholders.

And there are many such people, commonly termed 'stakeholders' to emphasize that their position is analogous to that of shareholders. A stakeholder is someone who has a commitment to a corporation that stems from the fact that they work for it, supply it, purchase from it, live near it, or are affected in some way by its activities. They can be employees, suppliers, customers, residents, and communities—anyone whose contractual relation to a corporation only at best partially reflects their total involvement in it.

We are typically simultaneously stakeholders in many organizations and activities. I have spent a significant fraction of my working life helping to build a business school in Oxford—the

Saïd Business School. If Oxford University decided tomorrow to fire me, then, while I hope that someone else might still be willing to employ me, I would have lost a great deal of my capital that I have invested in the university and the skills that are specific to that university. Likewise, I have devoted a considerable amount of time to building institutions outside as well as within the university and if those institutions closed down tomorrow, then the effort that I have expended on them will have been lost.

We invest in our families, in our local and religious communities, as well as our places of work. If they turn their backs on us or move elsewhere they impose costs on us that we cannot recover. We try to protect these investments through contracts—through employment contracts, supply contracts, marriage contracts, and social contracts—but ultimately they can only offer us partial security because of the complex and subjective nature of trying to attribute fault in the event of contract failure. We are ultimately exposed through the commitments that we make in the same way as shareholders are to their financial investments.

But are we really as committed as the shareholders who invest permanently without any contractual protection? The answer is in some respects more so because shareholders may be less exposed and permanent than we are. First, in the case of companies that are publicly listed on stock markets, they can readily exit by selling their shares and when they do so, they receive the full capital value of their investment. In contrast, if I get fired by Oxford University or one of the institutions that I have helped nurture ceases operations, then I cannot expect to be fully compensated for my past investments.

Second, in addition to transferring their shares to others, shareholders are in the aggregate taking capital out of corporations all the time—in fact more than they put in. The net amount of equity capital raised from stock markets in the last few decades of the 20th century was negative in both the UK and the US.[5] The way that shareholders are doing this is mainly through takeovers—every time a corporation is taken over by another for cash, then the acquiring corporation buys their shares for cash. The value of acquisitions is huge—around $3 trillion globally in 2009 of which typically perhaps 50 per cent is for cash.[6] In comparison, net new equity issued by companies was $700 billion in 2009 and over the period 2005 to 2007 it was actually negative, as companies directly bought back more of their shares than they sold.[7] So shareholders are regularly taking out more than they put in to their companies.

Employees cannot in general cash in the future expected value of their investments and live on the proceeds in the same way as shareholders. They are exposed to the whims of their employers and the labour market. So, far from shareholders being the committed, exposed parties, it is other stakeholders, including employees, who have most at stake. We can quickly get a rough idea of how much they have at stake from valuing the world.

Valuing the World

In 2010 the total market capitalization of all stock markets around the world was approximately $50 trillion.[8] So a stock market crash that wipes 20 per cent off the world stock markets makes the world poorer by around $10 trillion dollars. This sounds like a big number; but it pales into insignificance in comparison with the scale of lending. In 2010 the total amount of credit extended to the private sector was $90 trillion[9] and the stock of bonds issued by financial and non-financial corporations was somewhat less than $60 trillion.[10] So in stock market equity, loans, and corporate bond markets we have already clocked up about $200 trillion. Just to put this into perspective, the total global Gross Domestic Product (GDP)—the total value of goods and services produced in the world—was around $60 trillion per annum in 2010.[11] So the total stocks of debt and equity in the world amounted to more than three times the annual global GDP.

Of course this massively understates the total amount of equity in the world because, outside of the UK and US, the vast proportion of companies, including the largest ones, are not listed on stock markets. Even in the UK, amongst the largest 1,000 corporations only around one-quarter are listed on stock markets.[12] In France, Germany, and Italy the proportion is about one-fifth. Amongst smaller corporations nearly all equity is in private rather than publicly listed ownership. Since listed corporations are larger than unlisted ones, I will multiply the value of equity quoted on stock markets by a conservative estimate of three to get an approximation of the total world value of equity of about $150 trillion—approximately the same as private sector debt of $150 trillion—a total of $300 trillion. Those horrendous bank losses of $2 trillion in the financial crisis amount to small change in comparison to the total value of the corporate sector's financial liabilities. But even this considerably understates what we are worth.

There are approximately 3 billion people employed around the world. The International Labour Organization (ILO) estimates that the proportion of workers in 'vulnerable employment', defined as those in wage employment or less organized forms of employment, is approximately 50 per cent of total employment. So, 1.5 billion people essentially have little or no security of employment. Around 20 per cent of those in employment earn less than $1.25 a day and around 40 per cent less than $2 a day.[13]

So if I take $500 a year as the minimum income that employed people require, then there is around $750 billion of income a year that is earned with no security of employment, amounting over a forty-year working life to around $30 trillion of human capital that is exposed to no employment protection.

This is of course a massive understatement of the degree of exposed human capital. First, it excludes the 200 million people who are unemployed globally according to the ILO. Second, while $500 a year might be a minimum subsistence income, it is far off the average wage rate. If 50 per cent of total GDP is associated with labour income (i.e. $30 trillion of the $60 trillion),[14] then the average annual wage per employed person is around $10,000.[15] At this level, I am talking about an exposed value of closer to $600 trillion. Nevertheless, taking the most conservative estimate of exposed human capital, a rough account of the balance sheet of the private sector of the world on the liabilities side looks something like this:

	$ Trillion
Market Equity	50
Private Equity	100
Bank and Other Loans	90
Bonds	60
Labour Capital	30

We will refer back to these numbers at various stages in the book. The interests of banks and bondholders, unlike those of shareholders, are protected by contract. That puts the $150 trillion of creditors' capital (bank and bond finance) in a very different position to the $150 trillion of shareholders' capital (market and private equity) and, according to the proponents of shareholder value, justifies the imposition of specific obligations on directors to their shareholders. However, creditors are also exposed to risks—risks of failure of the businesses to which they lend, to service their interest, or to repay their loans. They too are stakeholders and the greater the emphasis placed on shareholder interests, the larger are the stakeholder exposures of creditors.

Suppose we follow the shareholder value principle to its logical limit and give shareholders complete discretion as to how they deploy the private sector financial capital of $300 trillion. Suppose that there is an investment available which will either double the value of the world's financial assets from $300 trillion to $600 trillion, or, equally likely (with the same probability), lose the entire $300 trillion. Not a very attractive proposition, you might well say—it delivers a return of either plus 100 per cent or minus 100 per cent, with the same probability so that the anticipated return is zero—investors expecting to lose as much as they might gain. But follow the shareholder value principle and leave the decision in the hands of shareholders and that is what they would choose to do with the world's wealth. From their perspective, it is an incredibly attractive investment.

If it turns out well, shareholders will have increased their $150 trillion to $600 trillion minus the $150 trillion due to creditors, namely $450 trillion—a 200 per cent return ($300 trillion increase) on their $150 trillion shareholding. If the investment turns out badly, they will have lost their $150 trillion—a minus 100 per cent return. So their expected earnings will be $75 trillion, namely a 50 per cent return on their $150 trillion shareholding.

Creditors will not be so happy. If the investment turns out well, their loans will be unaffected and they will just keep their

$150 trillion—a zero return. If the investment turns out badly, then they will lose the lot—a minus 100 per cent return. So their expected return is minus 50 per cent, exactly equal to the shareholders' gain, which is no surprise because this is pure 'wealth transfer', as it is termed—a simple expropriation of creditors for the benefit of shareholders.

Put the world in the hands of shareholders and that is exactly what will happen—they will transfer as much wealth as they can from creditors to themselves. Creditors protect themselves as best they can through contracts which impose restrictions on what companies can do with their money (covenants) and grant them rights over the assets of corporations that default on their loans (collateral). However, the collateral that the borrowers offer creditors as security for their loans will be of no value in the event that the world's financial assets turn out to be worthless. And restrictions imposed on what borrowers can do with creditors' money—the covenants—might provide them with little protection.[16] Who, for example, is to say whether the chance of the remarkable outcome is only 50:50 and therefore seriously against creditors' interests, as against what the borrowers might claim to be 99 to 1 and therefore almost certainly in the interest of everyone?

That is what shareholders will employ executives[17] to do. They will hire executives who will be paid handsomely to undertake the investment and promote it with complete conviction to creditors as a shoo-in low-risk winner. Executives will be rewarded irrespective of the performance of the investment, which in the above scenario is outside their control—they will be rewarded for picking what from the point of view of shareholders is indeed a winner. If the world is unfortunate enough to encounter the bad outcome, creditors will howl all the way to the government. The government for its part will accuse executives of outrageous conduct, subject them to public humiliation, urge shareholders to take a more active interest in the management of their corporations, and tell them to do a better job of aligning managerial with their own interests. Shareholders will duly respond by paying their executives still more to select even larger higher-risk investments in the future.

That is one interpretation of the financial crisis. You might take comfort from the fact that the losses in the crisis amounted to a mere $2 trillion in comparison to creditor claims of $150 trillion and therefore conclude that the above example is beyond the realms of plausibility. But you should not, because as the above suggests, this is Scene One of a drama whose tragic course is only just beginning to unfold before us—the spellbound and helpless audience of the world's population.

Creditors have been the victims of Scene One. The $30 trillion of vulnerable employees' capital will be in Scene Two. Subsequent scenes will include future generations, the environment, communities, and the animal species, because there is a lot at stake in the world beyond shareholder or even shareholder plus creditor capital. During the interval we will gasp for a drink and behind the bar will be someone who is always on hand to mix us the perfect cool cocktail, for a modest fee—a lawyer.

Doing One's Fiduciary Duty

In imposing a duty of care and honesty on the part of directors of a corporation to its shareholders, corporate law recognizes that business is inherently risky and grants directors considerable discretion in the exercise of their duty. Directors must be careful not to be in violation of relevant laws, for example in relation to employment, the environment, or bribery and corruption. But beyond that, unless there is clear evidence of negligence, misconduct, or incompetence, then the courts are unwilling to dispute judgements made by directors who claim that they acted in their corporation's best interests. Judges are not businessmen and they therefore grant 'business judgment' to those responsible for running businesses.

The duty of honesty and care could be extended to other stakeholders. Indeed, in many jurisdictions outside of the UK and the US it is.[18] In France, directors' duties are based on the general corporate interest of the company (*intérêt social*), which may be different from that of the company's shareholders. Directors have obligations to their shareholders, but these are less precise than the fiduciary responsibilities of directors to shareholders in the UK and US.

The concept of plurality of interests is more clearly embedded in German corporate law. As part of the economic and social fabric of the nation, corporations are expected to abide by commonly accepted legal and ethical norms, and directors are required to take account of the interests of parties in addition to those of shareholders. This is most clearly reflected in the rights of employees of German corporations, but it extends more generally to the interests of other parties. Unlike in the UK and US, these interests cannot be ranked, but give rise to a plurality of objectives that directors have to balance when making business decisions. The one exception to this is if, in so doing, the directors would put the financial viability of the corporation in jeopardy, in which case financial considerations take precedence.

Swedish corporate law lies somewhere between American and British on the one hand and French and German on the other. It retains returns to shareholders as the primary objective of the corporation, but allows directors to take account of other party interests and incorporate codes of conduct in the corporation's articles of association. It thus provides for directors to interpret the company's interests as extending beyond those of the shareholders, but does not require them to do so. It is enabling in allowing the company to take other parties' interests into account if it sees so fit, but it is neither prescriptive in requiring this, as in other Continental European countries, nor restrictive in prohibiting it, as in Anglo-American countries.

While these pluralistic approaches may assist with mitigating some conflicts between different stakeholders, they do not by any means resolve them. Employees, customers, and suppliers are as self-motivated as shareholders. They too will wish to see the corporation do its best for them even if this comes at the expense of other parties who have no protection. One author described Wal-Mart as at one time

> forcing employees to work off the clock, as well as discrimination against women and minorities in promotions to management positions. Wal-Mart workers generally receive lower pay and fewer benefits than workers at other retail stores. Because of the vast Wal-Mart work force of over 1.4 million, these policies have been blamed for driving down retail wages across America. On the other hand, the Wal-Mart philosophy squeezes suppliers and helps directly or indirectly save customers possibly over $100 billion per year.[19]

In this case, the benefits of one group of stakeholders—customers—came at the expense of another—employees.

Of course, we could impose obligations on directors to take regard of other stakeholders, most prominently employees as well as customers, but that will just leave other parties—local communities, the environment—unprotected. And as we try to extend the number of parties to whom directors owe a fiduciary responsibility, we increase the degree of discretion that they can exercise still further. Judges are already unwilling to intervene in business decisions, even when they are only asked to do so for the benefit of the company's shareholders. Extend the obligations to customers, employees, and communities, grant directors discretion over how to balance those conflicting claims, and there will be next to nothing that is legally enforceable.

The law cannot of itself solve the problem. Corporate behaviour is conditioned by incentives, and economists repeatedly tell us that incentives lie at the root of all problems. Get incentives right and the rest will follow; get them wrong and nothing that lawyers, governments, or anyone else can do will fix the problem. In the drama of the last section the incentives of shareholders and creditors were completely misaligned—the gains of shareholders came at the expense of creditors—and shareholders sought ways round legal provisions to exploit their creditors.

This ignores the fact that managers, shareholders, and creditors are in ongoing repeated relations with each other. Reckless behaviour by one party will undermine their reputations with the others and worsen the terms on which they will be able to do business in the future. For example, if corporations exploit their creditors, they will raise the cost at which they will be able to borrow from creditors in the future, namely the interest rate. Proponents of shareholder value suggest that it is our reputations that keep us honest and that it is to corporations' reputations that we should turn for the promotion of responsible behaviour and the protection of stakeholder interests. But before we leap too fast to that conclusion, we should perhaps heed the words of the Bard.

Chapter 3
Reputation

*'Reputation is an idle and most false imposition; oft got
without merit, and lost without deserving.'*
    Othello, Act 2 Scene 2, William Shakespeare

The Market Knows

Karstadt Quelle was formed in 1999 as a merger between two
venerable German family corporations, Karstadt Warenhaus AG,
the department stores, and Quelle Schickedanz AG, the mail-
order corporation, whose origins dated to the end of the 19th
century and the early part of the 20th century respectively. The
merger was not a success and shortly after it was consummated
the corporation was making losses. It expanded its tourist business by acquiring the large British travel firm Thomas Cook in
December 2000—not a very auspicious moment, months ahead
of 9/11—and its problems were compounded by other ill-judged
forays into alliances with Starbucks and Sony. Its losses continued
to mount in the face of Germany's worst retail recession since the

Second World War in 2002, forcing it to close stores and layoff staff.[1]

New CEOs came and went, but nothing reversed its fortunes until in 2005 Thomas Middlehoff was appointed as CEO. Middlehoff had previously transformed Bertelsmann, the former provincial media giant, into a new online business. Middlehoff sold off real estate assets in KarstadtQuelle, reduced its debt, and improved its cash flow. Between 2005 and 2007, KarstadtQuelle became a star of the German stock market. Its share price rose by a factor of over three during a period in which its rivals' share prices struggled to double. But it was a brief renaissance. The company expanded its tourist business and changed its name to Arcandor to reflect this, but its department stores and mail-order business languished. In August 2008 several of Arcandor's credit lines matured and it was forced to refinance its activities in the depth of the financial crisis and the collapse of Lehman Brothers on 15 September 2008. By the beginning of 2008 Arcandor's share price had almost returned to its 2005 levels, by the middle of 2008 it had halved from there, and by the end of the year it was hovering at around one-quarter of where it was in 2005. On 9 June 2009 the company filed for bankruptcy.

This 'rags to riches to rags' story illustrates the dramatic way in which the market can reward and discipline corporations in quick succession. It is a fickle master, evaluating corporate prospects on the basis of information available to it, and not hesitating to reverse its previous assessments when new information emerges. It is, as a consequence, one of the most powerful measures of an inherently nebulous concept—reputation. Your reputation is what determines your success, cramps your style, or opens unlimited opportunities to you. It takes years to establish and minutes to lose, and social media is radically intensifying its impact.[2]

However, measuring your reputation beyond saying that it is good, impeccable, tainted, or non-existent is extremely hard to do.

In contrast, in the case of companies, the stock market provides a quick guide to shareholders' views about the reputations of corporations. While it is by no means the only factor determining a corporation's share price, high reputation corporations command a premium in relation to their lower-status counterparts. Reputations allow corporations to charge their customers more or pay their employees and suppliers less than their not so reputable counterparts, and changes in reputation are reflected in movements in the value of corporations' shares. As a result, fear of loss of reputation is potentially a strong disincentive to engage in the abuses discussed in the previous chapter. Anti-social conduct, corruption, and violations of stakeholders, human rights, or the environment damage a corporation's reputation and will be reflected in its market value. For corporations concerned about their shareholders' interests, this threat of loss in value will discourage them from engaging in these activities in the first place. Reputational damage and its relation to share values is therefore an important sanction on corporate misconduct. This theory of reputation sounds good in principle, but unfortunately it has a serious defect.

A Fined Firm

There are many ways in which you are at risk when you hand over your money to someone to manage it for you. They may advise you badly, invest it poorly, steal it, lose it, not take sufficient care of it, and charge you excessively for doing all this for you. You are exceptionally exposed to those selling you financial services for the simple reason that gaining satisfaction from making other people rich is not a natural human instinct, whereas making oneself rich is. The interests of those to whom you entrust your wealth are therefore diametrically opposed to your own, and all that is stopping them putting their hands in your pocket and removing everything from it is fear of the consequences of doing it.[3]

That fear comes from the possibility of being caught. Historically the US has been strong on sanctioning misconduct and the UK has been weak. Here is the chairman of the Halifax Bank of Scotland (HBOS), Lord Stevenson, speaking at their annual general meeting in June 2008: 'There is a strong case for believing that the UK is exceptionally bad at dealing with white-collar crime. Only two weeks ago I was in New York and two people were convicted of insider dealing. We appear not to pursue things in the same way.'[4] Certainly the level of fines imposed by the UK's Financial Services Authority (FSA) has in the past paled into insignificance in comparison with those of the US's Securities and Exchange Commission (SEC)—approximately one-tenth on average.[5]

There is nevertheless a remarkable feature of these fines. While they may be modest in relation to their US counterparts they still inflict substantial damage on the offending corporations because of the reputational damage that they impose. When the FSA discloses that a corporation has engaged in some form of misconduct, the decline in its market value is approximately ten times that of the fine that the FSA levies. So the indirect reputational damage is ten times the direct financial penalty and compensation that the corporation has to pay.

This sounds deceptively good. The market is reinforcing the work of the regulator, the FSA, by inflicting a loss in share value that is far in excess of the fines that the FSA itself imposes. A corporation's reputation with its customers and investors is tarnished when it is penalized by the FSA and the market sanctions corporations that abuse their customers' and investors' trust. The corporation loses some of its custom, cannot charge its customers such high prices, and is unable to raise finance as cheaply as before, all of which adversely affect its market value.

That is the bright side of reputation and market discipline. The dark side is that this only works for certain types of misconduct— in particular where a corporation has been revealed to have acted against the interests of its customers or investors. Not unreasonably, customers and investors then lose faith in the corporation and are unwilling to trade with it on as favourable terms as before. That hurts the corporation and its owners.

However, where the corporation has abused some other party—for example the customers or investors of another corporation or the public at large through engaging in money laundering—then there is no such effect. Indeed, there is evidence that the share price of the corporation in question actually rises.[6] Why? For the simple reason that it has not hurt its own customers and investors—in fact they may have benefited from the wrongs the corporation has inflicted on others. So as you might expect, the stock market is a very selfish policeman. It only inflicts penalties on corporations which, by their actions, have damaged the corporation itself. Where the corporation has damaged other people or other corporations, then far from penalizing it, the stock market might even reward it for enhancing its profits.

On the morning of 29 September 1982, twelve-year-old Mary Kellerman died after taking a capsule of Extra-Strength Tylenol.

Her death was followed by the deaths of six other users of the same drug in the Chicago area. The capsules had been laced with cyanide. Having initially issued warnings, the manufacturers—Johnson & Johnson—decided to do a complete product recall. As a consequence, Johnson & Johnson suffered a share price decline of nearly 30 per cent.[7]

While this was a large share price reaction, Johnson & Johnson was not alone in suffering share price falls as a consequence of product recalls. More generally, if a corporation is found to have produced substandard goods or to have been at fault in accidents involving its products, then it suffers share price losses when these failures are revealed. In each of these cases, it is the corporation's own customers or related parties that have suffered as a consequence of the actions or negligence of the corporation.

That is not the case in environmental disasters. The victims there are 'third parties'—communities, wildlife, the atmosphere, not the corporation's own customers and investors. As a consequence, where corporations are found to have violated environmental regulations, the share price losses inflicted on corporations are no larger than the direct penalty imposed by the relevant regulatory authorities, without any further reputational effect.[8] In marked contrast to product recalls, and other failures that harm corporations' own customers, corporations are not sanctioned by the market for environmental failures that inflict damage on other external parties.

The revelation of misrepresentation of lending rates on the London Interbank Offered Rate (Libor) in June 2012 illustrates the nature of the problem. The announcement of a settlement between the UK and US regulatory authorities and Barclays Bank, the first bank to be sanctioned, came at 13.30 British Summer Time on 27 June 2012. By the close of trading on the

London Stock Exchange three hours later, Barclays' share price had risen! It was only the following day that Barclays' share price began a precipitous decline. What might have been regarded as a reasonable settlement for Barclays on 27 June became a public relations disaster with damning interventions by politicians and the press on 28 June. Cries for criminal investigations and accountability at the top of Barclays gave way to calls for the break-up of banks and the separation of commercial and investment banking. Suddenly, what seemed like a reasonably favourable outcome for Barclays became a major threat to its business. This is consistent with what has been observed elsewhere. The progressive downward adjustment of BP's share price after the Gulf of Mexico disaster in 2010 was not just a reflection of concern about consequential lawsuits, but also the damaging political interventions by, in this case, the US government. Without these public interventions, stock markets have marked disdain for the social as against the private costs of the actions of their firms.

The implications of this are striking. The market promotes good conduct in a very specific sense. It encourages good conduct in relation to things that it itself values. It values profits and it therefore responds abruptly to adverse information about the ability of corporations to earn profits. Anything that might inflict significant suffering on other parties but does not impact on a corporation's own profits is dismissed as an irrelevance. An irrelevance it might indeed be for shareholders, but an irrelevance it is far from being for the communities, employees, and animals that have suffered as a consequence. The market does its own thing with remarkable effectiveness and clarity. The only question is whether we share its values. To address that, consider the activity in which many of our smartest young minds are craving to be engaged—financial services.

You Too Can Be a Star Fund Manager

Want to be a star fund manager? Here is a simple prescription.[9] Set up a fund with the aim of beating a benchmark return of 4 per cent. The fund is a five-year fund from which investors can withdraw at the end of each year. As the fund manager you will be paid a standard fee of 2 per cent of funds under management and a 20 per cent incentive fee for the excess returns you earn on the fund over and above the benchmark.

This is what you do. Start off by raising $100 million. Feel you are not quite qualified to do this? Don't worry for a moment. You will be issuing a mouth-watering prospectus promising a good return well above what investors are earning elsewhere and they would simply look like fools not to snap it up.

Now look for a derivative[10] that involves taking a bet on an unlikely event, such as that the sun will shine in central London at midday on more than 50 per cent of days over the coming year— say a one in ten chance, so that it costs $1 to buy an option—a financial contract which pays $10 if this rare event happens and nothing if it does not. Now sell 11 million options on this event, which delivers you $11 million and requires you to pay $110 million if this event occurs and nothing otherwise. Take the $100 million that you have raised from investors, add in the $11 million from the sale of the option, and put the $110 million into 'safe' government Treasury bills yielding the benchmark 4 per cent. The remaining $1 million will be used for covering your costs of employing staff and computers to run this sophisticated asset management firm.

So the total amount that you earn for your investors is the $4,400,000 interest plus the $11 million from the options, namely a total of $15,400,000—15.4 per cent or 11.4 per cent above the benchmark of 4 per cent against which you are being compared. You are truly a genius, and to reward you for this remarkable performance they pay you $2 million on the funds under management and 20 per cent on the excess return of $11,400,000 over the benchmark $4 million, namely $2,280,000, a grand total of over $4 million. At least that is what you earn with a probability of 90 per cent provided that a freak turn of nature does not occur and the sun shines in London for a majority of the year.

The following year you do the same thing, earn similar amounts, and you keep doing this for say five years until you have enough to buy your stately home in the country and retire as a well-respected and wealthy member of the British establishment. A few years later, global warming speeds up, a freak year happens, and the sun shines for most of the year. But that is all to the good because you can sit safely in the beautiful gardens of your estate, enjoying the sunshine, reading about the turmoil in the fund management firm that you sold on to a friend of yours at a 'specially discounted price'.

This is in the class of the even simpler 'how always to win at roulette'—a technique that I invariably employ when I find myself in the unfortunate position of being in a casino, if only to provide myself with an excuse for exiting as soon as possible. Go into a casino, put $1 on red and wait for the wheel to spin round. If it lands on a red number, walk out of the casino with $2 and $1 profit. If it lands on a black number, put $2 on red. If the ball lands on a red number, you will get $4. You have spent a total of $3 so you can walk out again with $1 profit. If the ball lands on a black number again, then put $4 on red and keep going, doubling your stake until the ball lands on red. You will always therefore end up making $1 profit. Admittedly it will take you a bit of time to use this strategy to buy your country estate, but no doubt you will grow a little bolder and try it with larger stakes and profits before opening a fund that allows others to enjoy the fruits of your remarkable gaming talents.

Both these techniques use investment or gaming strategies that rely on large probabilities of small gains masking small probabilities of huge losses. In the case of the fund manager, it is the probability that you are forced to pay up on the option that you have sold. In the case of the casino, it is the small possibility of the ball landing on zero or that, due to a freak chain of circumstances, the ball continues to land on black sufficiently long that you end up running out of money before you are able to cash in your $1 profit.

What these examples illustrate is that it is very easy to devise strategies for earning 'abnormal' returns over extended periods of time before abnormal events that impose exceptional losses transpire.[11] They are not dissimilar to chain letters in allowing those at the bottom of the pyramid to earn profits before those at the top are left with its crumbled remains. The main difference is that while it is easy to identify most chain letters, it is very difficult to devise incentive arrangements that allow one to distinguish between genuinely talented fund managers and those who are just mimicking the behaviour of their more able counterparts, or at least to do so without discouraging the genuinely smart people as well as the charlatans.[12]

Perhaps the most serious consequence of the ease of constructing such schemes and disguising their downsides in the mists of time or the long tail of the distributions is the incentive that it gives to people to devote time to devising such schemes. One can quickly convince oneself that one is doing social good in helping others to make money, to correct distortions in the pricing of securities on stock markets and derivative markets, to direct investment to where it is most productive, when in fact one is doing no such thing. One is simply engaging in fraud. It is not necessarily fraud in a technical legal sense of stealing or even misleading. It is fraud in the sense of transferring wealth from future generations to the present. In each case, the current generation of investors, savers, gamblers, and fund managers are benefiting at the expense of the future and the more the loss is deferred into the future, the larger the number of generations who will be able to profit from it. In terms of the previous discussion, the stakeholders who are at risk from the activities of current investors are the next generation of investors.

In essence, there is a substantial element of 'Ponzi schemes'[13] in financial markets and, through financial innovation and the introduction of new financial instruments, these Ponzi schemes are becoming ever more complex and sophisticated. Since the new financial instruments are technically complex they can lure the best minds to engage in activities that are both intellectually demanding and far more lucrative than the conventional occupations in which they were employed. On the back of financial innovation, we are putting our scientists to work on devising new schemes that disguise the explosives stacked beneath our carefully accumulated financial wealth.

Financial Meets Mechanical Engineer

The obvious solution to these Ponzi schemes is to defer payment. Only reward people once their true performance has been revealed. So instead of paying out the 2 + 20 fund management compensation to you this year, let us wait and see and hold it back for, for example, ten years. Not now quite so attractive for you given that the likelihood of the scheme not blowing up before the ten years drops from 90 per cent to about one-third.

Alas, were it so easy, then we would all be rewarded with generous pensions and modest incomes during our lifetime. The only problem is that far from solving short-termism, it can create it.[14] To illustrate this let us just tweak the above example a little bit and suppose that instead of being a fund manager engaging in financial engineering, you are a very industrious mechanical engineer running a company into which shareholders have invested $100 million. The firm generates a very steady and predictable return of 6 per cent per annum on the shareholders' capital—modest in comparison to the 15.4 per cent that you would have earned them as a financial engineer but still a respectable 2 per cent above the 4 per cent benchmark against which you are being compared. You are paid a profit share of 10 per cent of the excess return that you earn above the benchmark—an income of $200,000—not quite what you could have earned as a fund manager, but a good income nevertheless and one that you expect to be able to earn for the next ten years up until your retirement.

Unfortunately one of your classmates from university chose to put their engineering skills to financial engineering instead of mechanical engineering and is working for a hedge fund. The hedge fund manager spots the $100 million in the company and says we know what we can do with that—we will purchase the firm, sell off the assets, invest the $100 million in Treasury securities, and write a low-risk $11 million option, yielding a total of 15.4 per cent. The shareholders cannot resist the offer or the explanation from your classmate that the reason they can earn so much more than you is that you are an unimaginative slacker who was just cruising into retirement. So they sell their shares to the hedge fund and are comforted to hear that the fund has promptly made you redundant. Of course with just a few years to go before retirement there is no prospect of you getting another job and your earnings come to a grinding halt. The more your income is deferred into the future, the greater the proportion that you stand to lose as a consequence of this.

A pity you might say, but not a tragedy. Oh yes it is, because you have already seen the same thing happen to all the classmates of yours who were dumb enough to become real rather than financial engineers. All their businesses have been 'financially engineered' and most are now redundant. So seeing this coming, would you set up the company in the first place? Would you trust your shareholders to support you against the hedge fund managers? Or would you, like your smart friends, choose to become a hedge fund manager instead?

The stakeholders exposed to these types of practices are not therefore just future investors, but all those currently engaged in activities with fewer opportunities to exploit future generations. In other words, market processes distort the allocation of resources in an economy to those that have the most opportunity to engage in the type of intergenerational transfers described above. More generally, if some commercial activities are able to operate to the detriment of other stakeholders—be they future generations of the same class of investors, or other current classes such as creditors, employees, or customers—then too many resources in an economy will be allocated to these activities.[15]

So not only do reputations fail to preserve the interests of certain stakeholders, such as future generations, but in the process they also reinforce the misallocation of resources to activities that trade to the disadvantage of these stakeholders. Faced with the failure of reputations to provide the right market incentives and protect our interests as, for example, employees in mechanical

SAIT - Library

engineering or investors in the hedge fund industry, we need to seek help elsewhere. We need someone to control the hedge funds from squandering our money or destroying our jobs. We need someone to restrain the systematic abuse of stakeholders by shareholders. We need an enlightened benevolent person with our rather than their own interests at heart. We need a regulator.

Chapter 4
Regulation

'Put not your trust in money, but your money in trust.'
Oliver Wendell Holmes

The Immoral Case for Regulation

In a recent survey of which professions people trusted the most, businessmen, politicians, and bankers came bottom. Alongside the clergy, doctors, and teachers, university professors came top. We might have no power, pay, or prestige, but at least people trust us to do nothing, earn nothing, and to take no credit for it.

Trust is clearly in short supply. Businessmen may be in the pits, but politicians have sunk as low as they could, bankers come close behind, and even regulators have lost our collective respect. In response to the past failures of regulation, there has recently been an avalanche of proposals concerning the governance of financial institutions. In the US, the Dodd–Frank Act is concerned with, amongst other things, corporate governance of banks. In the UK, the Walker Report, the Financial Reporting

Council, and the Financial Services Authority have all considered ways of improving corporate governance of financial institutions.[1] In Europe, the European Commission has produced a Green Paper on the Corporate Governance of financial institutions and more recently non-financial corporations.[2]

Behind all of these reports lies a belief that the collapse of financial institutions is at least in part attributable to poor corporate governance. A failure to measure, monitor, and manage risks is thought to have been widespread in the financial sector before the crisis. The required response is to improve the competence, training, and engagement of management. Rules on the appointment, training, induction, commitment, and independence of directors of financial institutions need to be strengthened. There should be greater authority in the hands of chief risk officers, more oversight by auditors and risk committees. There should be better alignment of managerial incentives with the interests of stakeholders, better communication between shareholders and management, more shareholder engagement, and better stewardship by investing institutions.

Why is this happening? The first point to make is that it is not unusual. The response throughout history to financial crises is to seek greater regulation. As Aesop said, 'never trust the advice of a man in difficulties'. One example is the South Sea Bubble, which in 1720 consumed the South Sea Trading Company along with 'a company for carrying on an undertaking of great advantage, but nobody to know what it is', and '"Puckle's Machine Company," for discharging round and square cannon-balls and bullets, and making a total revolution in the art of war'.[3] The response was the Bubble Act, which forbade the formation of all stock companies except those authorized by Royal Charter and set back the formation of corporations (incorporation) in the UK for one hundred years. Financial history is littered with examples of governments acting in haste in response to financial failure and repenting at leisure. As we are observing now, the political pressure to be seen to act in the face of failure is overwhelming and, as night follows day, we will see a significant extension and tightening of regulation that will undermine the operation of financial markets for years to come.

What is wrong with responding to financial crises with strengthened regulation? Numerous things: for one, the horse has bolted. Those people who were lucky enough to escape before the crash have made their fortunes; those who did not have suffered their losses. As one banker put it, 'this financial crisis has been worse than those terrible multi-million dollar divorce settlements—not only have I lost half my wealth but I still have my spouse'. Second, regulation is pro-cyclical. Just as a steady relaxation of regulation during the first part of this decade encouraged increased investment and asset price rises, thereby fuelling the bubble, so too a tightening of regulation will now raise the cost of capital, discourage investment, and exacerbate the downturn.

But there is a more fundamental problem with regulation. We associate regulation with the promotion of moral conduct. It prevents producers from abusing customers: it limits the extent to which firms can charge excessively high prices; and it encourages the delivery of high-quality services. In fact it does exactly the opposite—it promotes immoral conduct. No one drives at 30mph in a built-up area. Everyone drives at no less than 33mph or whatever is the speed limit at which, allowing for margins of error, one might get caught. Penalizing train companies for the late arrival of trains encourages them to trade off the penalties against the cost of ensuring punctuality. Forbidding the inclusion of certain harmful ingredients in products promotes the substitution of the cheapest permitted alternative.

Regulation therefore leads to instrumental behaviour that, far from enhancing moral conduct which embraces the welfare of others, focuses our attention on the regulations themselves and ways in which we can circumvent or minimize their effects.[4] Instead of worrying about the interests of pedestrians or cyclists, we stare at our speedometer; instead of being concerned about the impact of delays on their customers, train companies are concerned with indices of punctuality; and food producers advertise the health benefits of excluding harmful ingredients that they are forced to disclose, not the detrimental impact of others.

The futility of using regulation to promote moral conduct is illustrated by the response that it has promoted in the companies that it regulates. Corporations employ regulatory departments that are supposed to ensure compliance with regulatory rules and standards. They are, in fact, avoidance rather than compliance departments. They spend as much time trying to circumvent regulations as comply with them. For example, utilities, such as water, electricity, and gas companies, employ regulation departments to negotiate with regulators about the charges that they can levy on customers and to minimize the impact of regulation on corporate profitability. The futility of plugging a leaking container is not a bad analogy for regulation, except that the leaks that spring up elsewhere do not appear of their own accord but are deliberately punctured by highly paid compliance officers.

It is therefore not surprising that bankers have rewarded themselves grossly for failure, that banks have brought themselves to the brink of financial collapse, that regulators have been negligent or complicit, that credit rating agencies have been deficient in identifying potential corporate failures, that accountants are compromised by the consultancy services that they provide to firms that they audit, and that fund managers trade their clients' portfolios to no benefit except the large fees that they thereby earn. Nor is it surprising that Members of Parliament in Britain have flipped their homes, cleaned their moats, charged their mortgages, and made their charitable donations, all at the expense of the taxpayer. We are encouraged to do this by a system that confuses rules with standards, compliance with compassion, and obedience with integrity. We are no more immoral than our predecessors, but our response to immorality has encouraged us to be so, and the more that we try to plug the leaking vessel this way, the more immoral we will become.

Collateral Damage

Rules which look to improve the appointment, training, induction, commitment, and independence of directors give greater authority to risk officers, auditors, and risk committees, improve alignment of managerial incentives with the interests of stakeholders, strengthen communication between shareholders and management, and increase shareholder engagement and stewardship by investing institutions, all sound like motherhood and apple pie. How could they possibly be anything other than a good thing?

To answer that, it is first worth noting that the financial institutions that took the greatest risks and performed the worst in the recent financial crisis were those with the best corporate governance measured by the above criteria. Improving corporate governance would have led to worse performance in the financial crisis. How could this perverse result have occurred?

For this we need to go back to the relation between shareholders and stakeholders discussed in the previous chapter. As described there, a particularly important set of stakeholders in the economy is the creditors of financial institutions such as banks—people like you and me who deposit our money at banks. We invest our money in current or deposit accounts, sometimes in bonds, and earn generally modest rates of interest. We presume that our money is safe in banks, but just occasionally, during such periods as the recent financial crisis, we are reminded that it is far from completely safe.

To keep our money safe we want the banks to which we lend to be prudent, conservative, and invest cautiously. If things go wrong, then our money is at stake. If things go well, then we will not earn any more interest on our investments. The benefits of success accrue to shareholders, not those who lend banks money. There is therefore a direct conflict between the interests of shareholders and those of the depositors and bondholders of banks. Shareholders like banks to take risks because they enjoy the fruits of success; depositors and bondholders want banks to be cautious to avoid losing their money. So if one strengthens corporate governance and raises the authority of shareholders over the running of banks, then banks will take more risks to please their more powerful shareholders. That is exactly what happened in the run-up to the financial crisis.[5]

This conflict between shareholders and creditors of corporations afflicts all corporations. It is however particularly acute in banks because they have so much debt in the form of deposits and bonds. As a consequence, there is a particularly strong incentive on shareholders to encourage their directors to gamble with their money—if the gambles pay off then they profit, if the gambles fail then creditors lose—heads I win, tails you lose.

So given this, why are regulatory authorities advocating corporate governance rules that strengthen the rights of shareholders? The answer is that there is a large body of opinion which suggests that the most serious failure in corporations is a governance problem—a failure of the directors and managers of corporations to act in the interests of shareholders. Since no one shareholder in the large modern corporation listed on a stock market owns a significant fraction of the shares of a corporation, there is little or no incentive for them to do much monitoring of their corporations' performance. In other words there is inadequate governance of the running of corporations.

So, much work on corporate governance has sought to address this so-called 'agency' problem of aligning the interests of directors of corporations with those of their shareholders by improving their appointment, training, induction, commitment, and independence, giving greater authority to risk officers, auditors, and risk committees, and strengthening the relation of directors' incentives to corporate performance. The European Commission, and the Dodd–Frank and Sarbanes–Oxley Acts in the US are simply responding to this conventional wisdom by strengthening regulation. The difficulty is that in the process of solving one problem—the relation between shareholders and their managers—regulators are creating another—the relation between shareholders and creditors—the latter potentially being the more serious problem in some institutions, such as banks.

This is why attempts to impose regulatory solutions are often so misguided. What appear to be conventionally accepted wisdoms are simply wrong or incomplete, and when actions are taken in good faith to solve one problem, there are numerous unintended consequences which spring up elsewhere requiring further regulation to correct them. Still more seriously the experience of banks points to a widespread and damaging deficiency of the shareholder model of the corporation. It demonstrates the potential for shareholders to extract rents to their benefit and to the detriment of other stakeholders. In the case of banks, it was the creditors who in principle were the victims of shareholders promoting their own interests. In fact, since depositors were protected through public deposit insurance schemes and large banks were deemed too strategically important to be allowed to fail, it was not ultimately the creditors who bore the cost of bank failures but national governments and taxpayers. Furthermore, the scale of the required interventions from governments has been such as to threaten the solvency of entire countries, most notably Iceland and Ireland, let alone individual financial institutions.

This is a generic issue. Creditors and taxpayers were the stakeholders who were on the line in relation to banks. Employees are vulnerable to global recessions. The world's populations are the stakeholders who are exposed to corporations pursuing shareholder interests at the expense of the environment. To the extent that it is possible to rectify environmental damage, then it will be taxpayers who will bear the costs because the ability of corporations to absorb the costs themselves is seriously limited and, as in the case of the banks, many of the relevant corporations in industrial and energy markets will be regarded as too strategically important to be allowed to fail.

As another example, consider the possibility, however remote, that mobile phones are the cause of brain disorders, in particular amongst children and young adults, and that in twenty years' time a major international health crisis will be created as a consequence. Who will bear the cost of the provision of health care? It will be far beyond the capability of the mobile phone industry to cater with the scale of the problem and it will again fall upon the public at large.

Nanotechnology is one of the most exciting recent advances. Nanomaterials have improved industrial design and marketability of numerous products. Titanium oxide nanoproducts, for example, are used in sunscreens to block ultraviolet rays, but at the same time allow for their smooth application to the skin. Nanotechnology is used in bio-imaging, diagnosis, drug delivery, and therapeutics amongst many other purposes. Carbon nanotubes are exceptionally strong and hard, and have been used in atomic microscopes, hockey sticks, and wind turbines. However, there is very little known about the long-term effect of using or making these products. The factors that give them such remarkable physical properties may possibly also make them exceptionally toxic for humans. The needle-like features of carbon nanotubes may be similar to those of asbestos fibres, leading to concerns about their potential carcinogenic effects. No one knows at present how serious the potential risk is or whether it exists at all—which has given rise to a new field of study, 'nanotoxicology'—but one thing that we can be sure about is that if the problem turns out to be really serious, few companies marketing these products will be around or have the financial resources to compensate customers when the ill-effects are revealed.

In each case, the gains to successful commercial exploitation accrue to shareholders and the losses are borne by other parties, in particular ultimately populations at large and taxpayers. The problem is compounded by limitations on recovery for 'pure economic loss' sustained as a consequence of personal injury. If, for example, the founder of a business is forced to stop work as a result of ill-health caused by use of a mobile phone or nanotechnology products, then, even if causation can be established, the other owners of the business may not be able to claim compensation from the producers of the phones or nanotechnologies for their consequential loss of income. The limitation stems from the fact that pure economic loss beyond the injury to person or property would expose corporations to opening a 'floodgate' of claims against which it would be impossible for them to protect or insure themselves.[6] Judge Benjamin N. Cardozo, for example, describes it as a 'liability in an indeterminate amount, for an indeterminate time, to an indeterminate class'.[7] According to the 'neighbour principle', the relation between the relevant parties has to be sufficiently proximate and the potential for harm to the claimant reasonably foreseeable for the defendant to be liable for losses sustained by the claimant.[8] Two cases involving negligence on the part of auditors suggest that proximity may not extend as far as future as against current investors or creditors as against shareholders, neither party being able to recover losses from the auditors.[9] While economists and governments may wish to see the full effect of the actions of corporations reflected in compensation for all consequential damages, judges feel unable to impose costs for losses that are too remote from their original failures.

Knowing this to be the case it is perfectly rational for companies to pursue high-risk strategies since, as in the case of banks, shareholders will not bear the full costs of failure. Furthermore, it is equally rational for companies anticipating potential problems in the future to distribute as much as they can to their current shareholders so that there is as little as possible left in the business to pay out in compensation to the victims of the devastation that they have caused. In seeking to solve the agency problem between shareholders and managers, regulation that strengthens corporate governance and the relation between the two parties potentially exacerbates the conflict with other stakeholders.

Part I: How the Corporation is Failing Us

There are two senses in which the remarkable institution of the corporation is failing us. The first is the most obvious. While it has delivered extraordinary benefits in the form of products, services, technical advances, and prosperity to our lives, homes, and families, it has also been the source of unmitigated disasters—environmentally, commercially, and socially. While the scale of both will increase in the future, there is a still more significant sense in which the corporation is failing us.

The driving motive behind the corporation is the creation of shareholder value. It is the purpose of the corporation, its moral imperative, and its directors' primary obligation. However, in pursuing it, the corporation places the large stakes that other parties invest in the corporation at risk. In some cases, stakeholders seek to protect themselves through contracts, but there is a limit to the extent to which these are effective and in many other cases stakeholders do not even enjoy that degree of protection.

We might expect that time and the reputational damage which exposure of wrongdoing inflicts would encourage corporations to take appropriate account of the interests of stakeholders. Unfortunately this is not the case and reputations merely serve to reinforce the significance of shareholder interests, companies seeking to avoid only those activities that threaten to damage shareholder value and being willing to pursue those that do not. Indeed, future generations, including future investors, are merely other stakeholders who can be exploited to the benefit of current investors. The costs of this do not just come at the expense of the directly affected parties, but the allocation of resources in an economy which become skewed towards activities that transfer future benefits to the present.

Since neither incentives nor reputations can be relied on to align the interests of companies with those of society more generally, we turn to third parties, namely governments and regulators, to do this for us. However, all this does is to promote the development of another profitable industry, namely regulatory avoidance, and mechanisms for minimizing the impact of regulation on the pursuit of private gains. Indeed, regulation can create the very problems which it seeks to avoid by driving corporations in common, inappropriate directions that then have unintended side effects, such as the intensification of risks of systemic failures and greater burdens on the taxpayer.

The most significant source of failure is therefore that we have created a system of shareholder value driven companies whose detrimental effects regulation is supposed to but fails to correct, and in response we seek greater regulation as the only instrument that we believe can address the problem. We are therefore entering a cycle of the pursuit of ever-narrower shareholder interests moderated by steadily more intrusive but ineffective regulation. It is unsustainable and we need to break away from it, but, before we consider how to do this, I first need to explain why it is happening and, in particular, why it is happening now.

II

WHY IT IS HAPPENING

Chapter 5: Evolving Enterprises

The consequences of dispersion of ownership for the governance of corporations; why it has happened—three examples of the role of stock markets and takeovers in the growth of corporations and dispersion of their ownership; the evolution of ownership of Continental European corporations and the continuing presence of substantial family ownership there; the emergence of anonymous shareholders in the US and UK

Chapter 6: Bought and Closed

Why the market for corporate control has emerged; who benefits from it and its contribution to shareholder value; the association of the market for corporate control with changes in corporate strategy rather than the disciplining of bad management; shareholder activism as a more direct means of correcting poor performance; impediments to hostile takeovers and the widespread prevalence of controlling share-holders; the reasons for and advantages of diversity of corporate form; the adverse consequences of hostile takeovers for managerial commit-ment; and why some companies and countries discourage hostile takeovers

Chapter 7: Capital and Commitment

The significance of commitment for encouraging the participation of stakeholders; the relevance of capital to commitment; why local banking is important for the provision of corporate commitment, and why systemic concerns undermined local banking in the UK; the parallels of relationship banking with venture capital; the need to balance commitment and control, and why shareholder control can undermine the commitment of companies to stakeholders; differences in the degree of commitment of corporate systems in the UK and US from each other and from those in other countries

Chapter 5
Evolving Enterprises

I strut around my stately life
Hand in hand with lover and wife.
I even own a share or two
In a family firm my father grew.

Of course I have not the slightest view
On what this beast is supposed to do.
Nor have I any reason to care
Since in absentia I sit in a Chair,
Of a Board that yesterday I chose to hire
And tomorrow I've decided that I will fire.

Entrebrawneurial Britain. The Author

Man of Property No More

'In the time to come this volume may be proclaimed as the most important work bearing on American statecraft . . . and will mark a sharp turning point in fundamental, deep-thrusting thinking about the American State and American civilization.'[1] Few books receive reviews like that in the *New York Herald Tribune* and still fewer that are academic research monographs. But so a book that was destined to establish a new field of scholarship was greeted on its publication in 1932. 'This book will perhaps rank with Adam Smith's Wealth of Nations as the first detailed description in admirably clear terms of the existence of a new economic epoch', is how one review described it.[2]

These remarkable accolades were for a book entitled *The Modern Corporation and Private Property*, and its authors were Adolf Berle and Gardiner Means. The book created not only a new field, but also a new approach to research—an early form of interdisciplinary research between a lawyer, Berle, and an economist, Means. The impact of the book in part derived from its appearance in the depth of the 1930s depression, and a willingness on the part of many people to accept the criticisms of the corporation that were detailed in the book.

In fact the book nearly never saw the light of day because one of its early readers was not so receptive to it. It was originally published by an obscure Chicago publisher, owned by the Corporation Trust Company. An official of General Motors read the book and, offended by it, communicated his irritation to the Corporation Trust Company. Fearing the loss of General Motors' custom, the Company ordered the withdrawal of the book. Fortunately, the publishers offered the plates of the book to Macmillans, who took it over and promoted it far more actively than the original publishers could have done. 'Ironically, General Motors, whose harassment of Ralph Nader helped to catapult the corporate critic to national fame, also was responsible for launching Berle and Means's book. Like Nader, Berle and Means bear the imprint "Made in Detroit".'[3]

What created this stir was the observation that the modern corporation, as it was emerging in the US at the time of the depression, was not at all as people perceived it. The traditional view was of the local 'mom and pop' business which was a small-scale venture directly run by its owners. What Berle and Means documented as the state of the corporation in the US in the 1930s could hardly have been more different:

> The typical business unit of the 19th century was owned by individuals or small groups; was managed by them or their appointees; and was, in the main, limited in size by the personal wealth of the individuals in control. These units have been supplanted in ever greater measure by great aggregations in which tens and even hundreds of thousands of workers, and property worth hundreds of millions of dollars, belonging to tens and even hundreds of thousands of individuals, are combined through the corporate mechanism into a single producing organization under unified control and management.[4]

This meant that there was a fundamental disconnect between Adam Smith's classical economics description of the firm and the actual state of affairs in the US at the time:

> When Adam Smith talked of 'enterprise' he had in mind as the typical unit the small individual business in which the owner, perhaps with the aid of a few apprentices or workers, laboured to produce goods for market or to carry on commerce. Very emphatically he repudiated the stock corporation as a business mechanism, holding that dispersed ownership made efficient operation impossible [...] Yet when we speak of business enterprise today, we must have in mind primarily these very units which seemed to Adam Smith not to fit into the principles [...] he was laying down for the conduct of economic activity.[5]

The analysis of the book served two purposes. The first was to document the increasing concentration of wealth and power in the US in the largest 200 corporations, which by 1930 owned around one-half of all corporate wealth in the US.[6] The second was to show that those corporations were owned by a growing band of small individual investors. Popular capitalism had arrived in the US in the form of mass production owned by the massed ranks of the American population.

At first blush this might sound like a good thing. The moms and pops might no longer own the bulk of US business, but at least they participated in it and were rewarded by it through the small shareholdings that they owned in the newly emerging giant enterprises. But Berle and Means were less enamoured with this development, and indeed were deeply concerned about it. What they documented was that over time, the ownership of large corporations had become dispersed amongst an ever-larger number of investors, each with a steadily diminishing share of the corporation. This had continued to a point at which no one investor held a sufficiently large share of a corporation to have much interest in monitoring its performance or exercising control over how it was run. As a consequence, what had emerged were modern day acephali—headless monsters—in which the directors and officers of the corporation were accountable to no one.[7]

Berle and Means concluded two things: first, that the directors of a company had no right to control property that they did not own and, second, that share ownership was not really property at all because the owners had no control over their property. This 'separation of ownership and control' as it came to be known gave rise to serious economic inefficiency. It meant that the bulk of US corporate wealth was controlled by people with little interest in the welfare of their owners.

The resolution which Berle and Means proposed for this problem was for shareholders to re-engage with their property and to take an active role in its oversight and management. They were therefore early proponents of what is now widely advocated as shareholder activism or the engagement of shareholders in corporate governance—active oversight of their corporate investments, and an interest and involvement in how they are managed.[8] It is a theme that is now some eighty years later reverberating around the corridors of power in London and Washington as governments watch the consequences of Berle and Means' observations for the destruction of wealth in the financial crisis. So what Berle and Means recorded happening in the US has been extremely influential, but it was neither unique nor path-breaking. The move to dispersed ownership had in fact started several decades earlier on the other side of the Atlantic—in Britain. Some British corporate history is important in understanding the factors promoting dispersed ownership and the consequences of it.[9]

British Exceptionalism

There are not many engineering companies ranked amongst the largest 100 corporations in the UK and even fewer that are 250 years old. GKN is one of them, but the GKN of today is an almost unrecognizable descendant of the iron foundry at Dowlais near Merthyr Tydfil in South Wales that John Guest helped to establish when he became works manager in 1767. When his grandson became the company's sole owner in 1851, the Dowlais Iron Company was the largest iron works in the world, operating 18 blast furnaces and employing more than 7,300 people. The business was the first licensee of the Bessemer process, constructing the world's most powerful rolling mill in 1857, and producing its first Bessemer steel in 1865. As the later Guest, Keen and Nettlefolds, the company supplied the tracks of Brunel's Great Western Railway, the railways of America, Europe, and Russia, and the British Empire's First World War munitions effort, thus becoming one of the largest iron then steel producers in the world, with production firmly rooted in Britain. Today GKN is a major producer of aero-structures and powder metallurgy, sourcing production from all round the world. In between it moved into and out of car and helicopter component production.

This remarkable metamorphosis was primarily achieved through acquisitions. Guest, Keen, and Nettlefolds Limited was itself the product of mergers. Arthur Keen established the Patent Nut and Bolt Company in 1856 in Smethwick, England. In July 1900 Guest, Keen, and Company Limited was incorporated in Birmingham with the purpose of taking over the Dowlais Iron Company and the Patent Nut and Bolt Co., Ltd. In 1902 the company acquired Nettlefold and Company, one of the world's leading manufacturers of screws and fasteners set up in Smethwick in 1854, and so Guest, Keen, and Nettlefolds Limited was born and Mr Edward Nettlefold joined the board.

The 1920s were a crucial decade in the evolution of GKN. First, the company acquired John Lysaght Limited of Bristol in one of the largest tender offers of the decade. It then undertook two other major tender offers in November 1923, acquiring D. Davis and Sons and Consolidated Cambrian of Cardiff. At this stage, it was one of the largest manufacturing businesses in the world, involved in every stage of manufacturing from coal and ore extraction to iron and steel making, and finally to finished products including the nuts, bolts, screws, and fasteners for which it was renowned during this period. In 1930 it bought the Swedish fastener company Aug.Stenman, acquired Exors of James Mills, one of the world's largest makers of bright steel bars, and closed Dowlais, bringing an end to 170 years of iron and steel making at the works. In 1934 it purchased Henry Williams India, an Indian-based, British-owned maker of steel rails.

This demonstrates the remarkable power of takeovers in consolidating and redirecting corporate activities from declining to expanding sectors and from high-cost domestic to low-cost overseas producers. It allows corporate entities to enjoy effortlessly what their human equivalents relentlessly strive for—eternity and transmutation. Over a period of a century, through acquisitions Guest, Keen, and Nettlefolds was created, renamed, and remodelled as an almost unrecognizable image of its former self. And what allowed GKN to do this is a particularly important feature of the British corporate landscape—its large and active stock market.

Guest, Keen, and Nettlefolds primarily financed its acquisitions by issuing shares. It did this either directly in exchange for the shares of the companies it was purchasing or indirectly through raising cash to purchase the shares of the firms it was acquiring. For example, when Guest, Keen, and Company Limited was incorporated in 1900, the shareholders of the two companies received 250,000 ordinary shares, and 400,000 ordinary shares were issued via public subscription.

The effect of the share issues for acquisitions was to disperse shareholdings rapidly across a large number of investors. Before 1900 both Dowlais Iron Company and the Patent Nut and Bolt Company were 100 per cent owned by directors and their families. As a consequence of the mergers at the beginning of the 20th century, the number of ordinary shareholders rose to 546. By 1920 there were 1,000 shareholders, but it was the effect of the acquisitions at the beginning of the 1920s that was most significant, increasing the number of shareholders to 20,000 by 1924.

This is illustrative of a general point: the source of dispersed ownership in the UK is acquisitions and its active stock market, which allowed corporations to issue shares to finance those acquisitions. In fact, to be accurate it was stock markets rather than one stock market that allowed them to do this because unlike now, in the first half of the 20th century Britain was populated by stock markets in virtually every major town. There were eighteen provincial stock exchanges, which collectively were as large as the London Stock Exchange. By the middle of the 1880s, Sheffield, along with Oldham, was one of the two most important centres of joint-stock companies in the country.

Provincial stock markets played an important role in promoting new issues. Writing in 1921, one author noted that 'local knowledge on the part of the investor both of the business reputation of the vendor and the prospects of his undertaking would do a good deal to eliminate dishonest promotion and ensure that securities were sold at fair prices fairly near their investment values'.[10] Concentrating ownership among local investors was recognized as a method of reducing information problems as well as fraud. As one stockbroker said, 'the securities are rarely sold by means of a prospectus and are not underwritten, they are placed by private negotiation among local people who understand the [cotton] trade'.[11] As a result, securities were traded in the city in which most investors resided. For example, shareholders in Manchester were anxious that the shares of Arthur Keen's Patent Nut and Bolt Co. of Birmingham should be listed in Manchester where most of the shareholders lived. The reason was that proximity between brokers and directors was thought to create better-informed markets. In 1920 shares in Guest, Keen, and Nettlefolds were quoted in Birmingham, Bristol, Cardiff, Edinburgh, Glasgow, Liverpool, Manchester, and Sheffield.

GKN formally listed on the London Stock Exchange in June 1946. By then the directors owned a negligible stake and the largest shareholder of the period was the Royal Bank of Scotland, with 2.4 per cent of issued ordinary shares. In the second half of the century, Prudential Assurance, Norwich Union Life Insurance, Schroder Investment Management, and Scottish Widows Investment Management among others alternated as the largest shareholders, with stakes varying from 3 per cent to 5 per cent of issued equity capital.

The picture that emerges from GKN is of a corporation whose shares were traded on local provincial exchanges, expanded rapidly through acquisitions, broadened its shareholder base both numerically and geographically in the process, and, by the beginning of the second half of the 20th century, was widely held primarily by institutional shareholders. Its experience was replicated in another company that will shortly feature prominently in this book.

In 1794 Richard Cadbury, a prominent Quaker, moved from the West Country in Britain to Birmingham. Thirty years later, his son John opened a shop at 93 Bull Street, then a fashionable part of Birmingham, to sell tea, coffee, hops, mustard, and a new sideline—cocoa and drinking chocolate, which John prepared himself using a mortar and a pestle. In 1847 John Cadbury took his brother Benjamin into partnership, changing the name of the business to Cadbury Brothers of Birmingham, and renting a new factory in Bridge Street in the centre of Birmingham. Thanks to a reduction in tax on imported cocoa beans, the business expanded and received the first of a series of Royal Warrants of appointment by Queen Victoria.

The Cadbury Brothers moved their manufacturing operations to Bournville, UK, and established the Bournville factory and village, which became an important addition to the UK industrial landscape. By the time that Cadbury Brothers was incorporated as a limited company in June 1899, the Bournville factory had 2,600 employees. At that stage, Richard and George Cadbury, the sons of the late John Cadbury, owned 100 per cent of the ordinary shares.

The year 1919 was crucial in the company history when Cadbury Brothers merged with JS Fry & Sons of Bristol, whose product range complemented Cadbury's chocolates. After the merger, the new company was registered as British Cocoa & Chocolate. The two families shared both board seats and company ownership, with the Frys holding four seats on the board as well as the chairmanship and 45 per cent of ordinary shares, and the Cadburys holding the rest (six seats on the board, and 55 per cent of ordinary shares).

As the company's operations expanded, and factories opened around the world, the Fry family board representation declined, while Cadbury's increased. At the end of the 1960s, the Cadbury family held the chairmanship and seven of the thirteen seats of the board of directors, while only one Fry remained on the board. The Cadbury family held slightly more than 50 per cent of the ordinary shares, while the Fry family held just over 10 per cent. The rest was dispersed among more than 200 ordinary shareholders. That was the position when in 1969 there was a dramatic development in the life of Cadbury, which had its origins some 200 years earlier.

In 1783, 43-year-old German-born Jean Jacob Schweppe invented an efficient system for the manufacture of mineral water, and in 1790 he entered a partnership to expand the business and establish a factory in London. Around 1800 he changed his and the business name to Schweppes, while continuing to expand on a national scale. By 1831, J. Schweppes & Co. became the Supplier of Soda Water to the Royal Household. In 1834 John Kemp-Welch and William Evill bought J. Schweppes & Co., and extended the product range to include flavoured soda drinks such as lemonade. The following year the firm was awarded the Royal warrant by Queen Victoria, and in 1851 it won the contract to supply 'temperance' beverages at the Great Exhibition in the UK. By 1870 the firm's product range included Tonic Water and Ginger Ale. The former rapidly became popular with the British in India, as it contained quinine, which was used as a preventive measure against malaria. In 1877 the firm opened its first factory in Sydney, Australia, and seven years later a factory in Brooklyn, New York.

The sudden death of John Kemp-Welch in 1885 precipitated the formation of Schweppes as a limited company in the following year. At this stage, the company was 100 per cent owned by the directors until its public flotation in London on 6 March 1897. After flotation, the directors and their families held collectively 27 per cent of the 300,000 ordinary shares. The new company, Schweppes plc, was incorporated to acquire the business of J. Schweppe and Co. established in 1783.

The public flotation was extremely successful and probably over-subscribed. At the end of 1897, there were more than 1,650 ordinary shareholders and 750 preference shareholders. In 1919 the Kemp-Welch family relinquished the chairmanship (although two members remained on the board until the early 1940s), and under the new chairman, Sir Ivor Phillips, the company started a period of expansion. Overseas development was conducted through a newly formed fully owned subsidiary, Schweppes (Colonial and Foreign) Ltd. The strategy was to manufacture locally in the overseas countries, in order to reduce the group's reliance on exports. At the end of Sir Ivor Phillips' chairmanship in 1940, the company had more than 2,700 ordinary shareholders, and it was formally listed on the London Stock Exchange in December 1942. During the 1950s there were several major acquisitions paid in shares: L. Rose and Co. acquired in 1957 with 1,544,400 new ordinary shares, and Chivers & Sons, W.P. Hartley, and W. Moorhouse, all acquired in 1959 with together 4,000,000 new ordinary shares. In 1969 Schweppes plc merged with the Cadbury Group to form Cadbury–Schweppes.

The picture that emerges from all of these cases is of companies growing rapidly through acquisitions which allowed them to expand overseas and enter new lines of business. The acquisitions were financed through share issues that diluted the original family ownership of the firms amongst a large number of predominantly institutional investors so that, by the middle of the 20th century, formerly family owned firms were family no more. Acquisitions therefore contributed significantly to the emergence of dispersed ownership in the UK.

This is the story of the UK, but it is not what happened elsewhere in Europe. On the Continent, there was little or no progression to dispersed ownership. Contrasting the history of the UK with Continental Europe provides some insights into one of the most important features of the corporation today—the marked differences in the nature of its ownership across countries and its significance for the conflicts between shareholders and managers, and shareholders and other stakeholders.

Happy Family Firms

In 1863 Werner Siemens wrote to his brother, Carl, of his long-standing ambition to

> build up an enterprise which will last, which may perhaps one day under the leadership of our boys become an enterprise of world renown like that of the Rothschilds and make our name known and respected in many lands [...] For this great plan the individual, if he regards the plan as good, should be prepared to make sacrifices.[12]

Siemens AG would appear 150 years later, with some notable blemishes en route, to have fulfilled Werner Siemens's ambitions.[13]

The desire to perpetuate our names is a powerful one. We might love our daughters, but in many societies it is the sons that perpetuate names. There is one society in which the role of the male is particularly important and there is one family in which that role has had a particularly powerful effect. The will of the founding father of another firm could scarcely have been clearer:

> I hereby decree and therefore wish that my daughters and sons-in-law and their heirs have no share in the capital of the firm [...] Rather, the said firm shall exclusively belong to and be owned by my sons.[14]

His last commandment to one of his sons was his most powerful: 'keep your brothers together and you will become the richest people in Germany'. The biblical overtones were no coincidence, but their effect was more enduring than it had been for many of his forefathers.

Never has a father's last testament been carried out more conscientiously and more profitably [...] Since his death, any proposal, no matter where it comes from, is the object of collective discussion; each operation, even it is of minor importance, is carried out according to an agreed plan and with their combined efforts.[15]

The father was Mayer Amschel Rothschild, and his offspring were his ten surviving Rothschilds—five of whom were male.

Rothschild was quite justified in emphasizing the importance of family cohesion because across the Channel in England his wise words were not being heeded with sufficient care. British firms have been characterized as being founded by fanatical fathers and inherited by squabbling siblings who 'worked at play and played at work'.[16] One manifestation of this is the marked difference in the life cycle of family firms between Britain and the Continent. Whereas, as we have just seen, in Britain the ownership of families was rapidly diluted by share issuance as they grew through acquisitions, on the Continent families generally retained control of their firms.

The typical pattern of a UK family firm is that it does well to stagger through to the second let alone the third generation of family members. In contrast, in France, in Germany, and in particular Italy, family ownership persists from generation to generation. A family firm that was founded one hundred years ago and still survives today will typically remain family owned in France, Germany, and Italy, but not in the UK.[17] Many large family firms are quoted on Continental European stock markets while retaining a dominant family shareholder. Since Continental European firms are generally as large as their UK counterparts, this suggests that they have grown through means other than acquisitions financed from issuing shares. I will return to explain how this happened in Chapter 7.

For the moment, it is important to appreciate that as a consequence of this different evolutionary path, the ownership of corporations in the UK bears little resemblance to the rest of Europe. In 50 per cent of Austrian, Belgian, German, and Italian corporations, a single investor or group of investors controls more than 50 per cent of the voting shares in corporations. In 50 per cent of Dutch, Spanish, and Swedish corporations, a single shareholder controls over 30 per cent of the voting shares. In the UK, they control less than 10 per cent of votes.[18]

The stock markets of the UK have therefore carved out a pattern of ownership of corporations that is very different from elsewhere in Europe. Indeed the UK and US models are both very different from most parts of the world: in Asia, Europe, and South America, families and holding groups dominate the corporate landscape. The Anglo-American dispersed ownership pattern is the exception rather than the rule. Long, persistent holdings, frequently in the hands of families, dominate on the Continent to today. In the UK and the US they died out rapidly, giving rise to the phenomenon of the dispersed ownership corporation to which Berle and Means referred.

For Berle and Means the main consequence of this development has been the separation of ownership and control. Control has been transferred out of the hands of owners, the holders of the corporate property, into the hands of the executives and managers running the corporations. It has created the 'agency problem' to which so much attention has been given by policymakers over the last few decades, namely corporations run by executives for shareholders, none of whom have sufficiently large holdings to encourage them to devote effort to overseeing the running of their corporations. As a consequence by default, executives are given a free licence to operate as they see fit, frequently in their own interests rather than those of their shareholders. Many of the economic failings of the UK and US over the last few decades are put down to this deficiency of corporate governance—but quite incorrectly.

The problems of the world which have emerged over the last few decades have not been those of aligning managerial with shareholder interests, but exactly the opposite—making shareholders responsible for the corporations in which they invest. In fact, improving the alignment of executives with shareholders without shareholder responsibility has made matters worse because it has exacerbated the fundamental defect of aligning their interests with other stakeholders. What has brought this problem to a head is that as share ownership has become ever more dispersed for the reasons described in this chapter, owners have had progressively less responsibility for the corporations in which they invest.

As the one and only shareholder in Colin Mayer Ltd. (Limited), I am directly associated with its activities, and my personal reputation and future livelihood as well as my financial capital are at stake. If, in line with the world's balance sheet described in Chapter 2, the company's balance sheet has $300,000 of assets, of which $150,000 is equity and $150,000 is debt (bank finance and bonds) (i.e. one billionth of the world's balance sheet) then the investment described there, which doubled or destroyed existing assets, only looks attractive to me as the owner of Colin Mayer Ltd. if the cost to my reputation or future livelihood of the investment failing is less than $150,000 (in which case I stand to lose less than a total of $300,000 including my original invested capital, whereas I stand to gain

$300,000 with equal probability). Otherwise, as chairman of the board I will recommend its rejection.

In contrast, once the company has grown through issuing equity to become colinmayer plc (Public Limited Company) with 10,000 similar shareholders of whom I am just one, then no one will any longer be able to attribute its failure to me and I will be one of the other 9,999 recommending its acceptance at a shareholder meeting called to approve it. Furthermore, since I have invested the money that I have earned from selling shares in Colin Mayer Ltd. in buying one share in each of the 9,999 companies, I know that in total the investments will yield me overall a profit of $75,000 almost with certainty (assuming that the likelihood of the investment succeeding in one company is unrelated to the likelihood of its success in another). Dispersion of ownership has therefore rendered me irresponsible as well as indifferent to risk.

So in moving from a world with one giant company worth $300 trillion to many millions of firms with a small number of family owners, we began to solve a problem of irresponsible management by placing the reputation and livelihood of many millions of family owners at stake alongside their financial capital. But then, as we progressed further down the corporate evolutionary timeline to dispersed ownership, the irresponsibility reappeared with a vengeance, and worse than before, because not only could those involved hide behind a veil of anonymity, but now they could enjoy the benefits of portfolio diversification (holding a large number of shares whose earnings are not well correlated with each other).

The problem that Berle and Means documented of providing adequate incentives for dispersed shareholders to engage in good governance was one that the writer Tom Stoppard described as 'responsibility without power, the prerogative of the eunuch throughout the ages'. As owners, shareholders had responsibility for the consequences of the actions of their firms; but as increasingly dispersed owners, they had diminishing power with which to influence those actions and ensure that they were undertaken responsibly.

In response, the market developed a solution that at first sight provides a simple and effective way of re-establishing the authority of shareholders. It is a development that has shifted the balance of problems away from the Berle and Means one of responsibility without power to exactly the opposite—what a former British Prime Minister, Stanley Baldwin, described as 'power without responsibility, the prerogative of the harlot throughout the ages'. That phenomenon is hostile takeovers and the market for corporate control, and the country which best exemplifies it is the one where the hostile takeover market is most firmly established—the UK.

Chapter 6
Bought and Closed

An investor asks God how much he values a million dollars at. God replies, 'A cent'. He then asks how long does he regard a millennium as being and God says, 'A second'. The investor says, 'Could I please have a cent?' God says, 'Certainly – in a second'.

Chocolate Money

For Roger Carr, the Bank Holiday weekend of the summer of 2009 was a momentous turning point in his life. It started with what appeared to be an innocuous message on his mobile phone. It was from Irene Rosenfeld, the chairperson and CEO of Kraft, the US confectionary, food, and beverage company, who had just arrived in London from the US. She said that she would like to have a meeting with Carr. There was no agenda, but, unbeknown to Carr, Rosenfeld had come on a mission with a very specific agenda. Her mission was to acquire the British confectionary company, Cadbury, of which Roger Carr was chairperson.

Rosenfeld informed Carr that Kraft was willing to pay 745p for each of Cadbury's shares, 30 per cent above the price of its shares at the time. As far as Roger Carr was concerned the offer was unacceptable—'derisory' is the conventional term used by target management to capture their assertion that what was on offer seriously undervalued the partner they were courting. He had no hesitation in rebuffing the offer with the support of his board and advisors.

Although Kraft thought otherwise, as far as Carr was concerned, Kraft's approach appeared to be aggressive from the very first meeting. Failing to secure the backing of Cadbury's management, Kraft put out an offer letter directly to Cadbury's shareholders—a 'bear hug' as it is evocatively termed—in the hope that they would exert pressure on the management to accept. The normal war of words and substantial press coverage that surround a hostile bid ensued. Hopes of a counter bid from another firm ebbed and flowed and the share price gradually moved up well above the offer price to 800p per share, then 820p, and finally settled around 840p.

But the fate of the company was in reality determined by one thing. Here is Roger Carr's own account of what happened:

> Of course during a bid period, the loyalty of long term investors is severely tested as an increased share price provides an opportunity to sell some of their holding for short term profit as a precautionary move against the bid failing. This is called top slicing [...] Over the full 19 week period, some 26% of Cadbury was sold by long-term shareholders. Among the top 10 sellers, nine were North American shareholders and the other was European. Seven of the next ten sellers were also non-UK institutions. The long fund sales provided the opportunity for hedge fund purchases. The hedge funds were buying only for a short term

profit—so the greater the hedge fund holding the greater the likelihood of a transaction occurring to achieve the short term profit they were seeking. In other words, if they could buy enough shares, the deal would become a self fulfilling prophecy.

Carr continued:

It was the interests of this ownership profile that the Board was representing at the time of agreeing the 850p offer. Most of the short-term players acquired their stakes at share prices below 800p and would have taken a 20–30p profit for holding an economic interest in Cadbury for just a few weeks. Just to put that in context, a 30p gain on an 800p share price—in just six weeks— represents an annualised gain of some 33%,—a good return by any standards. Direct contact with shareholders throughout the offer period revealed that another 20% or so of the register would have accepted an offer in the range of 800–830p. After weeks of open warfare, Irene Rosenfeld, the Chairman and CEO of Kraft telephoned me on a Sunday evening—Day 44—to request a meeting—Chairman to Chairman—to offer improved terms. The strength of the defence, the support of the media and the comments of shareholders had delivered a message to the Kraft Board that the company was not to be stolen. They had decided to increase their bid. She opened the meeting with an offer of 830p. At that moment, I, my Board and advisors knew the battle for independence was lost. In the pursuit of shareholder value, the task became clear—however unpalatable—it was to negotiate for the best price possible for shareholders. Fighting to the end— however glorious—would deny shareholders their best price—so fiduciary duty had to overcome emotional instinct. In the event, the recommended offer at 850p meant that Kraft paid a 50% or £4bn premium to the undisturbed value of Cadbury on

4 September, and an additional $425m versus a revised Kraft offer that would have seen more than 50% acceptance.

In the final analysis, it was the shift in the register that lost the battle for Cadbury—the owners were progressively not long term stewards of the business but financially motivated investors—judged solely on their own quarterly financial performance. At the end of the day, there were simply not enough shareholders prepared to take a long term view of Cadbury and prepared to forgo short term gain for longer term prosperity. The short-term players that obtained their pivotal position in determining the outcome had reached that position by accumulating shares from long funds hedging their bets should the bid fail and the share price fall back for a period of time. At the end of the day, individuals controlling shares which they had owned for only a few days or weeks determined the destiny of a company that had been built over almost 200 years.[1]

There are many remarkable features of this account of one of the most important acquisitions of the decade. The first is the nature of the shareholders. The shareholder value view of the corporation sees the role of management as representing the interests of shareholders. But who are the shareholders? They start off being institutional, largely overseas, shareholders. However, they sell out in droves to hedge funds. While the institutional shareholders may or may not have an interest in the longer-term performance of Cadbury, the hedge funds certainly do not. In fact they have little interest in the underlying value of the corporation. All that they are interested in is the likelihood of the bid succeeding, because if the bid succeeds, then the share price of Cadbury will go up and if it fails, it will go down. So they are speculating on the prospects of the bid going through. They can equally well profit from the bid failing as well as succeeding by 'shorting' Cadbury shares.[2] Furthermore, as Carr notes, by their very actions they are also affecting the likelihood of the bid succeeding because they have no interest in holding shares in Cadbury for any longer than they have to. They want to sell their shares to the acquirer as soon as possible.

The second interesting feature of the bid is what Roger Carr saw as being his role. As described in the previous chapter, Cadbury is one of the oldest, most respected and famous companies begun by Quaker families during the 19th century. The firm was most distinctive in promoting the ethical values of enlightened entrepreneurs by building the town of Bournville for its employees. The town became the first factory in Britain to have its own resident doctor and dentist, and it prided itself on the amount of open space it incorporated for the recreation of workers. But the most significant innovation was the product itself. In the 1850s, chocolate was a luxury commodity. One of the reasons why cocoa and chocolate appealed to Quakers was that it offered a substitute for the evil ale which dominated British breakfast beverages until it was replaced by a nice cup of hot chocolate.

But Roger Carr did not regard his primary role as being the protection of this British establishment, the temperance society, the British manufacture of the product, or the employees of the company. It is not that he is an unsympathetic or callous individual; on the contrary he is an exceptionally thoughtful and respected businessman. It was that his role was first and foremost to represent the interests of his shareholders. If he had not done so then he would not have been fulfilling his fiduciary responsibilities. That meant seeking to maximize the terms of the offer that he could extract from Irene Rosenfeld and Kraft. That task he performed meticulously with extreme skill, determination, and success, extracting a further £1 per share approximately over the initial offer from Kraft.

However, the emphasis on shareholder value leaves other stakeholders exposed. In announcing the bid, Kraft stated, 'Our [i.e. Kraft's] current plans contemplate that the UK would be a net beneficiary in terms of jobs. For example, we believe we would be in a position to continue to operate the Somerdale facility, which is currently planned to be closed, and to invest in Bournville, thereby preserving UK manufacturing jobs.' Similar statements were made at various stages during the bid process. But one week after the bid was agreed, Kraft announced that it had reluctantly decided that it would be necessary to close the Somerdale plant after all and transfer its activities to Poland to the detriment of the British employees. Kraft was censured by the UK Takeover Panel for failing to satisfy expected standards of disclosure during a UK takeover bid. A report by a House of Commons Select Committee was even more damning:

> We believe that Kraft acted both irresponsibly and unwisely in making its original statement that it believed that it could keep Somerdale open. A company of Kraft's size and experience ought simply to have acted with better judgement. By making its announcement and the subsequent reversal Kraft has left itself open to the charge that either it was incompetent in its approach to the Somerdale factory or that it used a 'cynical ploy' to cast a positive light on Kraft during its takeover of Cadbury. We can neither prove nor discount either conclusion [...] What is clear is that Kraft's actions in respect of Somerdale has undoubtedly damaged its reputation in the United Kingdom and has soured its relationship with Cadbury employees. It will now have to invest significant time and effort into restoring both.[3]

Open for Auction

Hostile takeovers arrived in the UK in the first half of the 1950s. In the spring of 1953, Charles Clore, a self-made millionaire from business and property ventures, launched a bid for J. Sears & Co., the parent company of a shoe shop chain-store, Freeman, Hardy, and Willis. Instead of following the conventional approach of negotiating with target management, Clore mailed offer documents direct to Sears' shareholders over the heads of management.

> The Sears directors, who were taken entirely unawares, retaliated by announcing the tripling of the dividend. Shareholders were astonished by this sudden largesse, which was perceived as a desperate and irresponsible act on the part of the management. Faith in the incumbent board being thoroughly undermined, there was a rush to sell to Clore, who quickly acquired control of the company. 'We never thought anything like this would happen to us', were the Parthian words of the outgoing Sears chairman.[4]

In the autumn of 1953, Land Securities Investment Trust launched a similar 'hostile' bid for the Savoy Hotel Co., owners of the Savoy, Claridge's, and Simpson's in the Strand in London. So, hostile takeovers or the market for corporate control, as it is euphemistically termed, had come to Britain.

It is not entirely clear why the hostile takeover market emerged at this juncture in Britain. It might have had something to do with the rise of institutional in place of individual share ownership at around that time. Alternatively, the tighter financial disclosures required of company accounts by the 1948 Companies Act may have provided the basis on which corporate predators could for the first time make reasonably accurate estimates of asset values and earnings, and thus launch bids without the co-operation of the target.[5] In Charles Clore's takeover of Sears, it is reported that 'Clore launched his attack on being informed by a partner in the estates agent Healey & Baker that Sears' balance sheet under-estimated the real estate value of the corporation's 900 high street stores by £10 million'.[6]

The response of the corporate sector was to seek protection against the emerging takeover market. It initially received a sympathetic ear from the government and the Bank of England, who were concerned about the adverse effect that hostile acquisitions could have on the corporate sector and the government's policy of promoting restraint in dividend payments. All levels of government were involved, including in the case of the bid for the Savoy, the Prime Minister, Winston Churchill, who was worried about the possible impact of the bid on his favourite dining club at the Savoy. But while it found this form of buccaneering capitalism distasteful, the government felt impotent to do much about it and in any event, by the time of the next merger wave at the end of the 1950s, it had come round to the view that 'Mr Clore appears to have improved the retail shoe trade of the country'.[7]

Takeovers are now big business globally—over $3 trillion in 2011.[8] More than a third of that is accounted for by the US takeover market and about the same by European takeovers. The amount of takeover activity in Asia has been rising rapidly over the past decade to around one-quarter of total activity at present. Recall that I estimated total world equity at close to $150 trillion, including private unlisted firms. So, each year around 2 per cent of the total global value of equity is involved in mergers and acquisitions in one way or another.

Takeovers essentially come in two forms. First, there are mergers, where the management of the corporations involved agree that it would be a good idea for their two corporations to get together and create a new, single enterprise. They then seek the approval of their shareholders to this arrangement. That is definitely not what happened in the Kraft takeover of Cadbury. Instead, it was of the second type, acquisitions, where one corporation makes a 'tender offer' for the shares of another, sometimes with the agreement of the target firm's management or, as in the case of Cadbury, in the face of the resolute opposition of management. Offers are made directly to shareholders to sell their shares to the acquiring firm and acquisitions can therefore succeed even when management is opposed, as happened with Cadbury.

Why do corporations engage in such large amounts of takeover activity? The answer is ostensibly to make money. Markets for companies are like markets for oranges. If purchasers are willing to pay more than sellers require, there is a deal and an exchange of a company for cash or shares. The reason that purchasers are willing to pay is that they believe that they will be able to make more out of the firm that they are acquiring than the company itself—either because they think that they can run the firm better or because there is some opportunity that combining the two firms creates that individually was not available to them.

Kraft's acquisition of Cadbury was primarily motivated by the second of these considerations. It thought that acquiring Cadbury offered the possibility of creating a global confectionery business and extending Cadbury's markets in several parts of the world, most notably developing countries and North America. In addition, it saw considerable potential for saving costs of around $625 million on production, procurement, customer services, and research and development.[9]

One and a half years later, the idea of creating a globally integrated business did not seem such a good idea, and in August 2011 Kraft announced that it would be separating its North American grocery business from its global snacks business. In response, Roger Carr was reported as applauding the move and calling 'for the new company to be called Cadbury'.[10] Irene Rosenfeld defended it, saying that nothing had changed and that they were seeking to create two companies with sizeable scale in their respective markets.

Do acquisitions in general make money? The answer is for some people unquestionably yes and for some most certainly no. You only have to look at the Cadbury deal to see one group that made a lot of money—the shareholders of the target firm. They started off being offered a bid premium of 33 per cent and ended up earning a 50 per cent bid premium. On average, target shareholders earn a return of 30 per cent in hostile bids that are rejected by the management of target firms, and 20 per cent in friendly acquisitions and mergers.[11]

A second group that clearly does well are the consultants, lawyers, and investment banks that advise on, negotiate, and fund the deals. One of the consequences of the controversy surrounding the takeover of Kraft was that the Takeover Panel required companies for the first time to disclose fees paid to advising parties. One of the first major bids to be required to disclose advisory fees was the bid by the US fluid handling product firm Colfax for the UK engineering firm Charter. The fees on the £1.5 billion bid were estimated to be £90 million.[12]

The group that in general suffer is employees. 'Cost cutting' and 'rationalization' are common euphemisms for lay-offs in

M&A terminology. Typically post-acquisition there is a significant reduction in employment. For example, one study in the UK reports that there is a 19 per cent reduction in employment in UK firms that are involved in acquisitions by firms in related businesses to their own.[13] Evidence from the US suggests that employment losses are concentrated in head offices rather than in production establishments.[14]

In between, in a somewhat nebulous position, sit the shareholders of the acquiring firm. You might justifiably think it odd that, since the purpose of acquisitions is to further the interests of shareholders, acquiring firm shareholders do not benefit substantially from acquisitions. But in general they do not. In sharp contrast to the large step up in Cadbury's share price, Kraft's actually fell by around 5 per cent in the month of September 2009. Kraft's experience is by no means unusual in this regard— for the most part, shareholders of acquiring firms earn little or nothing and in many cases suffer losses rather than gains.

What is happening is that shareholders overall are benefiting substantially from acquisitions, but the gains are all accruing to the shareholders of the target firms. Acquiring firm shareholders and their management make little or no returns because they overpay for the target to the point that in many cases, they lose out from the acquisition. They get carried away in a bidding frenzy equivalent to what you might encounter when buying a house that you are so keen not to lose to a rival purchaser, you offer to buy for more than it is really worth. The seller walks away with a pile of cash while you are left to sleep on the floor to pay for the mortgage that you cannot afford. As the Cadbury case illustrated very clearly, shareholders of target firms look to their management to extract as much as they possibly can from the acquiring shareholders and the evidence is that in general they succeed in extracting at least the full value of the acquisition.

The attraction of hostile takeovers, such as the takeover of Cadbury by Kraft, is that they are effective ways of remedying the agency problem of the separation of ownership and control and disciplining managements that do not take adequate account of their shareholder interests.

One Good Hanging

The market for corporate control 'represents the most effective check on management autonomy ever devised. And it is breathing new life in the public corporation.'[15] So wrote Alfred Rappaport, a Professor at Northwestern University, in 1990.[16] What Rappaport meant was that takeovers were not just great ways of reducing costs and exploiting new opportunities, but they had a salutary effect on all management. Faced with the possibility that at any stage, a corporate raider could appear out of the woodwork and make a takeover offer for their firm, management will seek to represent the interests of their shareholders at each and every point in time. They will not relax their guard for one moment knowing that, in that moment, a raider would spot an opportunity for launching a bid and taking over their firm. So not only do takeovers redirect resources to where they can be most profitably employed, but, like corporal or capital punishment, where one good flogging or hanging sends shivers down the spines of the population at large, they can additionally promote shareholder value at all times for fear of the consequences of deviating from it.

What is particularly remarkable about the takeover instrument is that it requires no effort or input on the part of shareholders whatsoever. They can sit back and hold onto their shares, safe in the knowledge that if their management are not pursuing their interests continuously, some aspiring executive from another firm will seek out their shares and offer them what they should really be worth. It is as if you have a secret guardian continuously watching over your investments. This guardian is called the takeover market and those apparently exorbitant fees to investment bankers might be cheap at the price for the gains that the target shareholders reap from them.

Given this strong disciplinary role that takeovers perform, there is a curious feature of the Cadbury takeover. Cadbury's performance in the period prior to the acquisition was not by any account poor. Indeed in some respects it was better than that of Kraft. In the two months prior to the acquisition, Cadbury's share price outshone Kraft's.

The Cadbury bid is not unusual in this regard. Studies of takeovers suggest that the performance of targets of acquisitions is not particularly poor in the years before a bid. For example, a study in which I was involved of forty-two hostile acquisitions in the UK found that there was clear evidence of financial failure in only sixteen of the bids and some evidence of failure in ten of the bids. In sixteen of them there was no evidence of financial failure.[17] In a larger analysis of UK takeovers, another study found that the share price performance of targets of hostile bids was close to the market average.[18]

At the same time, this second study also found that a remarkable 90 per cent of the directors of targets of successful hostile bids lost their jobs in the two years after the bids were completed. In the case of Cadbury, the three most senior directors—the chairman, the chief executive, and the finance director—left within hours of Kraft taking control. So, one of the best ways of ensuring that you lose your job as a director of a firm is to become the victim of a successful hostile bid.

What is going on? Hostile takeovers should be disciplining bad management, but they do not target particularly poorly performing firms. Nevertheless, they still result in nearly all of the directors of the target firms losing their jobs, even though the targets have not performed particularly poorly. It is as if corporal punishment that was supposed to discourage bad behaviour was being administered haphazardly across the population. It does not sound as if it is performing a very efficient disciplinary function even though in principle it could do this very effectively.

What, then, are hostile takeovers doing? The Kraft–Cadbury case and the disappearance of the boards of target firms give a hint. Even though Cadbury had not performed particularly poorly, Kraft nevertheless thought that there were opportunities for improving its performance still further than the existing management had exploited. Cadbury's performance had been reasonable, but reasonable was not good enough. There was the potential for converting average into exceptional performance. The one thing that stood in the way of achieving that was the existing board of the firm and so a bid that drove out the existing management was required. Since the target management took a different view from the acquirer, they opposed the bid and sought to keep the firm independent.

But do not shed too many tears for the displaced management of the target firms who find themselves on the street after doing a perfectly reasonable if not exceptional job for their shareholders. Because alongside the shareholders of the target firms, the other group that does exceptionally well out of takeovers is the management of the target firms. The target management's relentless efforts to increase the amounts that they extract from the acquirers are not entirely altruistic for the benefit of their shareholders. They have equity stakes and share options themselves that mean that the higher the bid, the more that they will walk away with too. Indeed, their remuneration packages are designed to ensure that their interests are aligned with those of their shareholders so that in just such an event as a takeover, they do their very best to extract the highest price. It was, for example, reported that the CEO of Cadbury walked away with a pay-off of £17 million from the bid—there are many people who might 'reluctantly agree' to forgo their right to work for that sort of sum.[19]

So, hostile takeovers are not so much about correcting poor performance or disciplining bad management as changing the strategy of middle-of-the-road performers so that they become top performers. They therefore reflect disagreements over future strategy rather than past performance. Where there is really bad management, it is subject to a different type of treatment by the market, from activist fund managers.

Get Active

In ancient Greek mythology, Hermes was the messenger from the gods to humans. In modern British companies, he is the messenger from the shareholders to company directors, generally bringing news of the impending arrival of one of his father's, Zeus', thunderbolts. Hermes is the name of the fund manager established by the British Telecom Pensions Scheme to manage its assets. The Hermes Focus Fund is one of Hermes' funds that did something unusual by the normal standards of institutional funds—it engaged in the active management of the companies in which it was invested. In fact, it went out of its way to identify poorly performing firms in which it had good reason to intervene. It contacted the top management of the firm and made clear its wish to have implemented the changes it believed necessary to rectify the firm's problems: changes in the firm's financial policy—paying out more dividends to the shareholders or raising less equity from them; changes in the firm's investment policies—sales of underperforming divisions or disposal of unsuccessful acquisitions; or changes in the management, including replacement of the CEO or chairperson.

The Hermes Focus Fund did what governments and regulators around the world are currently urging financial institutions to do much more of, namely take an active role in the governance of their investments. Financial institutions frequently have corporate governance departments that oversee the companies in which they invest, but few have anything on the scale of or are nearly as active as the Hermes Focus Fund. The Hermes experience suggests that there might be good reason for them to take more of an interest in their poorly performing companies than they do at present because the results of its active engagement were impressive. The Hermes Focus Fund comfortably outperformed its peers, earned substantial returns for its BT pensioners, and significantly improved the share price performance of the companies in which it engaged.[20] However, for other institutions to be able to replicate this they need to note one critical feature of the Hermes Focus Fund which contributed to its success: it employed people who possessed industry as well as financial knowledge and expertise. It was therefore able to bridge the divide between investors and firms that afflicts most institutional investment—a lack of detailed understanding as to how to intervene in the management of firms that they own.

Shareholder activism targets poorly performing companies—hostile takeovers target averagely performing companies. Both would appear to be performing important functions in improving corporate performance. So, who could possibly object to takeovers that are designed to convert average into stellar performance? The answer is virtually every other country in the world.

Just Say Nein

What is interesting about the Cadbury case is that it could not have happened in virtually any other country in the world. In France, the government would have intervened. In Germany, a combination of banks, the local states (the Länder), and workers would have scuppered it. Even in the US, Cadbury could have employed a variety of defences. Britain has one of the most open markets for acquisitions by domestic and foreign companies of any country in the world. It therefore exemplifies what many economists extol, policymakers advocate, and international agencies exhort other countries to adopt.

The hurdles that exist to hostile takeovers in most parts of the world are formidable. From the end of the Second World War to the end of the 20th century there were just three hostile takeovers in Germany. The difficulties that the acquirers in these three cases encountered are illustrative of the impediments that exist around the world. In two cases, restrictions were imposed on the maximum number of votes that any shareholder could cast irrespective of how many shares they acquired. This meant that the acquirers could not gain control at shareholder meetings even where they held a majority of shares in the target company. When the Italian tyre manufacturer Pirelli tried to take control of the German tyre corporation Continental, it faced the concerted opposition of the German car industry that rallied to Continental's defence by buying blocks of shares in the corporation to prevent Pirelli from gaining control.[21]

Share blocks and voting right restrictions are just two of the mechanisms that shareholders employ to avoid unwanted takeovers. When the US social media company Linkedin listed on the stock market in 2011, it issued two classes of shares. The original shareholders who held shares in Linkedin before it went public received Class B shares, each of which had ten times the votes of the Class A shares that were sold to the public. This prevented an outside bidder from seizing control of the corporation without the agreement of the original shareholders, particularly its founder Reid Hoffman, even if a majority of the other shareholders wanted to sell it.

Google employed similar arrangements when it came to the stock market in 2004. Its founders, Sergey Brin and Larry Page, issued two classes of shares—Class A and Class B, where Class B had ten times as many votes per share as Class A—and went to the original shareholders who together controlled 61.4 per cent of the votes, 37.6 per cent of which were allocated to Brin and Page. In their 2004 Founders' initial public offering (IPO) letter, Brin and Page justified the share structure as follows: 'we have set up a corporate structure that will make it harder for outside parties to take over or influence Google. This structure will also make it easier for our management team to follow the long term, innovative approach.'[22]

In 2012 the English football club Manchester United filed for an IPO on the New York Stock Exchange in preference to the

London Stock Exchange. It did so to take advantage of New York's more liberal regulation of dual class shares, which allowed the owners, the Glazer family, to retain control of the club by holding shares with ten times the voting rights of the shares issued to the public.[23]

These dual class share structures are commonplace in the US, particularly in media companies. They are even more commonplace in Continental Europe. At one stage, the Porsche and Piëch families between them had total control of the Porsche car company, despite only owning one-half of the equity—the other half, which was held by the public at large, had no voting rights.[24]

Even if corporations do not issue two classes of shares to discourage takeovers, then they have several other means of defence at their disposal in the US. For example, they frequently employ what are termed 'poison pills'—arrangements that make it fatally expensive for acquirers to seize control of other companies. A poison pill is an issue of shares to all existing shareholders except the raider that has acquired more than a certain percentage of the shares of the firm, for example 20 per cent. So once the raider has acquired 20 per cent of the shares in a target firm, it discovers that all other shareholders in the target firm automatically receive new shares that reduce the proportion held by the raider. Anticipating this, raiders do not attempt to launch bids against firms with poison pills. Even if the firm does not have a dual class share or a poison pill at its disposal, then it might choose to be incorporated in a state in the US in which legislation makes it virtually impossible for a raider to take it over.[25]

Air Products, a Pennsylvania-based gas products company, is the world's largest supplier of hydrogen and helium. In February 2010 it made public its desire to take over another Pennsylvania-based gas company, Airgas, which specializes in industrial and medical gases. But it faced four hurdles in seeking to do this. First, Airgas's management did not want to be taken over and believed that the offer that Air Products was placing on the table at $70 per share seriously undervalued the company. It therefore rejected Air Products' bid. Second, Airgas had a staggered board of nine members, only three of whom were up for election in any one year. It could therefore take Air Products up to two years to be able to vote a majority of its nominees onto Airgas's board. Third, Airgas had a poison pill with a 15 per cent trigger, which meant that once Air Products had acquired 15 per cent of Airgas's equity, its shareholdings could be automatically diluted by the issue of new Airgas shares to other shareholders in the company. Fourth, Airgas's Certificate of Incorporation required that two-thirds of its shareholders had to agree to a merger with an interested party unless a majority of the directors on its board approved it. Airgas therefore had in place a range of takeover defences which protected it from Air Products' hostile bid.

At the Airgas annual meeting in September 2010, Air Products succeeded in electing three of its nominees to the Airgas board. But after the Delaware Supreme Court rejected an application from Air Products to bring forward the next meeting to January 2011, Air Products faced having to wait another year to gain majority representation on Airgas's board. So instead, Air Products appealed to the Delaware Court to order Airgas to remove its poison pill and other takeover defences. In February 2011 the Delaware Court ruled that Air Products' request was rejected and that the board of Airgas acted in good faith in retaining takeover defences. Air Products promptly withdrew its offer to acquire Airgas.

The case is especially striking because it is one where the arguments for Airgas shareholders' right of self-determination of the fate of their company appear particularly compelling. The offer from Air Products was all in the form of cash rather than the shares of Air Products so that Airgas shareholders knew precisely how much it was worth. Second, the offer was available to all the shareholders in Airgas on equal terms and there was no suggestion of some shareholders being offered a better deal than others. Third, the shareholders in Airgas had had a year since the offer was first put on the table and therefore plenty of time to establish whether a better one was likely to emerge.

How, then, could the Delaware court argue that takeover defences, which prevented the shareholders of Airgas from determining the outcome of the bid and instead handing the decision to its management, should remain in place? In summing up, Chancellor William Chandler said, 'this case does not endorse "just say never". What it does endorse is Delaware's long-understood respect for reasonably exercised managerial discretion, so long as boards are found to be acting in good faith and in accordance with their fiduciary duties.'[26]

What concerned the court was the role of arbitrageurs. Chancellor Chandler stated:

> both Airgas's expert as well as Air Products' own expert testified that a large number—if not all—of the arbitrageurs who bought into Airgas's stock at prices significantly below the $70 offer price would be happy to tender their shares at that price regardless of the potential long-term value of the company. Based on the testimony of both expert witnesses, I find sufficient evidence that a majority of stockholders might be willing to tender their shares regardless of whether the price is adequate or not—thereby ceding control of Airgas to Air Products.[27]

Chancellor Chandler went on to say:

> I find that the Airgas board acted in good faith and relied on the advice of its financial and legal advisors in coming to the conclusion that Air Products' offer is inadequate. And as the Supreme Court has held, a board that in good faith believes that a hostile offer is inadequate may 'properly employ a poison pill as a proportionate defensive response to protect its stockholders from a "low ball" bid'.[28]

In the case of both Airgas and Cadbury there was concern about the role of arbitrageurs in making the outcome of a hostile acquisition a self-fulfilling prophecy. The difference was that in the case of Cadbury, all the management could do was to protest in public about the iniquity of a system that allowed short-term investors to determine the long-term fate of a company.[29] In contrast, Airgas could seek protection in a range of takeover defences and a legal system that upheld the right of management to act in what they believed to be the long-term interests of the company, even where this conflicted with the short-term value of its shareholders' equity. The defences available to target management in the US are therefore significantly greater than in the UK.

So, most countries make it relatively straightforward for companies to protect themselves against hostile takeovers. In contrast in the UK, as the Kraft acquisition of Cadbury illustrated, there are very few defences available to a target firm even if there is widespread political and public opposition to the acquisition. The reason for this very open approach to acquisitions in the UK is that they are thought to promote efficiency. Whoever is willing to pay the most for a company presumably expects to derive the greatest benefit from owning it and should therefore have the right to control it. For example, the shareholders of

Cadbury clearly attached a greater value to the firm being controlled by the Kraft than the existing Cadbury management. So having a free and easy takeover market encourages capital to flow to where it can best be used by those who are most capable of employing it. In addition, as the Kraft case also illustrates, that capital frequently comes from overseas so that an additional attraction of the takeover market is that it encourages capital to flow into the UK. So given these benefits, why do other countries in the world take such a different view of the merits of takeovers from the UK? This takes us towards the heart of the matter—the corporation as a commitment device—and the potential conflicts that markets for corporate control may create with other stakeholders.

Corporate Islands

Return to the case of colinmayer plc and the problem that with 9,999 other shareholders I have no inclination to reject the investment that earns on average a 50 per cent return at the expense of the creditors in the company. I have no inclination to reject it because I suffer no personal costs from encouraging the corporation to accept it. However, it does come at a cost to the company since, while I cannot be personally associated with the decision, as an entity separate from me and the other shareholders, the company can be. It has a reputation that is distinct from the shareholders. So if the company suffers a loss in reputation worth $150,000 or more if the investment fails, then it will choose to reject it.

So, while as a small shareholder in colinmayer plc I cannot do anything to prevent the investment being accepted, I can appoint management to run the corporation who will be concerned about the corporation's reputation and seek to protect the creditors. We do not have to return to a world of family ownership to promote responsible corporations. We just need to appoint management whose interests are in the long-term success of the corporation, and I, as a shareholder, will then be pleased to delegate decisions to them. As a small individual shareholder, I cannot commit to uphold the interests of creditors even though I would like to be able to do so. But what a corporation as a distinct legal entity can do is to commit on my behalf. It is a commitment device.

At least it was until I introduced the phenomenon of this chapter—the hostile takeover. A hostile takeover by definition bypasses the management of the target firm; it is an approach by the management of the acquiring firms directly to the shareholders of the target in the face of opposition from the target management. In large part it freezes management of the target firm out of one of the most important decisions they have to take—whether or not to remain independent or merge with another firm. As such the hostile takeover is an anti-commitment device. The consequence, most vividly illustrated by the UK, is that we have created corporate acephali for whose destiny neither anonymous owners nor replaceable managers are ultimately responsible.

The choice between allowing hostile takeovers and preventing them is therefore one between being able to commit to other stakeholders and allowing shareholders to exert free control over the firm. It is therefore fundamental to the purpose and principles of the firm. It justifies why some companies might choose to implement anti-takeover provisions and others do not.[30] However, it does not explain why countries should choose to adopt them as a matter of national or state law and require all companies registered within their jurisdiction to implement them.

Indeed, if some companies have few creditors or other stakeholders, we might want them to abstain from takeover defences and
instead expose themselves to the discipline of the takeover
market. To understand why we might wish it to be a matter of
national or state as well as corporate policy, we should return to
the Galapagos.

As I described in the first chapter, what makes the Galapagos so
special is the fact that they are islands. As such, the indigenous
species were protected from the many predators that stalked the
neighbouring mainland and to which they would otherwise have
been exposed. In essence, although the iguanas and the giant
tortoises might not have called an extraordinary meeting to vote
on it, they had adopted an anti-takeover device, called the sea.
Without the sea, the creatures of the Galapagos could have
established whatever forms of co-existence they liked, but it
would all have been to no avail when the first beasts from the
surrounding areas stumbled across them as sitting prey.

That is what corporations which commit to their stakeholders
are—sitting prey to prospective hostile bidders. They have fleshy
stakeholders who can satisfy the most voracious acquirer's appe-
tite. So if the management of colinmayer plc is abstaining from
implementing the investment that expropriates wealth from creditors, an acquirer knows that it can take over the firm, implement
the project, and make an expected gain of $50,000. This does not
undermine the acquirer's reputation with its own creditors. It
may have an impeccable record of abstaining from undertaking
the investment itself; indeed, it might retain a bit of the money it
makes out of expropriating wealth from the creditors of the target
to provide further security for its own creditors.

However, like the actions of the first predators to make it to the
Galapagos from the surrounding areas, the effects of corporate

predators are devastating. Seeing what has happened to the unfortunate prey, the remaining animals discard all inhibitions, devour what they can, and resort, like their predators, to the laws of the jungle. So too while I earlier claimed that one good hanging was a salutary lesson to all underperforming management, it is also an inducement to hang the creditors and implement high-risk investments to their detriment. Unrestrained pursuit of shareholder value is no more a value in the ethical sense than consumption is in the animal kingdom. It is an outcome of the collapse of systems that encapsulate the interest of other parties in addition to those of the shareholders themselves.

We therefore create corporate Galapagos Islands to promote diversity of corporate systems.[31] We do so partly on the basis of different national values—some abhor the laws of the jungle; some are bored by the tranquillity of the Galapagos. But we also do it for reasons of economic efficiency. Just as the Galapagos have created an environment in which different species from the surrounding mainland have thrived, and each of the islands in the Galapagos has its own distinctive biological identity, so countries can promote different economic and industrial systems. Some are associated with strong protection of stakeholder interests and others with strong protection of shareholders. As in the world of species, so in the world of corporations—we should rejoice in diversity. As both states within the United States and countries within the European Union have demonstrated, we can promote corporate diversity quite simply by associating different corporate laws with different states and different countries. Some states in the US, such as California, have very few anti-takeover rules and others, such as Pennsylvania, extensive provisions. Some countries in the EU, such as the UK, discourage takeover defences while others, such as Sweden, permit them. Companies within the US are free to choose their state of incorporation, while operating anywhere within the US, and companies within the EU are free to incorporate in any member country and operate in any other.

The picture to emerge to date is of a world in which the corporation has made remarkable contributions to economic development and prosperity but also inflicted growing problems. The underlying principle of the corporation is perceived to be to promote shareholder interests, but these have come at the expense of other stakeholders who have significant interests in the corporation. Market incentives and reputations intensify the focus on shareholder interests and distort the allocation of resources in an economy to those that yield the greatest benefits for shareholders at the expense of other parties.

Regulation has been introduced to correct this and to encourage shareholders to take a more active interest in the management of their corporations. However, conferring more power on shareholders potentially exacerbates the conflict with other stakeholders. The irresponsibility of corporations has become worse with the decline of family ownership and the growth of dispersed ownership, at least in some countries in the world. Dispersed ownership economies developed a solution in the form of the market for corporate control and more recently activist shareholder funds, but these too have exacerbated conflicts with other stakeholders.[32]

Regulation, hostile takeovers, and shareholder activism have therefore all sought to address the agency problem between shareholders and managers by increasing shareholder control, in particular in countries such as the UK that have placed strong emphasis on market mechanisms. However, in the process they have undermined the position of other stakeholders. The primary deficiency of the corporation is its failure to protect these stake-holder interests. The correct response is not further regulation, which will only introduce other distortions, but to find mechanisms by which companies can demonstrate a greater degree of responsibility themselves without relying on others to do it for them. We need to establish the means by which corporations can demonstrate more commitment to their stakeholder community. To do that, we first need to understand the problem of commitment of the corporations' creators—mankind.

Chapter 7
Capital and Commitment

'Trust is good, control is better.'
Vladimir Lenin

Rational Sentiment

One of the greatest triumphs of mankind has been the invention of the rational man.[1] It is not quite clear when he first came into existence, but certainly by the middle of the 18th century he was frequenting the parlours of the most illustrious houses in Europe.

He was adopted with alacrity by economists and given the exulted title of *homo economicus*. Here is Adam Smith extolling his virtues in a *Theory of Moral Sentiments*:

> The qualities most useful to ourselves are, first of all, superior reason and understanding, by which we are capable of discerning the remote consequences of all our actions, and of foreseeing the advantage or detriment which is likely to result from them: and secondly, self-command, by which we are enabled to abstain from present pleasure or to endure present pain, in order to obtain a

greater pleasure or to avoid a greater pain in some future time. In the union of these qualities consists the virtue of prudence, of all the virtues that which is most useful to the individual.[2]

In comparison with his sentimental counterpart, rational man is an impressive animal. He is a calculating machine, evaluating the benefits and costs of alternatives and weighing them carefully against each other. On the enlightened basis of his decisions he dominates the less rational who embrace sentiment over rationality. As circumstances change, rational man adapts his chosen course of action to suit the current environment. He is forward looking, incorporating all relevant pieces of information relating to future as well as current circumstances. History is relevant in so far as it informs the future, but history is not a reason for clinging to past behaviour.

Rational man is like a gazelle leaping across the hills from one peak to another. He looks as far as he can ahead to where the next peak should take him and steadily ascends to greater and greater heights. Meanwhile, his counterpart driven by sentiment is locked in the valleys shrouded in mists, ploughing on his preconceived tracks. How fine rational man stands beside his sentimental counterpart.

So it would be if humans stood alone like the gazelle, able to make choices independent of the effects on others. But unlike the gazelle, rational man leads others along with him. And each time that his calculated planning leads him to change direction, he leaves a trail of followers who do not possess his physique or foresight behind. For some are suited to climb the bare pastures; others the rocky terrains; and others fear the heights themselves. So at each twist and turn he loses some of his faithful followers.

So be it. That is the price of progress and development. The world is not static; it changes and we must change with it. Those who cannot will, of necessity, be left behind. But meanwhile our sentimentalist who sticks resolutely to the valleys and pushes on relentlessly keeps his band of faithful supporters. And while they plough a difficult and opaque terrain, they do so together with the support that rational man has lost. They are bound together by a common belief that the sentimentalist cannot rationalize in a form that the rationalist cannot comprehend.

Who prospers most? No one can say with certainty. The presumption that rational man will win out ignores the strength that others can derive from the fixed point of sentiment. We may know the mind of the sentimentalist in a way in which we do not that of rational man. Were the great figures of history those who were carefully calculating, cautiously selective in their choices? Or were they those driven by emotion and gut feeling which instilled confidence and trust in others? Who should we trust the most— those who might cut the earth from under our feet for realization that circumstances have changed and the best alternative now dominates previously preferred courses of action? Or is it the leader who is blind to alternatives and will stick rigidly to where sentiment drives them?

Compelling Competition

As every individual, therefore, endeavours as much as he can, both to employ his capital in the support of domestic industry, and so to direct that industry that its produce may be of the greatest value; every individual necessarily labours to render the annual revenue of the society as great as he can. He generally, indeed, neither intends to promote the public interest, nor know how much he is promoting it. By preferring the support of domestic to that of foreign industry, he intends only his own security; and by directing that industry in such a manner as its produce may be of the greatest value, he intends only his own gain and he is in this, as in many other cases, led by an invisible hand to promote an end which was no part of his intention. Nor is it always the worse for the society that it was no part of it. By pursuing his own interest, he frequently promotes that of the society more effectually than when he really intends to promote it. I have never known much good done by those who affected to trade for the public good. It is an affectation, indeed, not very common among merchants, and very few words need be employed in dissuading them from it.[3]

This powerful idea defined the course of nations after it was first expounded by Adam Smith in 1776. Not only is rational man an impressive animal, but also through the pursuit of his own self-interest he achieves an outcome that furthers not just his own well-being but that of society as a whole. Furthermore, this is more likely to promote social well-being than its self-conscious pursuit—an endeavour that is in any event not commonly observed.

The invisible hand that guides our self-interest towards the common good is competition. As each of us seeks to gain more from working, consuming, and investing we confer more on those who employ us, supply us, and borrow from us. Just as rats rushing to leave a sinking ship re-establish its buoyancy, so in the individual pursuit of our own self-interest we collectively confer benefits on those who lie on the other side of the market. All that interference by monarchs, governments, or well-meaning do-gooders can do is to undermine the efficacious property of markets.

General acceptance of this concept has resulted in a steadily increasing focus of public policy on the promotion of markets and competition. Elimination of barriers to international trade, to the free flow of international capital, to restraints of trade by cartels, and to abuse by monopolists is what has dominated the economic and political agenda since the Second World War. The more choice we have and the easier it is for us to move between suppliers, purchasers, employers, employees, borrowers, and lenders in an informed way, the more effective will be the power of markets to direct our self-interest towards the common good.

Most of the criticism of rational man has focused on his failings and limitations. His ability to predict the future, to evaluate the implications of different courses of action or to determine the right one is seriously limited. What is more worrying is that he makes systematic mistakes, is influenced by what should be irrelevant considerations and fails to take account of highly relevant ones. Rather surprisingly, he is therefore human. This relatively recent remarkable discovery has given rise to a whole area of academic enquiry—what is known as 'behavioural economics'. This is concerned with identifying human failings and determining their consequences for an economics community which previously had presumed humans, if not quite infallible, at least sufficiently smart learners not to make the same repeated mistakes.

As you can imagine, the implications of the 'bounded' nature of human rationality are pretty far reaching. Our gazelle no longer ascends quite so magnificently from peak to peak, but periodically stumbles, falls back, and erroneously heads downhill. But however serious are his limitations and no matter how significant these are for his progress, they do not diminish rational man's intent or attempt to pursue his own well-being. He remains a self-interested, albeit now more imperfect, creature and he is just as willing to cut the earth from beneath those who follow him as his more capable counterpart was. In fact, the consequences are potentially even more serious: so long as we attributed remarkable properties of foresight to rational man, we could at least justify his self-interest on the grounds that it benefited him and pointed others in the right direction of the next peak, but we can no longer presume this of his more human counterpart. His self-interest may be positively damaging for his own as well as others' well-being.

The concern here is less with the reasoning ability of rational man, which is what has almost exclusively dominated recent economics debates, but his preoccupation with his own self-interest. Even if they could, would humans select the course that was suited to their own interest? It has become such a firmly embedded notion that as soon as one questions it and asks whether humans might have broader goals than their own self-interest, then one is categorized as being an idealistic sentimental-ist, unwilling to confront the realities of human nature. However, in actual fact we go out of our way to stop ourselves from pursuing our own self-interest and there is a very good reason why we do this. It is not in our interest to pursue our own interests.

That would of course be a nonsensical sentence if we were islands operating on our own; however bad we were at it, we would still be best off pursuing our own interests. But we are not. We rely on others at least as much, and frequently more, than we do on ourselves to promote our interests. We need others to help us to achieve what we want to do, and if their willingness to assist us is dependent on what we do to or for them, then the world becomes more complex. No longer can we simply act selfishly, indifferent to the impact on others. We need to worry about how our actions impact others if only because what they do will in turn affect us. So our self-interest may well be furthered by restraining ourselves to consider the interests of others who in turn will then benefit us more than they would otherwise do.

How can we restrain ourselves? We impose self-discipline on ourselves in restraining what we might otherwise naturally be inclined to do through being reflective individuals who adopt accepted norms of behaviour. The Nobel prize-winning economist and philosopher Amartya Sen in particular has argued that it is naïve to presume a simplistic view of rational man that assumes him to be egoistical or even altruistic in the purely selfish sense that his altruism only extends as far as he derives pleasure from it.[4] Sen believes that we are more reflective in adopting codes of behaviour that go beyond those from which we derive personal satisfaction. We are thus willing to accept social norms that conflict with our individual preferences.

I do not want to enter into a debate about the degree to which it is meaningful to consider rational beings as displaying self-restraint or adopting moral codes. All I would assert is that, however much individuals demonstrate self-restraint, it is not sufficient, once we consider our dependence on others to help us deliver what is in our own self-interest. The reason that I can state this with confidence is that, however much I can restrain myself to encourage you to help me today, it will be inadequate tomorrow when you have already done so and I derive no further benefit from displaying continuing self-restraint. Once you have given me what I want, then I will adopt my naturally self-centred persona and dismiss any concerns that I might previously have had about you. Knowing that that is what I will do, you will not help me in the first place. To stop this from happening, and from all such interactions unravelling through similar forms of backward reasoning, I need someone credible to help me tie the knots that will bind me to you, even once it is no longer in my interest to do so. That someone, I will argue, should be the corporation.

Banking on You

You might not associate Pingyao in the remote inland Shanxi province of China with being one of the great financial centres of the world. But during the Qing dynasty, that is what it was. It is credited with having established the first draft bank in China—the Rishengchang bank—which, by the end of the 19th century, was one of the largest in China.

The bank had its origins in a successful dye business that was headquartered in Pingyao and had branches in many parts of China, including Beijing. A problem that afflicted the firm, like others in China, was how to transport silver safely in payment for dyes over the long distances between its branches and Pingyao. A flourishing network of escort agencies therefore developed to protect the bullion as it was transported across China. To demonstrate safe delivery of their consignment, the carriers were responsible for bringing the seal of the recipient back to the sender on the paper bearing the seal of the sender.

Even though the guards were experts in the martial arts, they could not provide complete security, particularly when they began to be confronted by attackers with guns. In response the firm started to use paper remittances in place of the expensive and risky transportation of silver. The expertise required therefore changed from the martial arts to calligraphy and the production of carefully designed watermarks to avoid the hazard which replaced that of bandits, namely the fraudulent creation of remittances. As the firm increased its use of remittances, others sought to employ its services to assist them with transfer of their monies across China. As a consequence, over time the firm found itself steadily developing from a dye business with some money transfer functions on the side to a bank with some associated dye activities, and in 1823 it formally established itself as the Rishengchang Bank.

Having done so, there was a second risk that a newly established bank with distant branches faced and that was how to ensure that the branches were well managed.[5] What the bank did to achieve this was to reward the managers through shares that paid a dividend which depended on the annual performance of the bank and the branch, and continued for a period after the manager retired. The shareholders did not interfere in the running of the bank, but retained the right through exercising the bank's voting shares to replace the management if their performance was poor. Management's commitment to the bank was therefore assured on two scores—first, because their earnings depended on its performance and second, because their continuing employment and livelihood was at risk if they failed to perform adequately. This system operated successfully for the best part of a century until it was abused at the beginning of the 20th century by owners of the bank, who assumed the powers of management, and exercised executive authority themselves.

What the bank was very successful at doing prior to its decline was to introduce control mechanisms that minimized risk of failure by silver carriers (through the double seal system), fraudsters (through elaborate paper designs and watermarks), and managers (through monitoring their performance and employing a combination of incentives and threats of dismissal). In other words, those who invested in developing skills in the martial arts, in calligraphy, and in management were carefully constrained by the bank to avoid the malpractices by which they might otherwise have been tempted. Had the bank not been willing to invest in the processes that were required to ensure the necessary controls and had the employees not been willing to be constrained in these ways, then their skills might well not have been employed. When the owners finally abused the controls and assumed executive power themselves, the bank collapsed.

Conventionally economics views prices as being the mechanism by which demand is brought into line with supply in different markets. If there are too many people willing to supply the services of carriers, calligraphers, or managers, then their wages will fall so that banks demand more of their services. However, if the banks cannot or do not constrain temptations on their employees' part to steal, defraud, or exploit them, then they will not employ them in the first place. Furthermore, declines in wages might well make the problem worse not better because employees will then have less to lose from being caught and dismissed. Some forms of unemployment are a product not of excessively high wages or inadequate skills of employees, but a failure on the part of firms to provide employees with mechanisms to constrain their conduct. In the absence of these controls, firms will see a pool of untrustworthy individuals, and potential employees will perceive an inadequate demand for their services. And both parties will be right: there will be both insufficient supply and inadequate demand for the services of employees.

Where the firms do not employ the controls necessary to prevent abuses by their employees, they need to raise, not lower wages. By raising wages they increase the value to employees of employment and discourage them from engaging in activities that might result in their dismissal. In essence, employees have more capital at stake. Wages will be higher and employment lower in economies in which firms employ poor mechanisms for controlling their employees' lack of self-restraint. It will look as if workers are pricing themselves out of the market when in fact they will be pricing themselves into a market in which firms are not giving them any other means to exercise the restraint that they would like to demonstrate.

Economic poverty does not necessarily result from incompetence, idleness, or dishonesty on the part of workers as much as from inadequate opportunities available to them to show the degree of restraint which they need to and wish to be able to exercise. The rationality of humans is not so much bounded by their information processing capabilities as by their exercise of self-interest. We wish our pursuit of self-interest to be constrained by more than we can ourselves achieve, but the world frequently does not offer us the means by which to do it. One of the reasons for this failure is the difficulty of raising the capital that is required for us to be able to demonstrate commitment. Where finance is available, then economies have thrived. Where it is not, they have declined. The contrast between early 19th-century and 20th-century Britain is a good illustration of both of these developments.

Revolutionary Finance

For the first half of the 19th century, British industry dominated the world. The Industrial Revolution saw the introduction of new forms of production that reduced costs and raised output to levels that were unimaginable a few decades earlier. Canal, river, road, and sea transportation was transformed and economic activity shifted from agriculture to industry and trade. For a brief period Britain was the 'workshop of the world'.

The Industrial Revolution was not financed by the stock market but instead out of the private capital of individual entrepreneurs and their families and by lending from banks. As manufacturing enterprises subsequently developed in textiles, coal, and iron, they funded their investments largely through retained earnings.[6] Local banks in Britain were also critical to this success and funding of the Industrial Revolution. The majority of British banks in Georgian Britain were partnerships, many deliberately small to avoid the 1708 Act that restricted banks with more than six partners from issuing bank notes. Many bankers were originally engaged in a business for which banking was a sideline. Thomas Smith, a cloth merchant in Nottingham, began operating the earliest known provincial bank in the 1650s. Others were established from the mid-18th century with the purpose of funding industrial and commercial activities.[7] The bankers were therefore knowledgeable about both borrowers and the trades in which they were engaged, so that between 1784 and 1810 the number of local banks increased in Britain from 119 to 650.

The existence of a large number of small, private banks, empowered to engage in note issuance, caused serious stability problems. Over the period 1809 to 1830 there were 311 bankruptcies of country banks. In particular, there was a serious failure in 1825. English businessmen noticed that the Scottish banking system, which had long permitted joint-stock banks, was much less affected. In response, in 1826 joint-stock banks were legalized in a 65-mile radius from London and, from 1833 within London as well to increase capital and spread risks in the banking sector.

Within ten years, over one hundred joint-stock banks had been established.

Competition in banking intensified appreciably, banks engaged in riskier lending, and, despite the greater capital of the joint-stock banks and the Bank Charter Act of 1844, which created the supremacy of the Bank of England, banking crises persisted; there were further crises in 1847, 1857, and 1866. With the introduction of limited liability in joint-stock banks in 1858 and 1862, national networks of branches were established, eliminating the private bankers in the process. Banking in Britain therefore moved in a very short space of time in the second half of the 19th century from being highly fragmented and localized to being concentrated and centralized in London.

The final nail in the coffin of local banking occurred on 2 October 1878 when the City of Glasgow Bank failed. Since the shareholders had unlimited liability, it was a traumatic experience for the City of Glasgow: 'nearly 2000 families suffered severe loss; many were ruined'.[8] The failure had repercussions not just in Scotland but also throughout England. This was a turning point in the relation of banks with industry when they realized that their exposure to local industries left them at the mercy of crises. The failure of the Bank of England to provide lender of last resort facilities lay at the heart of the realization by banks that it was in the London money markets not the Bank of England that they had to seek liquidity. 'It was explicitly the aim of the Bank [of England] to teach the market that all financial intermediaries had to look after their own liquidity, even in an emergency, by restricting themselves to "sound banking practices".'[9]

The small local banks, which dominated the first half of the 19th century, gave way to the national banks with their headquarters in London. They were less willing to invest longer term in activities without adequate collateral. They were discouraged from engaging in risky lending: 'reject... everything that is not readily convertible into money. In short, turn over a new leaf, and mind your own business.'[10]

Some people have argued that British banks failed to provide finance in the form or on the scale of their German counterparts.[11] One determinant of this was the policy of their respective central banks. The 19th-century German central bank's willingness to support long-term lending was critical to the willingness of German banks to provide such lending.[12] British banks' unwillingness to do likewise stemmed from the reluctance of the Bank of England to support banks when liquidity was needed. Other people believe that these alleged differences between banks in different countries are exaggerated, there being 'an unexpectedly large degree of similarity in the lending practice of banks from many parts of Europe', and that 'a case can be made for the greater sophistication of British financial markets'.[13]

The disappearance of local banking from Britain was to have a dramatic effect on the course of British industrial development in the 19th and 20th centuries. As the economic historian Peter Mathias has noted:

> This consolidation brought a consolidation of conservative lending policy with it. Many local country bankers in the eighteenth century were much more unstable, much more risky in their lending policy. But the growth of national joint-stock banks eventually spread more conservative banking principles. Branch managers' freedom of action became limited by their London head offices. The banking system became a very stable, very efficient instrument for short-term accommodation without being an important instrument for financing investment, unlike in Germany where the banks initially sponsored the growth of

great new industries. In Britain, the City to a large extent had its back turned to industry.[14]

As a consequence,

the able, ambitious man, frustrated from rising to positions of power within a family firm, could perhaps more easily have found the finance for launching his own company had banking traditions been closer to those in France and Germany. In later times the problem of financing the development of new innovations and small firms needing to cover large development costs and wanting to expand more quickly than is possible out of profits much exercised public policy.[15]

The history of banking in the US was very different from the UK. The US has had a highly fragmented banking system with a large number of small banks without extensive branches. As one academic has noted,

American federalism fostered fragmented banking, as each state chartered and protected its own banks, excluding branches from other states' banks and often preventing their own single-location banks from branching [...] Entrepreneurs affiliated with banks could go national, but the bankers, because of branching restrictions could not. The commercial paper market—short-term IOUs from a debtor—was the way financiers and industry 'contracted around' the geographic restrictions.[16]

State banks were the main source of external finance for small companies lending short term to finance their working capital requirements.

The decline of local banking in Britain had a dramatic effect on the nature as well as the performance of its industry. Towards the end of the 19th century, the family companies that were to dominate much of the British corporate landscape during the 20th century were established.[17] Companies such as Beechams, Bovril, Cadbury, Colman, Crosse and Blackwell, Huntley and Palmer, Lever Brothers, Mackintosh, Peek Frean, Reckitt, Rowntree, Schweppes, and Yardley, many of which had a strong Quaker family connection, became household names. In the absence of a supportive banking system, they, like other firms in Britain, increasingly turned to the stock market to provide their external financing needs. Equity was issued, growth occurred through acquisitions, ownership became dispersed, and family ownership declined in the way that was described in Chapter 5.

Those industries, most notably, chemicals, electrical equipment, and metals, that relied heavily on large-scale investments did not do nearly so well. They failed to flourish in relation to their US and German counterparts and by the 1930s there was an acute awareness of the problem of the financing of British industry. In the wake of the stock market crash of 1929, the British government established a committee, the MacMillan Committee, named after its Chairman Hugh MacMillan, to respond to a growing concern 'that great difficulty is experienced by the smaller and medium sized businesses in raising the capital which they may from time to time require'.[18]

The Committee noted that from the beginning of the Industrial Revolution to the end of the 19th century, British industry developed with little assistance from the City of London and 'insofar as it required banking facilities, it found them from the independent banks, often family banks, which in general had their headquarters in the provinces, and particularly in the Midlands and the North, where the new industries flourished'. With the demise of independent local banking, the Committee concluded that 'the only other alternative would be to form a company to devote itself particularly to the smaller industrial and commercial issues'. In response, fifteen years later in June 1945, the Industrial and Commercial Finance Corporation (ICFC) was established.

For a brief period in the 20th century, ICFC provided Britain with a financial institution that matched its German counterparts in the funding of industry.[19] Its success reflected its distinctive features. It was owned by the UK clearing banks and the Bank of England but created in the face of considerable opposition from the banks, which regarded it as a competitive threat rather than a complementary institution. It focused on the financing of small manufacturing companies in their early development stage and frequently took equity stakes in firms, but did not have direct representation on their boards. It undertook active screening and monitoring of borrowers and, unusually for British clearing banks, its loan officers had a high degree of technical competence and commitment to long-term lending. Like the successful activist fund managers, it developed a degree of industrial expertise that allowed it to bridge the gap between finance and business which had emerged when the British banking system lost its local roots in the 19th century.

ICFC was an immense success. Following losses in its first three years to 1948, it made substantial profits in every year subsequently. The number of its investments went up by a factor of ten between 1954 and 1984, and investments by ICFC were regarded as signals of quality certification. After it was permitted by its bank shareholders in 1959 to raise external funds, ICFC expanded to become the largest provider of growth capital for unquoted companies in the UK. In 1973 ICFC acquired Finance Corporation for Industry, a sister company also formed in 1945, and in 1983 the combined group was renamed Investors in

Industry—*3i*. Its investments were increasingly concentrated on venture capital, initially focused on start-ups, early stage, and development capital, and by the end of the 1980s it became by far the largest provider of venture capital in the UK.

True to the British custom of selling off successful institutions, the banks and the Bank of England sold their stakes in the *3i* Group in 1987. This was, after all, the era of privatization in the UK when it was thought that the market knew best. In one sense it did and in 1994 the company was floated on the London stock market with a market capitalization of £1.5 billion. But in another sense it most decidedly did not. Steadily *3i* shifted from being a funder of small and medium-sized enterprises (SMEs) and a main provider of venture capital in Britain to being a management buy-out firm. The repositioning of its activities contributed significantly to the switch in UK venture capital from early stage in the mid-1980s to management buy-outs and buy-ins by the end of the 1990s. As a consequence, by the beginning of this century, Britain had once again returned to being a country in which there was little serious long-term funding of SMEs and limited venture capital to finance seed-corn, start-ups, and early stage ventures.

The inadequate provision of long-term bank finance for SMEs has now been a problem in the UK for more than a century. It became acute after the financial crisis in 2008. Despite repeated government exhortations and attempts to pump money into the banking system through what was termed quantitative easing, the funding of SMEs dried up completely. As would be expected of an arm's-length banking system that had limited long-term engagement in the funding of small companies, SMEs were perceived by banks to be excessively high risk. And as had repeatedly been the case since before the failure of the Bank of

Glasgow, the primary concern of the Bank of England and the UK government was the protection of the payments system.

The Independent Commission on Banking, which the government established in 2010 in response to concerns about the financial stability of the UK's banking system, produced recommendations that were solely concerned with enhancing the safety of UK banks. Its remit was not to address the fundamental deficiency of the banking system, namely to finance high-risk small and medium-sized enterprises. Its proposals to ring-fence retail from investment banking were designed to protect and preserve what were regarded as key components of banking from another financial crisis. In the process it was hoped that SME lending which was included in the ring-fence would be enhanced, but there were no specific recommendations to this effect and, by requiring activities within the ring-fence to be low risk, it was destined to have exactly the opposite result.

With much of the British banking system in public ownership following its failure during the financial crisis, this was a golden opportunity for the government to restructure British banking in a form in which it would perform a valuable social function. Its failure to do so is all the more surprising given that its record thus far has been better than at least one other country in this regard.

Silicon Chaps

The Deutsche Wagnisfinanzierungsgesellschaft is not perhaps a name that immediately springs to most people's, at least non-German speakers', minds. Fortunately it has an acronym WFG and even more fortunately, the German government decided to launch it in 1975 at around the time that ICFC was rising to prominence in the UK. I say fortunately not on account of its fortunes—in fact it was a disaster—but because of its intended functions which were exactly the same as that of ICFC in the UK, namely to address a shortage of equity funding for small companies—an equity gap.[20] In marked contrast to ICFC, the WFG made losses in each of its first nine years. Most of the firms it supported recorded net losses, bankruptcies accounted for a high proportion of them, and entrepreneurs were ashamed to admit that the WFG had a stake in their firm. The contrasting fortunes of two organizations with almost identical purposes are instructive if only because ICFC is a rare example of a British corporate financing success.

Twenty-nine German banks founded the WFG, with a government guarantee of 75 per cent of any losses that the banks might incur. The board of the WFG comprised representatives from industry and government, scientists and consultants. The WFG initially focused on early stage investment, in particular in manufacturing and information technology. The criteria for selecting investments were the degree of innovation of products and processes, their potential markets, the quality of entrepreneurs, and the shortage of alternative sources of finance. The WFG took minority equity stakes, granted entrepreneurs a buyback right over the equity, and took no control rights in their investments. In many respects this sounds very similar to ICFC.

The difference came in terms of the degree of external interference. The banks and the government both meddled in the activities of the WFG in Germany, whereas the Bank of England kept the government and the banks at bay in ICFC in the UK, at least until it decided to extricate itself at the end of the 1980s. ICFC was able to take long-term positions in companies, whereas the WFG was subject to short-term commercial and political interference.

In many respects, the operation of ICFC until the end of the 1980s resembled that of venture capital firms. Venture capital comprises two parties—the limited partners, who are the institutional and individual investors, and the general partners, who are the venture capital firms investing in individual companies and entrepreneurs. The general partners manage portfolios of companies and are frequently successful entrepreneurs themselves who have chosen to control larger portfolios of investments. They provide business and technological expertise that both the entrepreneurs and investors might otherwise lack and they connect entrepreneurs with others who can assist them commercially, financially, and technically. Silicon Valley is a large networking and mentoring laboratory in which experienced entrepreneurs help to coach and connect their aspiring protégés.

Entrepreneurship in other countries, including the UK, frequently lacks the pool of experienced entrepreneurs on which to draw to provide this intermediary function. As a consequence, investing institutions complain that there are not enough viable projects in which they can invest and entrepreneurs complain that there is not enough money available to finance their high-potential projects. From the institutions' perspective there is insufficient supply of investments and from the entrepreneurs' viewpoint there is an insufficient supply of funding. And both parties are right. Without experienced entrepreneurs to reassure financial institutions about the business and technical judgements that they need to make, entrepreneurship looks to be a wildly risky activity; and from the perspective of entrepreneurs who lack the support of those more experienced than themselves to help develop their concepts, insufficient finance appears to be the major constraint on their aspirations.

What ICFC then *3i* did for a brief period in the UK was to bridge the divide. In the US, around one-quarter of venture capital funds are invested in early stage firms. In the UK, start-up and early stage investments also accounted for around a quarter of venture capital investments in 1984, but with *3i* withdrawing from the market, by the end of the 1990s this had fallen to less than one-twentieth. The business of private equity firms had changed from venture capital financing of new businesses in their early stages of development to buy-outs by management of existing businesses.

Only one-fifth of private equity capital in the UK currently goes to venture capital, the rest being invested in the buy-out sector. Venture capital as a proportion of GDP is twice as large in the US as the UK and the invested amount per company is approximately eight times larger.[21] The low levels of investment in venture capital in the UK relative to the US mirror the low returns that investors have historically earned on venture capital investments in the UK, particularly on early stage investments.[22] It is not surprising that true early stage venture capital funding has all but disappeared in preference to the funding of buy-outs by management of existing firms, since that is where the profits lie.[23]

So from a banking system that used to be a locally based source of funding of industry to one that was concentrated in the City of London and more concerned with fee generation than with growing companies; from a private equity business that used to fund early stage investments in new start-ups to one that prefers to reorganize the ownership of existing ones; from local stock markets that sustained relations of trust between shareholders and firms to institutional investors that hold global portfolios at arm's length, the UK financial system systematically deserted the funding of its start-up, small and medium-sized enterprises in search of more lucrative, safer fee generation from established larger businesses. It has done so because a concern about financial stability encouraged the concentration of banks in London at the expense of local banking, which previously was the bedrock of small firm financing. As a consequence, firms increasingly turned to equity markets instead and in the process steadily dispersed their ownership as they funded their investments and in particular acquisitions. This in turn exposed them to threats of takeovers and in particular the market for corporate control, which undermined their ability to commit to long-term interests and other stakeholders. From a financial industry that was committed to the growth of new enterprises, we have moved to one that is concerned with controlling existing ones.

Outside of the UK and US, external financing has primarily come from banks that allowed firms to grow without diluting share ownership. Shareholdings remained concentrated in the hands of predominantly family owners who could commit to other parties but also pursued their private interests to the detriment of the commercial performance of firms. In the UK, a combination of weak relationship banking and the absence of defences against hostile takeovers promoted the financial performance of firms, but at the expense of both shareholder and managerial commitment. In the US, the presence of local banking, takeover defences, and equity finance established shareholder commitment in some firms, managerial commitment in others, and the absence of either in a third group of firms. While the UK and the US are generally categorized together as market-based systems, they are therefore in fact very different: the US combines features of the weak commitment observed in the UK with both strong ownership and managerial commitment. I will argue that this diversity has been a source of considerable economic advantage to the US over other countries, including the family firms of Continental Europe.

Au Lait

Collecchio is a town just south of Parma in Italy, probably most renowned for its dairy products—Parmigiano-Reggiano or Parmesan cheese, and Prosciutto di Parma or Parma ham. It is the town where in 1961 a young entrepreneur, Calisto Tanzi, established a dairy business. Two technological developments—the introduction of Tetra Pak milk cartons to replace glass bottles and the ultra-heat treatment (UHT) of milk—provided Parmalat with significant product innovations which it exploited to considerable advantage in the 1960s. These were followed in the 1970s by the lifting of monopoly restrictions on milk distribution, which gave the firm new lines to market.

Parmalat diversified into other dairy products, food products, and overseas into Europe and South America. By the end of the 1980s it had become one of the largest food companies in Italy, large enough to attract the attention as a potential takeover target of a food company that has already featured as an acquirer in this book—Kraft. In fact, the Tanzi family decided not to sell the business to Kraft but instead to go public on the Milan stock exchange—a fatal decision that led to the inexorable collapse of the business in December 2003 as Europe's largest corporate bankruptcy, with outstanding liabilities of €13bn and the jailing of Calisto Tanzi for fraudulent bankruptcy.

The sequence of events leading to the collapse has been extensively documented.[24] The pervasive nature of the failures, frauds, and conflicts of interest which afflicted numerous parts of the Italian corporate and financial system from auditors to banks to credit rating agencies to regulators is well summarized in an Italian government report which appeared shortly after the collapse: 'The most alarming finding... is that all the structures set up to protect the system, albeit at different levels, failed: both internal corporate control functions, and external regulatory and supervisory authorities clearly failed with regard to certain financial market activities and the conduct of specific individual banks.'[25]

In particular, far from being the means to uphold sound long-term principles, Parmalat's family ownership was a vehicle that facilitated the embezzlement of funds and the exploitation of a web of controlling interests and political connections. Funds were diverted to family members and their private companies and used to service personal debts. Subsidiary companies, most notably Bonlat, helped to disguise the corporate losses and, between 1990 and 2002, Parmalat diverted €500 million to the family's tourism company Parmatour of which Tanzi's daughter was a board member.[26] The potential stability that concentrated shareholders offer other stakeholders is therefore also a possible source of diversion of resources to the private benefit of the families. In critiquing dispersed share ownership, we should be careful not to glorify family ownership.

Commitment and Control

As the military and political control that the British Empire once exerted has declined so the control that the City of London exercises over corporate assets around the world has expanded.

Britain may produce and invest progressively less itself, but increasingly control of the world's assets is exercised by corporate headquarters and financial institutions that are based in London. Nowhere does one observe such free and unimpeded exercise of corporate control and allocation of company assets as in the UK. Over the last two hundred years Britain has progressively thrown off inhibitions about unleashing corporate capitalism and has embraced its most unrestrained manifestations. The imperialists of the 21st century are no longer the commanding officers of armed battalions in the colonies, but the chief executive officers of arm-chaired boardrooms in the City.

The form of capitalism that has emerged in Britain is the textbook description of how to organize capital markets and corporate sectors—dispersed shareholders with powers to elect and remove directors with or without cause before expiration of their terms of office, large stock markets, active markets for corporate control, a good legal system, strong investor protection, a rigorous anti-trust authority—the list goes on. It is what many countries around the world aspire to, what economists recommend, and what international agencies such as the IMF and World Bank encourage developing and emerging economies around the world to adopt. Against this background it is surprising to observe how mediocre the performance of the British economy has been and how dissatisfied much of its population is with its economic and social conditions.

It is as if the most ardent followers of lifestyle, nutrition, and well-being prescriptions suffer the most chronic symptoms of ill-health and depression. In response, we should encourage them to be more attentive to the recommendations that they have not wholeheartedly adopted—the approach that the international agencies take when presented with uncomfortable examples of failures of their economic policies—and not allow them for one moment to question the infallible judgement of the experts. We should in other words flog them until they feel better.

What could conceivably be wrong with the progressively greater control that banks, private equity investors, stock markets, and takeovers have exerted over the corporate sector? They finance, own, and oversee the assets that they have entrusted to those running and working for their firms and they are therefore perfectly within their rights to penalize, remove, and dismiss at a moment's notice anyone who does not perform to the highest standards. Indeed if they do not do this they are abdicating their responsibilities as financiers, property owners, and guardians of corporate assets to ensure that their money, property, and assets are deployed in the very best way.

We should therefore admire the British as exemplary in promoting the highest standards of care, honesty, and loyalty amongst those who are fortunate enough to work in the companies which they fund, own, and manage. The well-ordered class system of due deference by the lower orders to the landed gentry lives on in the guise of the modern corporation, with the shareholder replacing the land owner, the fund manager and private equity investor replacing his land agent, and the workers filling the tills rather than tilling the fields. No wonder the British feel so comfortable with this state of affairs—it is what they have endured since time immemorial.

However good its pedigree, it has a serious downside and that arises because the converse of control is commitment. Exemplary as a form of control the British financial system might be, it systematically extinguishes any sense of commitment—of investors to companies, of executives to employees, of employees to firms, of firms to their investors, of firms to communities, or of this generation to any subsequent or past one. It is a transactional island in which you are as good as your last deal, as farsighted as the next deal, admired for what you can get away with, and condemned for what you confess.

While incentives and control are centre stage in conventional economics, commitment is not. Enhancing choice, competition, and liquidity is the economist's prescription for improving social welfare, and legal contracts, competition policy, and regulation are their basic toolkit for achieving it. Eliminate restrictions on consumers' freedom to choose, firms' ability to compete, and financial markets' provision of liquidity and we can all move closer to economic nirvana. Of course, economics recognizes the problems of time inconsistency in us doing today what yesterday we promised we would not conceive of doing today; of reputations in us continuing to do today what we promised to do yesterday for fear of not being able to do it tomorrow; and of capital and collateral in making it expensive for us to deviate from what we said yesterday we would do today and tomorrow. But these are anomalies. Economics does not recognize the fundamental role of commitment in all aspects of our commercial as well as social lives and the way in which institutions contribute to the creation and preservation of commitment. It does not appreciate the full manner in which choice, competition, and liquidity undermine commitment or the fact that institutions are not simply mechanisms for reducing costs of transactions, but on the contrary means to establish and enhance commitment at the expense of choice, competition, and liquidity. Commitment is the subject of soft sentimental sociologists, not of realistic rational economists. The sociologists' are the words of Shakespeare's 'Love all, trust few. Do wrong to none', the economists' those of Lenin: 'Trust is good, control is better'.

Where economics errs is in failing to recognize our dependence on others to assist us with realizing what we seek to achieve and the dependence of other people's willingness to do so on our commitment to them. It is not that contracts could not be written or terms of exchange of our mutual assistance agreed, it is simply that if we are not committed to abide by them, they are of no significance. My trust in you derives not from the piece of paper that I hold in my hand but from the sacrifice that I see you making on my behalf. What will you forgo if you deceive me; what will I endure from abusing your confidence? What is the capital that we have both invested to secure the relationship and without which no price, contract, incentive, or punishment is of any significance? How durable is your commitment in the face of adversity—is it resilient in difficult times or vulnerable to alternative temptations? With your commitment, I will make a corresponding sacrifice and without it I will walk away.

Commitment has substance. I can measure the volume of it from the depth of capital committed, the length of time for which it is committed, and the breadth of activities to which it applies. A large amount of capital that can be withdrawn instantaneously is of little value, as is a negligible amount of capital committed for a long time or a lot of capital for activities of negligible significance. I can give substance to my commitment by allocating a sufficient amount of capital for a relevant range of activities over an adequate length of time. What is sufficient, relevant, and adequate depends on the degree, nature, and duration of our relationship. Too much, for too many things, for too long leaves me unnecessarily exposed to you; too little, for too few things, for too short a period leaves you uncertain about my intent.

Corporations are commitment devices. They achieve this by making the capital that their owners invest in them permanent.

Once invested it cannot be removed. At least that in principle is how they create commitment. However, the original designers of the corporation did not anticipate a recent development that I have described in this book which undermines this—the acquisition. The permanent capital of the firm is no longer permanent; it can be extracted in acquisitions that are paid for by cash. An acquisition fully financed by cash can extract not just the book value of invested capital but its total market value, thereby rendering it impossible for shareholders to commit to the provision of permanent capital.

While acquisitions make it impossible for shareholders to commit capital themselves, perhaps their executives can do it for them by pre-committing to reject acquisitions. That is where the still more recent phenomenon of the hostile acquisition enters the picture because, by allowing predators to appeal directly to the target shareholders over the heads of the target management, it also prevents executives from being able to pre-commit. What was once an important commitment device has therefore been systematically undermined by takeovers and in particular hostile takeovers.

To illustrate these features of commitment and control, go back to Colin Mayer Ltd. It has $150,000 of debt and $150,000 of equity. It employs some people who between them have invested $30,000 in the company in the sense that if they are fired they will over their lifetime be $30,000 worse off as a result of being deskilled or finding it difficult to obtain alternative employment—part of the vulnerable workers of the world. If Colin Mayer was entirely under my control I would leap at the prospect of investing the firm's assets in the activity that will double or destroy the company because I will earn the 50 per cent on my shares. Now, however, that decision not only expropriates returns from my creditors, but also leaves my employees $30,000 worse off as well if the risky investment fails. Anticipating that this is likely to happen, if they are unable to protect themselves adequately through contracts, they will be unwilling to accept employment with me in the first place, seeking securer alternative forms of employment elsewhere.

I would like to be able to commit to my employees, but on my own I am unable to do this; with the assistance of Colin Mayer Ltd., I can. I hire a manager who is paid in relation to the total earnings of the business, the performance of the combined equity and debt capital. My manager will have no incentive to implement the investment that benefits me, the shareholder, at the expense of the creditors. Appreciating that Colin Mayer Ltd. is much less likely to engage in high-risk investments that expose them as well as the creditors to risks of losses, potential employees will be more willing to accept employment with my company than with me as an unincorporated business.

Furthermore, if they still feel exposed to me interfering in the running of the firm and overriding the decisions of the management, then they may be more comfortable being employed by my widely held equivalent colinmayer plc with its 10,000 shareholders rather than just me. They know that the incentives for any one shareholder to intervene in the running of the firm are small and they are therefore less exposed to shareholders pursuing their own self-interests at the expense of the creditors and the employees. In an exact reversal of the problem suggested by Berle and Means of dispersed shareholders, from the perspective of firm commitment, the separation of ownership and control is a benefit, not a cost.

In this regard, the emergence of activist shareholders like Hermes is a mixed blessing. It might target bad management and correct failing firms, but it might also allow shareholders to expropriate the vested interests of other stakeholders. Hostile takeovers are a still more extreme version of this because they allow shareholders to reassert their authority without lifting a finger. As soon as the market catches wind of the fact that colinmayer plc is hesitating to implement the risky investment, a predator will appear and proceed with it. The creditors and employees of colinmayer plc will therefore welcome the independence that its dispersed ownership confers on its management but worry about its exposure to shareholder activists and, in particular, hostile predators.

The commitment of the firm is not restricted to financial capital. The values and goals of family firms reflect the personal sentiments of the family members about the organization and their interests in it. We normally regard these 'private benefits' as diminishing the efficiency of organizations and indeed at first sight they would appear simply to undermine more rational value propositions. The anonymity of shareholders in dispersed ownership firms in this context is beneficial in dispelling the sentiment that an investor may feel about the corporation and replacing it with a collective rationality. However, in the context of commitment to other stakeholders, the supremacy of reason over sentiment in the dispersed ownership firm is less clear-cut.

Even if no capital is invested in the firm, then family values create stability and commitment to other stakeholders that dispersed shareholders cannot provide. So as the one shareholder of Colin Mayer Ltd., my fanatical interest in, for example, bookshops means that employees in my bookshops know that I will not close them even when it is financially rational for me to do so. As one of 10,000 shareholders in colinmayer plc my personal interest in books is of no significance, and employees know that collective rationality will prevail and the shareholders will close or sell off the bookshops when it is financially advantageous for them to do so. colinmayer plc could overcome this by reemploying me as chief executive and giving me the authority to make decisions about continuation or closure of bookshops—my sentiment about bookshops would prevail once again over pure rational value propositions. However, in the presence of hostile takeovers and shareholder activism vehicles, even that ability to provide fixed points of sentiment for other stakeholders is extinguished.

This relates to a second feature of the corporation and that is as a control device. Since capital is so critical to the process of making commitments, some people, namely the financially and intellectually well endowed, are much better placed to make credible commitments than those who have less access to it. Insufficient committed capital is a primary source of exclusion of individuals from the market place, from employment, from financial markets, and from participation in economic activity in general. Not only do most people not have the resources to spend what they wish, in addition they do not have the capital to demonstrate their commitment to others and thereby to gain access to the economic activities that would allow them to escape from their current state of impoverishment. They are locked into a world in which they cannot credibly signal their desire to contribute to rather than steal from society. They are in the economics jargon 'credit-constrained', 'unable to make their notional demands effective', 'discouraged workers', 'unemployed', or just plain 'screwed'.

What institutions such as the Ltd. Company and the plc do is to allow people to escape from economic exclusion. They achieve this by enhancing the potential of those working for them, supplying them, or purchasing from them to make credible commitments through restricting their future range of options. They are control devices that limit the possible courses of conduct that can be undertaken and without which people would be incapable of restraining themselves from pursuing activities that are to the detriment of others. Institutions do this by constraining the ways in which people act and disengage, imposing rules and conventions that limit their choice, alternatives, and liquidity. By restricting behaviour in this way, they encourage other people to make commitments to them that otherwise would not be forthcoming and thereby enhance rather than diminish the current capabilities of those whose actions they constrain.

The employees of colinmayer plc are a case in point. If there is an active labour market and it is easy for them to obtain alternative employment at any time, then it is the firm not the employees which is exposed. The employees have made no commitment, whereas it may be costly for the firm to train new workers every time that an existing one resigns. Now it is the potential employees who would like to be able to demonstrate commitment to gain employment but are incapable of doing so on their own. The firm offers a means of achieving this. It can do it financially by delaying payment of their wages, thereby making it costly for them to depart prematurely before the firm has recovered its investments in training them. Alternatively, it can encourage commitment by making employment in the firm a valued attribute in its own regard, reflecting strong employee affinity with the goals and values of the organization. Critical to both forms of control of firms over their employees is their corresponding trust in the firm—trust that the firm will not expropriate their deferred payments by, for example, engaging in reckless investments and trust that it really will uphold the values to which it aspires. That is why the balancing of commitment and control in the firm is so vital to its successful operation.

The corporation can simultaneously demonstrate commitment and control. As employees gain experience and reputation in the corporation, then the degree of latitude that they are allowed to exercise increases. Their commitment to the corporation can be cemented by deferring some of the earnings that they have accrued to the future. But for them to be willing to accept this, they must trust the corporation not to squander or expropriate it. That is where the declining ability of owners of corporations to be able to commit is so damaging. It means that those who would otherwise be willing to make commitments will abstain from doing so. The growth in executive compensation over the last few years is a manifestation of the lack of trust of executives in the corporation to look after their longer-term interests. The collapse of defined benefit pension schemes is an illustration of how their distrust is justified—corporations have systematically eroded pension schemes by reducing contributions ('pension holidays') during profitable periods, thereby undermining them during less profitable times.

The changing nature of the corporation has meant that it has become progressively less a commitment mechanism and increasingly a control device. We no longer trust the corporation to look after our interests and with considerable justification, because the corporation can no longer offer commitments in the way in which it could when finance came from local banks, ownership was concentrated, capital was permanent, and executives could uphold the interests of other stakeholders. We must value the corporation's values and trust it to uphold those values, even in the face of adversity. For it to be able to do this, the corporation needs to have control over its own destiny and protection from external forces that seek to influence it, including its owners. The corporation needs values and it needs to be able to exercise its own governance over those values.

This in principle is the remarkable contribution that institutions are capable of making to our welfare, but of course in practice their potential for doing exactly the opposite is enormous. The history of the world is of some institutions enslaving, subjugating, and persecuting those over whom they have exercised authority, not liberating and enriching them. Institutions ranging from government to religion have frequently done more in the name of personal and social well-being to diminish than enhance individual capabilities by curtailing freedom and limiting options. They therefore threaten rather than protect our liberty and prosperity.

That is where the corporation has an advantage because it offers the potential for individual choice that other institutions do not provide. Employees can choose the companies for which they work. Customers can choose the corporations from which they purchase products. Shareholders and banks can choose the companies in which they invest. Societies can choose the companies that they wish to support and those they wish to restrain. If we can choose to abide by the restrictions imposed by the corporation then we can enhance our commitment to the welfare of others while avoiding the curtailment of liberties that other institutions impose. It is a distinction between voluntarily agreeing to restrict our freedom to achieve desired outcomes in the future and having our liberty involuntarily curtailed to no benefit to us now or in the future.

It is an important distinction and it means that the corporation holds out greater potential than other institutions, such as government, for establishing the commitment that we are individually unable to demonstrate. However, for it to be accepted in this role, then it must expound and uphold values with which we feel much more comfortable than we have to date.

Part II: Why It Is Happening

Corporations have evolved in some countries from closely held, family owned to widely dispersed, largely institutionally owned entities. This has occurred in the process of corporations growing and financing their activities through issuing equity. It is particularly associated with growth through acquisition funded by stock markets. Where this has happened, it has created a separation between the ownership and control of corporations which has weakened the governance of corporations and the accountability of management.

Markets for corporate control and shareholder activism emerged as mechanisms for correcting this failure. They have yielded large benefits for the shareholders of targeted companies and they have allowed shareholders to circumvent management in implementing more profitable strategies. However, they have come at a price, namely the ability of the corporation to provide commitments to its stakeholders.

The benefit of being able to commit is the trust that it engenders in others and their willingness in turn to make investments and sacrifices which in the absence of such commitments they are reluctant to do. By separating ownership and control of the corporation, shareholders are able to delegate authority to directors who can make commitments to other parties that shareholders would like but are unable credibly to provide themselves. The significance of the corporation as a distinct legal entity is its ability to commit in a way in which other organizations cannot.

Bank finance is critical to this. It is a primary source of capital for owners who wish to retain control of corporations. Where it is readily available, such as in 18th- and 19th-century Britain, in the US, and in many other countries in the world, then it has allowed corporations to grow without dispersing their ownership; where it has been more restricted, such as in 20th-century Britain, then equity markets have provided alternative sources which have dispersed the ownership of founding families. Dispersed ownership has had the benefit of restricting the damaging influence that families can exert on the commercial activities of corporations, but it has also undermined the ability of families to provide the long-term commitments which dispersed anonymous shareholders are incapable of offering.

Commitment and control lie at the heart of the corporation and achieving the right balance between the two is critical to its success. To date, little attention has been given by business or economic historians to the factors shaping the balance between the two. This is a serious omission, as policies that shift it in one direction or the other can have widespread ramifications and a failure to appreciate this can have unintended consequences. One example of this is the adverse effect that the promotion of bank consolidations in response to their financial distress had on their provision of funding for small and medium-sized enterprises. In seeking to correct these mistakes we need to appreciate not only their underlying causes, but also the full potential for the corporation to address a variety of issues that we have been unable to resolve to date.

III

WHAT WE SHOULD
DO ABOUT IT

Chapter 8: Value and Values

What we should be valuing in the corporation and the measures of it; shareholder value as an outcome not a goal, and its potential adverse effects on corporate and industrial performance; the relevance of the financial structure of corporations; the importance of dividends; limited liability as a restriction on shareholder commitment; the significance of incorporation and the separation of ownership and control for upholding corporate values; the benefits of diversity in corporate form and the way in which regulation can undermine this; the need for regulation in the context of systemic risks; longevity and the survival of the corporation as indicators of corporate success

Chapter 9: Governance and Government

The trust firm; its role in exercising governance and protecting stakeholders; the relation of the trust firm to existing organizations and the circumstances in which it is appropriate; the maturity of shares and commitment of shareholders; the need to balance commitment and control, and its implication for different classes of shares; the public purpose of the corporation and what the trust firm can do to fulfil this; the tragedy of the commons and what the trust firm can do to resolve it; the significance of the trust firm for economic development and the lessons that should be learnt for the success of mobile money

Chapter 10: Without End

The amoral nature of the corporation and the importance of values; what role the board of trustees can play in upholding values; the structure of shareholdings and long-term interests; public purpose and the protection of our heritage; the process by which the proposals in this book should be scrutinized, disseminated, and implemented; their implications for practitioners and policymakers

Chapter 8
Value and Values

'What is a cynic? A man who knows the price of everything and the value of nothing.'

Oscar Wilde

Death Value

In 1987 Jeremy Edwards, John Kay, and I published a book with a title of limited popular appeal—'The Economic Analysis of Accounting Profitability'[1]—it was perhaps not surprising that it did not make it to the airport bookstalls or the bestseller lists.

Nevertheless, it had a significant impact on the way in which policymakers in the UK thought about the performance of firms and used profits and value to regulate companies and control monopoly abuse. The book made the straightforward point that value and profit have no absolute meaning, but can only be considered against a well-defined alternative. There is no absolute value to a company any more than there is to a painting or a house. The value that you attach to purchasing 32 Maynard

Close, Milton Keynes is relative to buying 16 Maynard Close or a house in nearby Precedent Drive. In the case of regulation and anti-trust investigations we suggested that the most relevant alternatives are the cost and value of entry and exit from an industry.

One of the supposed merits of shareholder value is that it is measurable and precise. There is no confusion as in the case of the stakeholder firm of trying to pursue multiple and frequently conflicting objectives. Firm values are available for all to see on stock markets and in their company accounts. In contrast, there is no observable basis on which to measure the value that other stakeholders attach to a firm.

In fact, the reliance that people place on stock market values is spurious. That they are based on the assessments of a large of number of investors does not lend them any particular reliability. On the contrary, the outcome of a large number of people making assessments about the uncertain distant prospects of a firm's earnings is likely to be particularly subjective and, as the behavioural economics literature has argued, prone to systematic biases and mistakes.

Market values are informative about the assessment that investors make of the benefit of investing in a firm as against investing in another firm or another security of similar risk. They are particularly useful in evaluating how investors respond to the arrival of a new piece of information about a firm. For example, some studies have examined the stock market reaction to the unexpected news of the death of firms' chief executive officers (CEOs) and often report that the stock market reacts positively to the news.[2] It must be comforting to CEOs to know that their untimely death will at least bring joy to their investors. In fact, given their fiduciary responsibility to their shareholders, perhaps ritual suicide should become a statutory requirement for CEOs.

Even if market valuations were accurate, that would not justify basing the objectives of the firm on them. They should provide no more of a guide to future corporate prospects than long-range weather forecasts do of the desirability of holidaying in Britain and they should certainly not exert any more control over how corporations allocate their resources than a meteorological office does over where tourists take their holidays. We should start at the other end and determine what we want firms to do and then establish the metrics by which we evaluate their performance. After all, as John Maynard Keynes reputedly said, 'it is better to be approximately right than precisely wrong'.[3]

Social Value

One of the most enduring legacies of the post-Second World War era was the programme of privatizations that Margaret Thatcher's government set in train in the UK in the 1980s. Whole swathes of the UK economy that were formerly in the public sector were sold to the private sector. The UK privatization programme prompted similar programmes throughout the world. There were privatizations in Africa, Asia, and South America as well as in Europe, most notably Eastern Europe, and North America.

Once in the private sector, the formerly public enterprises were subject to regulation. Regulation was designed to ensure that the privatized enterprises, which were sometimes monopolies or oligopolies in their industries, did not exploit their customers by charging excessively high prices, and delivered the quality and quantity of services that were expected of them. The questions that the regulatory bodies had to address were how to determine the activities that the privatized corporations should be encouraged to perform and how to reward them for those services. What emerged was a new industry—regulatory departments and regulatory offices—that were designed to answer these questions.

Key to this was to attach values to the services provided. For the most part these were cost based—the projected minimum capital and operating expenditure required to make utility services such as electricity, gas, and water available to a country's population—and then unit prices were estimated on the basis of projected levels of demand that would just cover the costs. The value which capital markets attached to the companies that provided these services reflected the degree to which they were able to deliver services at less or more than the projected costs. In essence, regulatory departments determined the values that society attached to the quality and quantity of services that the utility firms were expected to provide and then companies sought to deliver them at the lowest cost.

The main deficiency that emerged in this arrangement was in its practical implementation. As described in Chapter 4, the separation between regulatory departments and corporations repeatedly placed regulators in conflict with and at an information disadvantage to their regulated companies. It was relatively easy to bring down the operating costs of the privatized utilities, but much harder to ensure, on the one hand, that they invested adequately for the future and, on the other, did not over-invest to excessive standards or levels of capacity at the expense of customers. Nevertheless, methods of valuing services and ensuring their efficient delivery are now quite well established in the utility sector.

Elsewhere, attempts to determine social values have been less successful. Environmental pollution has been one of the least successful. Proposals to project the environmental effects of corporate activities and attach values to them have made virtually no progress. Determining likely future impacts is hard, attaching values to them still harder, and evaluating the appropriate rate at which to discount the future costs back to the present well nigh impossible. So the valuation of environmental degradation is extremely subjective and has been infeasible to implement with anything like the required degree of precision. As a consequence, there are essentially no mechanisms for ensuring that companies internalize the effects of their costs on the environment.

The reason that environmental valuation has failed is that it starts from a very different position from the regulation of utilities. Instead of looking at the problem from the perspective of the cost of pollution avoidance, it attempts to attach values to the effects of pollution. This is destined to fail. A more promising approach is to define the public policy as one that has no net impact on the environment or a maximum 10 to 20 per cent increase in particulate emissions, and then determine the lowest-cost way of achieving this. In other words, values should not be defined by unreliable and subjective discounted future environmental costs, but by the lowest costs at which any level of pollution can be avoided.

The application of this approach can be illustrated in relation to our 'natural capital'—the stock of the world's ecosystems. How should we value our plants, wildlife, fish, air, and rivers? How should we account for the diversity of our ecosystems? How should we ensure that they are sustainable and continue to be replenished? To date, the answer is we have not done so, and we have consumed them as if they were a free good whose exploitation was of no consequence. So long as their rate of depletion was modest, then that might have been a reasonable assumption.

But that is manifestly no longer the case and our failure to account for the depreciation of the world's stock of natural capital is having devastating consequences for our well-being and the survival of our descendants.

To stop this abuse, it has been suggested that we should start to include the value of natural capital in our national accounts alongside that of such man-made assets as buildings, equipment, and infrastructure.[4] By so doing it is argued that we would take proper account of our natural resources and the cost of exploiting them for alternative uses. Admirable though this sounds in principle, it suffers from two serious deficiencies. First, valuations of natural capital are highly subjective and contentious. The value that I attach to preservation of the Sumatran rhinoceros might be quite different from yours and both our valuations will be different from those of people in other parts of the world or other generations. Second, the concern that valuation of natural capital raises amongst its opponents is that it legitimizes precisely the threat from which the ecosystem should be protected, namely its treatment as a marketable commodity which can be consumed or transferred to alternative use at an appropriate price.

On the other hand, we have clearly not served our ecosystem well by failing to account for it at all. A more appropriate and practical approach is to determine how much it costs to sustain it and avoid its degradation and destruction. How much do we have to spend to protect species, to preserve rainforests, and to keep our rivers, lakes, and seas clean? These are quantifiable numbers about which there can be a measure of agreement. Furthermore, they do not presume that there is a value to these assets which can be realized by transferring them to alternative uses or owners. They recognize that unlike private goods, natural capital is neither alienable in being transferable to other owners nor appropriable in having enforceable legal property claims. And unlike public goods such as defence, parks, and policing, in its purest form it is not even controllable in being capable of improvement by human intervention. Instead, it is just vulnerable to neglect and exploitation, and needs to be preserved and protected. The costs of sustaining the ecosystem appropriately evaluate the resources that are required to ensure that that happens.

Another illustration of this approach is the proposal to introduce 'payment by results' in the health service. What this attempts to do is to value public health services and reward providers in relation to their measured performance outcomes, for example the extent to which they succeed in curing drug addicts of their addiction. In fact, what it does is produce a host of unintended and undesirable outcomes, for example a focus on curing relatively mildly addicted patients in comparison with their hard-core counterparts. Instead, again the focus should be on defining the services that should be provided and the minimum cost at which we can legitimately expect those services to be supplied, and not on incentivizing through attaching values to particular outcomes.

In all the above cases it has been perfectly possible to provide reasonable estimates of the value of services that go well beyond normal market activities. It has been perfectly possible to do so once the services that are being sought have been defined. In fact, the reliability of current costs of providing pollution abatement or health care services is greater than market estimates of the present value of future earnings, as reflected in the share price of corporations. If measurability and precision were the relevant criteria, then we should all be proponents of stakeholder rather than shareholder economies. But they are not; the challenge lies not in determining values of activities that are traditionally regarded as immeasurable, but in identifying the things that we really value. To date, some countries appear to have been quite unsuccessful at doing that and two examples illustrate why.

Shared Values

There were few more admired members of the British industrial establishment than Arnold Weinstock. He joined Radio and Allied Industries in 1954 and through his single-minded focus on cutting costs and improving productivity, he turned it into one of the most profitable British television set manufacturers. When the General Electric Company (GEC) took over Radio and Allied in 1961, Weinstock became a substantial shareholder in GEC and in 1963 he was appointed managing director, a post that he held until he retired in 1996.

In 1967, with the support of the British government, GEC took over Associated Electrical Industries (AEI) and in the following year English Electric, to create an electrical engineering giant, ranking alongside General Electric in the US, Philips in the Netherlands, and Siemens and AEG in Germany. Rationalization of the acquisitions resulted in a spectacular increase in profits.

> The secret is to see what the market will pay for a product. You then see if you can manufacture at that price. You then work out what you can get off the costs by squeezing a discount out of the suppliers, producing in bulk, reducing your manpower—and that is your profit.[5]

In 1989, in conjunction with Siemens, GEC engineered a hostile acquisition of one of Britain's major electronics companies, Plessey. By the time that Weinstock retired in 1996, GEC had profits of just over £1 billion on sales of £11 billion, with cash reserves of £1.1 billion. His successor, George Simpson, spurred by the stock market's enthusiasm for telecoms, moved GEC away from its traditional activities in defence, making two large telecoms-related acquisitions in the US. Renamed Marconi to reflect its break from the past, the stock market value of the company soared until the technology bubble burst in 2000, leaving it with crippling debts and a perilous financial situation. After narrowly avoiding insolvency, it staggered on until a majority of its assets were sold to the Swedish corporation Ericsson, leaving Telent, a company that delisted in 2007, to become a private company, as the only British remnant of the once world-dominant electrical and electronics engineering firm. The rest of British electronics—Ferranti, Racal, and Thorn–EMI—went the same way, with Vodafone, a mobile phone service provider carved out of Racal in the early 1990s, as the brightest surviving star.

What Weinstock did brilliantly was to exert financial control over an industry in which control was sorely lacking. What he failed to do was to build on the major acquisitions that he engineered to establish a world-dominant business. He created immense financial wealth for his shareholders, but success for the City did not equate to success for the British electrical and electronics industries that he came to lead.

The Arnold Weinstock story is one that was replicated elsewhere in the UK. The City promoted conglomerate mergers as the saviour of British industry in the 1960s, then focus and demergers in the 1980s, then the technology boom in the 1990s, and finally the technology collapse in the 2000s. Weinstock was actually less in awe of the stock market and his share price than many of his other business colleagues and certainly his successor, but even he could not ignore their powerful influence.

Arnold Weinstock's counterpart in the US was Jack Welch in the namesake US firm General Electric (GE). In the year before Welch became chief executive officer (CEO) in 1981, GE had revenues of $27 billion; in the year before he left in 2001 they had increased to around $130 billion and its market value had risen over the period by a factor of nearly thirty. In 1999 Jack Welch was named as 'Manager of the Century' by Fortune magazine.

Like Weinstock, Welch's success in large part derived from his focus on costs and efficiency, for which he famously earned the nickname 'Neutron Jack'—a reference to the power of neutron bombs to eliminate people while leaving buildings intact. In particular, GE was far more successful at controlling its working capital costs than its arch-rival, Westinghouse Electric.[6] So much so that, while over the period of Welch's tenure GE's fortunes thrived, Westinghouse took on a large amount of debt, encountered serious financial difficulties in the 1990s, steadily sold off all the industrial activities with which it was previously associated to purchase a number of media companies including CBS, and eventually, in 2000, ceased to exist as a separate business when it was acquired by another media company, Viacom.

Success in the UK and US electrical and electronics industries was thus in large part determined by cost control and the ability of their CEOs to impose it. Very welcome as this clearly was to their shareholding communities, the focus on costs was not necessarily the recipe for industrial success. For in creating shareholder value, both Weinstock and Welch were overshadowed in the development of their industries by the newly emerging giants, first in Japan, then in Korea, and most recently in China. And the focus of corporations in these countries was quite different from that of their UK and US counterparts.

In a survey of between fifty and one hundred middle managers in each of France, Germany, Japan, UK, and US, Masaru Yoshi-mori assessed the views of people in the five countries about the purpose and policies of their companies.[7] In the UK and US, 71 per cent and 76 per cent of respondents respectively saw it as being run for its shareholders rather than its stakeholders more broadly, while just 22 per cent in France, 17 per cent in Germany, and 3 per cent in Japan viewed it in this way. The purpose of the corporation is therefore regarded very differently in different countries. So, too, are its policies. In response to a question about whether their CEO attached greater significance to main-taining their dividends than retaining their workforce, in both the UK and US 90 per cent of respondents thought that the CEO regarded dividends as more important than employment, whereas 60 per cent of respondents in both France and Germany and 97 per cent of respondents in Japan thought that their CEO viewed job security as more important than dividends.[8]

UK and US CEOs are unusual in putting shareholders before other stakeholders and dividends before employment. Their cor-porate preoccupation with cost cutting, financial performance, and share value is not shared by their counterparts elsewhere. In most countries, it is the success of the business that CEOs worry about; in the UK and US it is the financial performance.

The preoccupation with finances in the UK and the US is misconceived and damaging. Shareholder value is an outcome, not an objective. It should not drive corporate policy but be treated as a product of it. Setting a company's objectives in relation to its share price is like determining an individual's lifestyle and medication on the basis of their body temperature.

If you try to maintain your temperature permanently at 37 degrees Celsius, you will certainly get sick. If you do not inflict serious physical damage on yourself from drowning in liquids or enduring freezing conditions, you will definitely suffer immense psychological damage from your neurotic preoccupation with your thermometer.

A company's share price is no more than a partial and imprecise meter of corporate performance that like your thermometer should be examined occasionally and disregarded more frequently than it is actively considered. No lesser a figure than Jack Welch recognized this when he said in an interview with the *Financial Times* in March 2009 about the financial crisis: 'On the face of it, shareholder value is the dumbest idea in the world. Shareholder value is a result, not a strategy . . . your main constituencies are your employees, your customers and your products.' Perhaps not all of his employees recognized this when they worked for him, but at least that is what, with hindsight, Neutron Jack professed to practise.

However, there is one important distinction between personal preoccupation with thermometers and corporate focus on share prices. While we are at liberty to ignore our thermometer, a CEO is not similarly free to ignore their corporation's share prices, at least not in the UK or, in some cases, in the US. It is as if the angel of death is lingering above the CEOs' heads, waiting to pounce the moment they allow their body temperature to deviate from 37 degrees Celsius. That angel of death is the corporate predator, the acquirer, who on perceiving the slightest deviation of a firm's share price from what they regard as an attainable level can launch a hostile bid against the unsuspecting target management. Like it or not, the British and in some cases the American CEO has no option but to worry, continuously and feverishly, about their corporation's share price. That is why, quite rightly, middle managers in the UK and US saw their CEOs as being preoccupied with different concerns from their counterparts elsewhere. And what in part drove their CEOs' concerns about dividends was their schooling.

Trivial Pursuits

'Name me one proposition in all of the social sciences which is both non-trivial and true.' When faced with this challenge from the renowned Polish mathematician Stanislaw Ulam, the one response that the Nobel laureate economist Paul Samuelson could eventually give was the principle of comparative advantage from international trade—the gains from trade that a country derives from specializing in those activities in which it has a relative advantage, even if it has an absolute advantage in none. 'That it is logically true need not be argued before a mathematician; that it is not trivial is attested by the thousands of important and intelligent people who have never been able to grasp the doctrine for themselves or to believe it after it was explained to them.'[9]

Applying the same criteria in finance, the one contender for Stanislaw Ulam's challenge is the irrelevance of capital structure, advanced by the Nobel prize winning economists Franco Modligliani and Merton Miller—the proposition, that under certain conditions, the value of a firm is unaffected by how it is financed through debt or equity or a combination of both. That it is logically true under its assumptions is evidenced by the fact that it has not been falsified in the fifty years since it was first advanced; that it is not trivial is attested by the fact that men and women of indisputable intelligence in all walks of life have been unable to grasp it, even after they have sat through hours of classes patiently explaining it to them. As a lecturer in finance, I can vouch for the second part of that sentence.

Some of the inability of the audience of the lectures to grasp the proposition might derive from their reluctance to do so. The assertion that the activities for which they earn unimaginable sums of money is of no value is not one which immediately endears itself to them. Since the logical derivation of the proposition from its assumptions is incontrovertible, they prefer instead to seek to rubbish its assumptions. That is not hard to do since the assumptions, literally interpreted, are demanding. However, the importance of the proposition that finance does not matter for the value of the firm derives less from its validity than from identifying the conditions under which it applies. Like Isaac Newton's laws of motion, it is evident that there are frictions that undermine its practical application but, without understanding the frictionless world of Modigliani and Miller, it is impossible to appreciate the significance of the frictions. What the Modigliani and Miller theorem clarifies is the importance of the frictions for the actual forms of finance that companies choose to adopt.

The first friction is taxes. In the absence of taxation, the composition of finance does not matter for the value of the firm, but if the tax authorities treat some forms of finance differently from others then a substantial amount of resources will inevitably be devoted to avoiding those forms that are treated less favourably. So, for example, tax authorities around the world treat the interest payments on debt borrowings in the form of bank loans and bonds more favourably than the equivalent dividend payments on equity finance from shareholders. There is, therefore, a strong tax incentive to use debt in preference to equity.

A great deal of analysis has demonstrated that important though taxes are in principle, they do not provide an adequate explanation for the capital structures that firms around the world choose. The second friction that the Modigliani and Miller proposition highlights is the paucity of information that investors have about what the firm is doing. If it is difficult for investors to be able to evaluate accurately the likely future performance of the firms in which they invest, then information communicated through firms' chosen capital structure will affect their stock market value. For example, the proportion of their earnings which firms pay their shareholders as dividends is thought to reflect managers' degree of optimism about their future prospects. Again, plausible though this is, it has at best only provided a partial explanation for how firms structure their finances.

Fifty years since the Modigliani and Miller proposition was first formulated and despite a huge industry being devoted to researching the financial decisions of firms, there remain fundamental inconsistencies between what firms do and what it would appear rational for them to do.

Dividend Puzzles

It was the depth of the British recession at the beginning of the 1980s. Of all the British industrial companies, Imperial Chemical Industry (ICI) was probably the most eminent and successful. In its heyday it was the largest manufacturing company in the British Empire and regarded as the bell-wether of the British economy. So when the recession hit, it was not surprising that

ICI's earnings fell and it found itself short of cash. It was, therefore, also not surprising that it sought to retain a greater proportion of its scarce earnings in the business and pay out less to its shareholders as dividends.

You might think so, but its shareholders did not agree. Its announcement that it was cutting its dividends sent a shockwave round the City of London, its share price plummeted, and it was prevented from accessing the stock market for funds for the best part of the decade. Ten years later it was subject to a hostile bid from the serial predator, Hanson plc. Starved of funds it progressively sold its pharmaceuticals division and then its commodity chemicals business until it was left with nothing but Dulux paints, which it sold to the Dutch firm Akzo Nobel in 2007.

'Shareholders are stupid and impertinent. Stupid because they give their money to somebody else with no effective control over what this person does with it and impertinent because they ask for a dividend as a reward for their stupidity.' With these words, Carl Fürstenberg, the famous German banker (1850–1933), attacked the shareholder fraternity and raised questions about corporate dividend policy which persist till today.

Why do firms pay dividends? Why do they pay their shareholders dividends in the year in which they raise new equity from the very same shareholders, thereby incurring substantial fees to investment bankers for arranging the new issues and income taxes on their shareholders' dividends, when they could instead have simply withheld the dividends? Since shareholders own firms, they own the earnings that firms retain on their behalf. They should not therefore care whether money is retained in the business or paid out to them and they certainly should discourage firms from imposing unnecessary income tax on them or fees on their firms by paying dividends when the funds are needed in the business.

What underlies the Modigliani and Miller proposition, and thereby the whole of modern corporate finance, is the direct identification of the corporation with its owners, its shareholders. It is not just that the corporation is run in the interests of its shareholders; the corporation is its shareholders. They own the corporation and therefore what it retains to fund its activities is their property and indistinguishable from the property they live in, drive in, or sleep in. It really makes no difference whether the corporation holds property on their behalf; it is theirs and only delegated to others to manage because it is believed that they are particularly competent at doing it.

The basic proposition of this book is that this principle is fundamentally wrong. By design as well as legal construct, a corporation is a separate entity from its owners just as you are different from me. Just as I might have certain legal rights over you as my employee or supplier, so too I have certain legal rights over the corporation as my property. But my rights are deliberately constrained, deliberately because if they were not then there would be no purpose in establishing a company as against being an unincorporated business. This inverts the underlying premise in Chapter 2 of shareholder value requiring managers to uphold the interests of vulnerable shareholders. The justification for the separate legal construct is that it creates opportunities which in its absence would not exist, just as your separate existence creates opportunities that would not exist if we were one and the same person.

In particular, the separate existence of the corporation allows its owners to provide commitments to others which, in its absence, would not be possible. Some of these are contractual but most are not and, where they are not, the separate nature of the company provides a basis on which owners can make commitments that would otherwise not be credible.

This distinction between the corporation and its owners has fundamental implications for all aspects of corporate activities, including finance. To take dividends as an example, since the corporation has a separate legal persona from its owners, what is retained in the corporation is not the same as what is in the possession of its shareholders, any more than what you possess is my property too. This is not a distortion or a deficiency of the corporation; it is quite deliberately structured to allow shareholders to establish outcomes that they would otherwise be incapable of achieving.

Once the separation of corporation and owners is recognized, then the significance of dividend policy becomes transparent. Reducing dividends and raising new equity issues are now no longer equivalent ways of increasing the corporation's capital resources. Retained earnings are under the control of the corporation; new equity issues come from funds that are under the control of shareholders. The larger the corporation's dividend payments, the more frequently it has to come back to its shareholders to raise equity finance and the greater the control that is transferred to shareholders.[10]

This is reflected in the way in which investors exercise control over poorly performing management. Interventions typically come in response to financial difficulties which necessitate the raising of additional funds from lenders or shareholders.[11] The power of the investors in such circumstances derives from their ability to make the provision of new finance conditional on management implementing the changes that their investors deem necessary to rectify the underperformance. The more control in the hands of investors, the less in the hands of the corporation, and the less commitment that the corporation can credibly give to other parties.

We can illustrate this with the example of colinmayer plc. The company has $150,000 of debt and $150,000 equity and employees are exposed to the tune of $30,000. The management has thus far resolutely resisted implementing the risky investment that offers shareholders an expected return of 50 per cent. But the management now decides to pay out its equity capital as a dividend or to buy back its shares. After all, it is shareholder capital, and according to Modigliani and Miller it makes no difference whether it is in the hands of shareholders or retained in the business. Having paid it out, the management seek to raise it in the form of a new equity issue. The shareholders agree, but are only willing to do so if the corporation implements the risky investment that threatens creditors' and employees' interests but significantly benefits shareholders. The degree of commitment that shareholders can credibly demonstrate to other stakeholders is critically influenced by the corporation's dividend policy and is undermined by the apparently innocuous recycling of funds through dividends and new issues.

This is just one example of how financial policy affects the ability of a corporation to commit to its stakeholders. The most dramatic illustration came in the recent financial crisis.

Resurrecting Capital Structures

Between 2000 and 2008 the four main banks in the UK (Barclays, HSBC, Lloyds, and Royal Bank of Scotland) doubled the ratio of debt to equity capital on their balance sheets from sixteen to thirty-two.[12] The banks' cushion to protect them against the type of financial shock that struck in 2008 had been eroded, with devastating consequences when it came. Why did they allow this to happen?

The amount of equity that a corporation has on its balance sheet is an important determinant of its resilience to financial difficulties. The larger the proportion of equity, the greater the depth of capital that is committed to the business and the more immune it is to adverse financial developments. A large amount of debt and little equity (a high level of 'leverage') leaves corporations exposed to financial failure with insufficient capital and thus stakeholders to the termination of the corporation's business.

In the case of Colin Mayer Ltd., the leverage of the corporation—the ratio of debt to equity—is one to one ($150,000 of each of debt and equity). With this capital structure, from a shareholder's perspective the risky investment offered the attractive prospect of an expected return of 50 per cent. If the corporation replaced its debt (bank and bond) finance with equity by issuing shares, then this would no longer be the case. If the corporation was all equity financed, then the investment would offer a zero expected return to shareholders and at considerable risk. It would therefore be rejected by shareholders. If, on the other hand, like banks, it was 90 per cent debt financed with $270,000 of bank and bond capital, then the expected return to shareholders would rise from 50 per cent to 450 per cent—nine times as much—because shareholders have captured the same gains with a fraction of the capital previously invested, exposing much more debt to the risk of loss.

The incentive to act recklessly is far greater at higher levels of leverage. It is not only creditors who are adversely affected by this but also other stakeholders. The willingness of employees to expose their $30,000 of vulnerable employment to the 90 per cent leveraged corporation will be much smaller than to the unlevered corporation. They will correctly perceive a lower level of commitment by shareholders to the protection of their livelihood in high than low leveraged corporations.[13] From the perspective of a Modigliani and Miller corporation, it does not make any difference whether I borrow $150,000 personally as Colin Mayer or corporately as Colin Mayer Ltd.—it leaves me overall with the same level of leverage either directly on my own account or indirectly through my corporation. From the point of view of employees and other stakeholders, it is critically important. Debt in the company affects them and their livelihood in a way in which debt on my personal balance sheet does not.[14]

Leverage affects stakeholders' faith in the company because it determines the depth of capital committed.[15] If the corporation has too much debt relative to equity, then it will be too financially vulnerable to sustain credible beneficial relations with other parties; if it has too little debt, then it will be over-exposed to other parties, such as trade unions, and excessively vulnerable to them.[16] There is therefore an optimal proportion of equity capital that reflects the capital commitment which the corporation should be providing to its stakeholders.[17]

Following the elimination of the separation between stock broking and market making with 'Big Bang' in the UK in 1986 and between commercial and investment banking with the repeal of the Glass–Steagall Act in the US in 1999, the 1990s and 2000s were periods of rapid expansion of investment banking. Fee-based transaction activity increased relative to traditional commercial margin lending and borrowing. Investment banking involved shorter-term relations with customers than commercial banking and demanded less capital to protect customers. Leverage therefore grew naturally as the outcome of the change in the composition of banking, but when the financial crisis struck, it was not just investment banking that was exposed.[18] The crisis resulted in commercial as well as investment banking failures.

In itself the combination of businesses with different levels of commitment was not a problem or unusual. It happens routinely in conglomerates operating in several industries and some banks chose not to follow the trend to universal banking by retaining independent commercial banks. But what made banking different was the degree of interconnections between financial institutions. Nearly two-thirds of the rapid increase in banks' balance sheets prior to the crisis was attributable to lending not to the rest of the economy but amongst banks themselves.[19]

The reduction in capital commitment in commercial banking therefore had serious national and international repercussions for financial systems as a whole, as well as for investors in individual institutions. The threat that the failure of large universal banks posed for countries' financial system meant that they could not actually be allowed to fail—except of course in the case of Lehman Brothers, and the disastrous repercussions of that made a repeat of it inconceivable. They were protected by governments which bailed them out at huge cost to the public purse. In effect, the public sector provided capital commitment to the banks through deposit insurance and rescue funds such as the Troubled Asset Relief Program (TARP) in the US, and these public commitments substituted for private commitments, resulting in a withdrawal of private sector capital.

Avoidance of a recurrence of this 'crowding out' of private commitments in the future will require governments to desist from being the guarantors of the banks and shareholders to resume their proper function of performing this instead. There is a role for public commitments in protecting financial systems, but only against system-wide failures, not those of individual institutions. The imposition of requirements on banks to hold sufficient capital to extinguish their individual risks of failure makes them excessively exposed to their stakeholders, in particular their borrowers. As happened in the post-financial crisis period, it therefore results in a withdrawal of banks from the provision of lending to the corporate sector, with devastating consequences for economic activity.

It is not just the amount of debt which matters in a commitment context, but so too does its form. It matters whether corporate lending comes from local banks, which are committed to their borrowers, or international banks that are not, or from bond markets where lenders' commitment is particularly weak. It matters whether the lending is short term and can be withdrawn with little notice or long term where it cannot. It matters whether inflation rates and interest rates are high, causing repayments to be 'front-loaded' to the early years of loans or back loaded to later years through being indexed to the price level. It therefore matters for a vast array of corporate activities that have been difficult to rationalize to date. And in particular it matters for what was probably the most significant innovation in the corporation.

Limited Liability

There was not a man who was practically concerned in any large commercial undertaking, who was not convinced that the measure, if passed, would not only be most useless, but most mischievous [. . .] The only effect of the Bill would be to induce ignorant

persons to enter into the most delusive and disastrous undertak-
ings [. . .] Men having small capital would invest it in undertak-
ings of the nature of which they would be totally ignorant, and
would have to entrust the sole management of their property to a
body of directors, who, instead of being the servants, would be the
masters of the Company [. . .] He objected to the Bill, because it
was not founded on a sound principle, and because he believed
that, instead of serving the working man and persons of small
capital, it would mislead them, and would deceive society itself.[20]

The Bill to which the Right Honourable Mr Muntz objected
so strongly was one before the House of Commons in London on
26 July 1855 relating to the proposed introduction of limited
liability for companies.

Limited liability—the provision by which in the event of a
company failure, the shareholders are only liable for the capital
they have invested in the corporation, not for any further call on
their personal assets—had been encountered in various forms in
Britain in the 17th century, including in the East India Company,
but it was not widespread. Attempts by parties in England to
establish limited liability agreements between themselves were
struck down by the courts on the grounds that they 'militate
against the principle of partnership . . . that every person engaged
in a partnership is liable solidarily, as they say upon the Continent, for everything'.[21] Until the introduction of limited liability
in 1856, limited liability was only granted through Acts of Parliament that were restricted to public investments in, for example,
the canals and railways.

The original pressure for its introduction came neither from
investors nor entrepreneurs, but from a group of middle-class
philanthropists, the Christian Socialists, who saw limited liability
as a way of encouraging working-class people to save and thereby

alleviate poverty. The cause was subsequently taken up by those advocating freedom of contract, most notably Robert Lowe. But it was really a pragmatic response to developments across the English Channel that finally forced Parliament to accept limited liability. The Vice President of the Board of Trade, E. P. Bouverie, stated in June 1855 that 'during the last two years at least twenty companies have been formed in France solely for the same purposes. They are, in truth, English companies, both as to capital and directors, and all this expenditure is just much money taken from this country and paid to France as a consideration for the use of her laws.'[22] The laws of France that were so troublesome to the Board of Trade were derived from the Napoleonic Code de Commerce of 1807, which established the *société anonyme* and the *société en commandite par actions* as limited liability organizations.

As the *Economist* recorded in 1926, 'the economic historian of the future [. . .] may be inclined to assign to the nameless inventor of the principle of limited liability, as applied to trading corporations, a place of honour with Watt and Stephenson, and other pioneers of the Industrial Revolution'.[23] Nevertheless, according to traditional corporate finance and the Modigliani and Miller theorem, limited liability is almost an irrelevance. The risks that shareholders avoid through limited liability are simply transferred to the creditors, who bear all of the losses in the event of corporate failure and demand higher interest rates to compensate them for this.

In contrast, limited liability is fundamental within a commitment context because it creates a restriction on commitment, which in its absence would be infeasible. Limited liability imposes a limitation on the exposure of shareholders to losses that otherwise would be unlimited. It therefore allows shareholders to impose an upper bound on the level of commitment they provide to other stakeholders, and it is critically important as a way of balancing the commitments between different parties to the corporation.

As Colin Mayer Ltd. I have a strong incentive to engage in the risky investment. As an unincorporated business I do not. If the risky investment fails, then creditors will come banging on my door demanding that I sell my house to be able to repay the $150,000 that they have lost. Without limited liability, the risky investment is exactly what it is: a zero return, high-risk prospect with no attraction to me as a shareholder. In this regard, elimination of limited liability is one way to discourage frivolous investments. However, without limited liability, exposures of different parties are reversed. Knowing that there is a bottomless pit that is available to bail out the failing corporation, it is my employees not me who will wish to implement the risky investment. I gain nothing on average from it and take considerable risk. Their $30,000 of vulnerable employment is protected by my obligation to bail out the firm if the investment fails. If it succeeds, then they will be working for a more valuable firm from which they will expect to extract higher earnings. I will therefore with some justification mistrust the way in which the firm is managed on my behalf.

The need to balance commitments explains why companies use complex structures with limited liability subsidiaries within larger group organizations.[24] These allow the corporation to display different levels of commitment to different parties. To return to the example of banking, one way in which banks can demonstrate a higher level of commitment to their commercial banking than their investment banking stakeholders is through a holding company structure, in which commercial banking is undertaken in a subsidiary with a higher level of capital than investment banking, and this is what the Independent Commission on Banking has recently proposed for the UK.[25]

If the inventor of limited liability deserves a place alongside Watt and Stephenson, the inventor of the corporation should sit beside Galileo and Newton. While limited liability allowed for a greater diversity in forms of commitment than previously existed, incorporation provided the basis for diversity in the first place. And it is the innovation of incorporation that is currently under threat.

Affirmative Assets

There are five key features of a corporation: (i) a legal personality distinct from its owners and its managers, (ii) centralized management by a board of directors, (iii) shared ownership of capital, (iv) transferable shares, and (v) limited liability. This is the order in which the features of the corporation emerged in England over half a millennium. The corporation developed out of the guilds, which were a pre-Norman Conquest creation that were granted the right to possess and manage property.[26] They took on a trading function that in turn developed into craft guilds and companies of merchants. They established a governance structure involving governors and assistants for the purpose and the rights to enact statutes and ordinances for the exercise of their duties. It was with the expansion into overseas trading in the 16th century that a need to raise capital arose and shared ownership emerged.[27] In the middle of the 17th century the capital of English East India Company became fixed and in return its shares became transferable. It was only in the middle of the 19th century that limited liability was granted.

In Continental Europe the ordering was different. The *societas*, *compagnia*, and *commenda* were legal contracts designed to promote merchant and trading activities. Financing was provided by investors who had a claim on a share of the profits, often with limited liability. The English structure therefore emphasized administration of a public function with the financing of commercial activities developing on the back of this. The Continental European company was from the outset concerned with the financing of trading ventures and the creation of contractual arrangements to achieve this.

There are two forms of separation that are critical to the creation of the legal personality of the corporation. The first is the separation of the assets and liabilities of the corporation from those of the investors. The second is the separation of the management of the corporation from its ownership. The first is achieved by a combination of what are termed 'affirmative and defensive asset partitioning'.[28] Affirmative asset partitioning (or as it is also termed 'entity shielding') protects the assets of the corporation from the creditors of the shareholders of the corporation. It prevents shareholders from using the assets of the corporation to settle their personal liabilities. Defensive asset partitioning is limited liability, which protects the shareholders from the creditors of the corporation. Together they ensure that the assets of the corporation are available to meet the claims of the creditors of the corporation and the personal assets of the shareholders can be used to satisfy their personal liabilities, unencumbered by the debts of the corporations in which they invest. They enable corporations to establish contractual arrangements distinct from those of their owners.

The second form of separation is that of management from ownership. This is achieved by the creation of a body, the board of directors, which is distinct from the members of the corporation. The directors are authorized to manage the capital of the corporation subject to limitations on its activities set out in its charter or memorandum of association. They do not have authority to manage the personal capital of shareholders that has not been subscribed to the corporation. Shareholders have rights to manage their own personal capital, but only very limited rights over the capital in the corporation, in particular over its withdrawal from the corporation.

That in principle is the nature of the corporation. The practice over the past fifty years has been rather different. Affirmative asset partitioning is particularly important for the operation of the corporation. Without it, the corporation becomes an appendage of its owners because, irrespective of the administrative control that the directors are granted, the owners can take on debts that become the responsibility of the corporation. But that is what excessive shareholder control threatens. Instead of doing it by contract, shareholders can set up investment vehicles, let us call them hedge funds for example, which buy shares in a company with a view either to taking it over or to exercising control as an active investor, thereby encouraging it to pay out more of its earnings and assets to its shareholders. This is not done by contract but through the exercise of voting rights, and the effect is very similar. Is it being done for legitimate reasons such as incompetent management or because some of the shareholders have cash requirements to meet their personal liabilities?

In essence, shareholders with immediate cash needs, what we might term 'short-term' shareholders, are extracting cash from the corporation at the expense of other stakeholders. They can do this because the non-shareholding stakeholders have no voting control over the corporation. Anticipating that this will happen, stakeholders will be less willing to invest in the corporation. Shareholders would therefore like to be able to bind themselves from this happening, but once stakeholders are committed it is always in the interest of short-term shareholders to extract cash from the business at their expense. That is the dilemma that markets for corporate control and shareholder activism present and observations that they yield positive share price gains for shareholders tell one nothing about their desirability. This is what would be expected of a mechanism that extracts rents at the expense of non-shareholding stakeholders.

Avoiding this dilution of the benefits of incorporation requires either directors to be granted greater independence than they have at present, which raises agency concerns about self-interested directors pursuing personal gain at the expense of the corporation, or more committed owners and less control in the hands of short-term shareholders, which raises concerns about disempowering shareholders to the benefit of self-interested management. So a resolution of the problem requires corporate governance mechanisms that promote commitment and stronger managerial oversight, and ownership arrangements that encourage both longer-term and more active shareholdings. These are the subject of the next chapter.

Proposals to date have gone in the opposite direction and the reason for this illustrates why we should worry about whether economics provides an adequate description of corporations and financial markets. Being concerned about the validity of economics may appear a highly introspective activity; after all, the world will go on even if economic theory is entirely inadequate. The trouble is it just might not. Practitioners and the public at large may be highly dismissive of economic theories, but there is one group of people that is not.

The Value of Diversity

As described in Chapter 4, the financial crisis sent policymakers and regulators into overdrive. Confronted with the accusation of being caught sleeping on the job, they responded with a vengeance. Consultation documents, recommendations, and reports concerning all aspects of the governance of financial institutions appeared with such speed that one might have been excused for thinking that they had been in the minds of policymakers all along.

The driving principle behind these recommendations is the prevailing economic wisdom that poor corporate governance contributed to the financial crisis, that there is a serious 'agency problem' in aligning the interests of directors of corporations with those of their shareholders, and that regulation needs to be put in place to strengthen corporate governance and ensure a better alignment of interests. For example, there should be a separation of the roles of chairperson and chief executive officer, more non-executive directors on the boards of corporations, and a closer relation between executive remuneration and corporate performance.

Within the context of conventional economic models, these may be sound recommendations. Within the context of the commitment view of the corporation, they are not. Aligning the interests of directors with shareholders makes perfect sense if shareholders are the most vulnerable party, as I have already described conventional theory as suggesting. However, it is the wrong policy if they are not. If, for example, creditors are the main stakeholders at risk, then deepening the capital commitment of shareholders is a prerequisite and strengthening shareholder control without it undermines rather than enhances the soundness of banks.

There is now some recognition amongst policymakers of the inappropriateness of conventional prescriptions in this particular area, but there are wider implications of the commitment view of the corporation. The first proposition is that generally applicable policy proposals concerning the governance of corporations simply do not exist. The balancing of commitments and control is a delicate activity that will be highly specific to the particular nature and context of the corporation. The optimal governance of corporations, as reflected for example in the degrees of capital commitments of different parties, will vary across corporations within industries, let alone across industries and countries. The search for uniform rules of governance is both pointless and damaging.

To illustrate, while I have questioned the emphasis on shareholder value in conventional economic models, there are circumstances in which low shareholder commitment, a high degree of share liquidity, and the anonymity of dispersed ownership will be entirely appropriate. Threats of bankruptcy and takeovers were two means available to British manufacturing corporations to counter militant wage bargaining by trade unions during the 1960s and 1970s, and high dividend distributions and acquisitions were two methods to limit control of regulators over price setting by British utilities during the 1990s and 2000s. Funds that engage in short-term restructurings may be needed to counter entrenched interests in failing organizations, and short-term institutional investments to facilitate removal of entrepreneurs of start-up firms when their useful service is over. However, there will be other circumstances in which a failure to commit is highly damaging to the long-term interest of firms.

As a result, there is not a universally superior form of ownership and governance of firms which is suited to all firms at all times; instead, some arrangements are better suited to certain activities at particular points in time. For example, industries that employ large amounts of skilled labour (for example, machinery and shipbuilding) and those that require a great deal of external equity finance (for example, instruments and electrical machinery) are found to grow particularly rapidly in countries where there are high levels of concentration of ownership. Corporate structure is especially relevant to investment in research and development. Ownership and governance therefore confer comparative advantage on some activities, not absolute advantage on all.[29]

Regulations that impede firms' choice of their appropriate arrangements undermine their performance. For example, one of the most important contributions to the growth of venture capital and Silicon Valley in the US was the relaxation in 1978 of the 'prudent man rule' in the Employee Retirement Income Security Act (ERISA). This had previously restricted investments of pension funds in private equity as too risky, and its relaxation (to allow risks to be measured in relation to portfolios rather than individual investments) made available a major source of funding for US venture capital firms from which until then they had been excluded. There should be divergence of governance arrangements within and across industries and countries, and care should be taken to ensure that regulation does not impede this.

The second proposition is that, while regulation concerning the governance of individual corporations is not appropriate, the regulation and management of economic and financial systems as a whole is essential. Just as managers of individual divisions or subsidiaries of a corporation cannot define the appropriate governance of the corporation, so corporations cannot determine the appropriate governance of economic and financial systems. That is the correct responsibility of national and international authorities. The failure of regulation of the crisis has been to distinguish adequately between individual institutional problems, which are not the proper remit of governments or regulators, and systemic risks, which are.[30] This is the equivalent of distinguishing between the control of pandemic crises, which are the proper concern of public health authorities and beyond the remit of individual doctors, and medical health problems of individual patients, which are not.

Guided by incomplete economic models, the focus of corporate governance and regulation to date has therefore been on the wrong issues—harmonization at the micro, individual corporation level instead of the macro, systemic level. It is not just in relation to policy formulation that the right economic models matter. Achieving diversity at the level of individual corporations is critical for the performance of corporations and their potential to thrive and survive.

Age Cannot Wither Her

The oldest continuously trading independent family firm in the UK today is RJ Balson & Son. Actually there have been a lot of sons since John Balson established the company trading meat at the local market in Bridport, Dorset in 1535 and the business passed through generations of Balsons down to Richard Balson today.[31]

Longevity is not necessarily a virtue, but when it comes to business it says something about the trust and loyalty that customers and employees place in it. Of course there are many British institutions that are much older than the oldest family firms (not least the university of which I am a member), but unlike some of these other organizations, firms have to compete to survive and live by their reputation in the market. The test of time is a trusty sign, particularly so in the UK where, as we have seen, family firm duration is exceptionally short.

Of the three oldest continuously trading family firms, Balson is a butchers (now selling its esteemed sausages in the US as well as the UK), Durtnell and Sons is in its thirteenth generation as a building company standing on the same land that the family owned since its establishment in 1591, and Hoare and Co. is the oldest surviving English deposit bank in its eleventh generation since it was founded in 1672.

What marks out these and the other oldest surviving independent firms is the emphasis that they place on product quality and reliability. While I have not examined their relative pricing, I suspect that Balson does not produce the cheapest sausages in the UK, Durtnell and Sons the cheapest buildings (at least when it came to the refurbishments of Buckingham Palace and Clarence House in London), or Hoare and Co. the cheapest banking services. But equally I suspect that they have been able to provide some of the highest quality products and services on a consistent basis in their industries.

These firms will have done very nicely for their families over a long period of time, but almost certainly not earned nearly as much as some other retailers, construction companies, or financial institutions in the UK at particular points in their history. As a consequence, had they been widely held listed corporations, they would in all probability not have survived, at least as independent firms. They would have been deemed to be failures at various points, failing to generate as large returns for their investors as some of their more racy competitors and would therefore have been taken over by these rivals.

This is illustrated by another group of British corporations that were prominent internationally rather than domestically. The chartered trading companies, such as the East India Company discussed before, were superseded in the 19th century by the merchant trading companies, such as Jardine Matheson and John Swire & Sons, which played a key role in the organization of British international trade. The trading companies remained important elements of British multinational enterprises until the beginning of the 1980s. They survived two World Wars, the Great Depression, and the end of the British Empire, and then, just when liberalization of international trade around the world seemed to create new opportunities for them, they suddenly disappeared. What finally proved to be their downfall was a very domestic problem: the British stock market. With conglomerates falling out of fashion, they were forced to focus and divest their diversified holdings to a point that by the turn of the century few remained in existence. Those that survived, such as the Jardine Matheson and Swire groups, had one thing in common: they were family owned and therefore immune to stock market pressures. 'Curiously, therefore, whilst family ownership and management is sometimes used to explain the conservatism of earlier British trading company, in the final years of the twentieth century it was only to be the family owned firms that survived.'[32]

Financial benefit is a product of quality and reliability, but quality and reliability are not a product of financial benefit. If the latter are the corporation's values, then the former do not follow, but if the former are the corporation's values, then the latter might well (but not necessarily) follow. The deficiency of the dispersed ownership corporation is that it forces financial benefit to be the driver (for fear of a loss of control if it is not pursued) and in the process it drives out quality and reliability as the primary objectives.

What is required is the re-establishment of values which customers, employers, suppliers, and communities value as the primary objectives of corporations. These values are, in most cases, self-evident and how much they are worth can be determined from how much people are willing to pay and invest in them. The values can be restricted to the quality and reliability of goods and services the company provides. They can extend to the conditions of employment of its personnel or its relations with its suppliers.

Equally, they can include a broader set of social and public issues that go beyond the corporation's direct functions. They can, for example, relate to the corporation's involvement in the communities within which it operates; the quality of public as well as private services that it provides at local and national levels; the prices at which it provides these services; and its respect for the environment and future as well as current generations. The values of the corporation can and should be many. The condemnation of multiple targets confuses simplicity of execution with completeness of principles. We live by many principles, but we execute them through a narrow set of applications. Likewise, the corporation should have a simple set of objectives but a broad set of values by which it judges their implementation. The mistake of those who try to apply, for example, payment by results in the health service is to seek to impose a narrow set of values on a broad range of activities. That is the wrong way round and generates the cynicism and instrumental behaviour to which it is subject.

Our failure to promote the corporation as a commitment device has resulted from an inadequate appreciation of its potential to be one. Theory and policy have both seen it as a vehicle for promoting the interests of shareholders. The problem is not one of how to define or measure values to which we attach significance, but how these values can be re-established in markets where patterns of ownership are no longer conducive to the promotion of interests other than those of the shareholders. Companies need to be able to determine the appropriate balance between commitment and control in circumstances that range from the smallest start-up to the largest established corporations; from high technology to traditional industries; from emerging economies to highly developed ones; and from corporations with a purely private to those with a public and social purpose. Achieving the appropriate balance under these varied conditions does not require uniform or stifling regulation, but enlightened forms of governance and government around the world.

Chapter 9
Governance and Government

'Nothing so impairs your judgement as the sight of your neighbour getting rich.'

J. P. Morgan

Fractious Families

One of the most successful companies in the world is the Indian Tata Group. As a salient symbol of the reversal of economic fortunes, it owns, amongst many other organizations, what were previously British Steel, the iconic British car companies Jaguar and Land Rover, and the most British of British establishments— Tetley Tea.

Under its current chairman, Ratan Tata, it is in its fifth generation of family stewardship. In fact, the ownership of the firm is not primarily in the hands of the Tata family but the many trusts to which the family have bequeathed their wealth. Today the trusts control two-thirds of the shares of the firm. They do not run the business. The businesses have their own boards, which are concerned with the formulation and implementation of the companies' strategies. What the trusts do, in addition to making substantial philanthropic donations, is to lay down the values of the business and the principles by which the individual businesses operate. They are therefore the guardians of the company's philosophy.[1]

As such, this structure has provided a vehicle for the implementation of the types of values that were discussed at the end of the last chapter. It does not undermine the commercial nature of the organization. The businesses compete with ruthless and highly effective efficiency around the world, but the trust ensures that they abide by a set of principles and codes of conduct that uphold the name and reputation of the firm.

Trusts and foundations are by no means unusual features of corporations. They are commonplace in the US. Andrew Carnegie created the Carnegie Endowment for International Peace on his 75th birthday in 1910. The Ford Foundation was established in 1936 for 'scientific, educational and charitable purposes'. The Rockefeller Foundation received its charter in 1913 'to promote the well-being of mankind throughout the world'. But what distinguishes the Tata trusts from their American counterparts is that, not only do they perform charitable functions, they also control the corporations which fund them.

This is a feature of some German foundations. ThyssenKrupp AG, one of the largest steel producers in the world and one of the largest German companies, is owned by a charitable foundation, the Alfried Krupp von Bohlen und Halbach Foundation. Control was transferred to the Foundation in 1966 in response to Alfried Krupp's concerns about whether his son's 'ostentatious and hedonistic' lifestyle made him suited to uphold the family traditions and inherit the family firm.[2] The charitable ownership of

Krupp and other German firms, such as Bosch, provides them with a defence against hostile takeovers and the possible adverse consequences of these for their employees. However, as Tata demonstrated, it does not weaken their commercial orientation. For example, it did not prevent Krupp from embarking on an active campaign of hostile acquisitions of other firms. In 1991 Krupp launched one of the first hostile bids in post-Second World War Germany against the steel company, Hoesch. Hoesch's management and workers were resolutely opposed to the bid, but ultimately failed to prevent it and a loss of sixteen thousand jobs from taking place.[3] In 1997 Krupp attempted another hostile acquisition of the steel company, Thyssen. This one failed in the face of strong opposition from its management and workers, but was consummated as an agreed merger between the two companies the following year.

Foundations and trusts are also employed in countries such as Germany as ways of preserving the interests of family members in the running of a business without requiring control to be retained within the family. This is an alternative to the Japanese solution to the problem that genetic offspring of brilliant entrepreneurs are not themselves necessarily outstanding businessmen. What Japanese fathers who have not produced their own commercially minded children do is adopt a son who takes the family name in a legal adoption process, transfer control of the family firm to him, and bypass their less gifted natural offspring! The Mitsui and Sumitomo families are two examples of where this has happened.[4]

Family firms have advantages over dispersed ownership firms. In particular, they benefit from the comparatively long-term horizons of their family owners. However, they also have drawbacks. In particular, they are at the mercy of family members who may be more interested in deriving personal benefits from owning and controlling the firm than in its commercial fortunes. These personal interests give rise to family disputes and internecine battles.

Family succession is one area where conflicts are common. A parent's enthusiasm to transfer ownership to their offspring and maintain the family line may cloud their judgement about their offspring's capabilities.[5] Financial policy is another area of dispute. Families may be excessively cautious in approving expansion plans for fear of losing the capital that they have accumulated to date, or they may want to extract earnings from the company in the form of dividends at the expense of its future investment and growth. Family ownership, while prevalent around the world, is not the resolution to the 21st-century corporation's problems.

It is also important to recognize that while stock market ownership creates its own problems, it has considerable merits as well. It is the source of substantial and flexible capital for corporations. It provides a form of funding that is a major cushion against the risks that a corporation faces, and against which other forms of finance provide no protection. Dispersed share ownership allows shareholders to hide behind a veil of anonymity which, while not good for upholding commitment—it is difficult to have a relationship with the anonymous—does avoid the lobbying and political pressure that other investors may have to endure. While inadequate bank finance may have contributed to excessively dispersed ownership in some countries, deficient equity markets may have perpetuated concentrated family ownership unduly elsewhere.[6] What is therefore required is an approach that addresses the defects of dispersed ownership systems while recognizing their strengths and working with rather than against them.

There are two instruments that are available for achieving the appropriate degree of commitment and control in organizations. The first is the structure of the board of directors of corporations and their degree of independence from their shareholders. The second is the nature of ownership and the degree of control that resides with different shareholders. The degree of independence of the board can vary from continuous accountability to their shareholders to the type of independence that is associated with arrangements that are specifically designed to protect the interests of third parties.

Trust Firms

In trust law, the property of one party (the settlor) is managed by a second (the trustee) on behalf of a third (the beneficiary). The trustee owes a fiduciary duty to the beneficiary, who is the beneficial owner of the trust property. It therefore differs from the agency relation of a director to a shareholder in a company, by which the director owes a fiduciary responsibility to the shareholder as the owner as well as beneficiary of the property, i.e. the settlor and the beneficiary are one and the same. In view of the separation of the roles of settlor and beneficiary of property in a trust, the potential for failure are particularly high and the fiduciary obligations on the trustee especially onerous.

The application of trust law to the corporation is not conventionally viewed as appropriate because of the association of the corporation with its members, namely its shareholders. The directors owe duties of loyalty, honesty, and care to the corporation which, as we have seen, may reflect the wide body of stakeholders, but only in so far as that is consistent with the interests of its members. To the extent that a degree of separation between the owners and the directors is important in allowing the directors to take a judgement in the interests of the corporation broadly defined, this is enshrined in the notion of 'business judgement' in which courts presume in favour of directors. There is no perceived need to create a formal obligation of directors to other stakeholders and to do so would be regarded as creating confusion in the purpose of the company.

However, a combination of the growth of takeover activity, shareholder activism, short-term shareholdings, and shortening executive contracts have in practice weakened the separation between shareholders and the corporation, notwithstanding the position taken by courts in formal judgments. It has therefore become increasingly difficult for directors to do anything other than reflect what is perceived to be in the immediate interests of their most influential, frequently short-term shareholders. The calls for greater shareholder activism only serve to reinforce this. The ability of directors to act in what is deemed to be the longer-term interests of the corporation more broadly defined has largely been eroded.

At the same time, the potential for directors to abuse their fiduciary responsibilities has intensified. Directors' and shareholder interests are increasingly viewed as being at odds. A damaging cycle of shareholder mistrust prompting greater shareholder activism, which in turn prompts a more self-interested response on the part of directors, has been set in train. A resolution needs to be found to both the excessive mistrust and interference by investors.

Directors need to be able to balance the interests of owners and other parties. Initially, dispersed ownership raised the attractive prospect of achieving this by freeing management from the suffocating control by family owners to which they were previously subject. But the liberty was abused both by directors and by owners who saw potential gains from greater interference. The hoped-for benefits of the dispersed ownership corporation therefore proved to be illusory and the publicly listed corporation is in retreat. For example, the number of companies listed on the main market of the London Stock Exchange has halved in just 13 years from 1,890 in 1998 to 990 in 2011. Increasingly, corporations are seeking protection in private rather than public ownership. That will come at a price as the deficiencies of excessively interventionist private owners and inadequate access to financial resources become evident.

Instead, a solution should be sought in addressing both the need to protect the interests of shareholders more effectively than at present by strengthening corporate governance and appreciating that commitments to other parties have to be upheld for these parties to be willing participants in the corporation's activities. One approach to this is what I term the 'trust firm'.[7] A trust firm is a corporation that has a board of trustees who are the guardians of the corporation's stated values and principles. As in the case of the trustees of the Tata Group, they do not interfere in the day-to-day running of the firm, but do ensure that the firm has clearly articulated values and principles and abides by them.

This serves two functions. First, it strengthens existing governance arrangements by providing oversight that is distinct from the executive. The confused role of non-executive directors between providing oversight for shareholders and dispensing advice to the executives is a primary cause of many board failures (frequently expressed in terms of 'not wishing to rock the boat' or 'undermine the harmony of the board'). A degree of separation allows for some but by no means entire independence.

Second, it allows the corporation to commit credibly to the principles and values that are in the interests of shareholders as well as stakeholders but to which shareholders would otherwise fail to adhere. It is therefore a means by which companies are able to provide commitments to others who will in turn make commitments to the corporation.

The values that the board of trustees uphold will be those of the corporation's customers, investors, and employees.[8] They can, as in the case of Tata, extend to a broader set of philanthropic activities. Charitable functions are best achieved by organizations that have both the knowledge and resources to deliver them. So, too, are public services. As will be discussed further below, one of the attractions of the trust firm is that within one organization public and private values can be integrated instead of, as at present, relying on separate regulation or public–private contracts to align private with public interests. The trust firm can assume the functions of public interest groups without the current dysfunctional confrontational relations that exist between regulator and regulated firm, or between public contractor and private supplier.

There should be no presumption that trust firms should be applicable for all activities. Companies should be free to choose. The benefits of a board of trustees are most likely to arise when a firm moves from the status of being a private limited company with a small number of investors to a public limited company with a larger shareholding. Until an organization of substance is created then there is little for investors or stakeholders to commit to, except the vision of the founding entrepreneurs. The values of the firm are synonymous with those of the founders. It is when the firm has reached a significant stage of development and has broadened its investor base to the point that it takes on the status of a public limited company that the need for a board, which reflects the values of the company, arises. Those values could be defined by the founding shareholders and therefore provide a means by which the founders' goals are perpetuated, or they could incorporate broader social objectives in a corporation with a public as well as a private function.

As Colin Mayer Ltd. and a dominant shareholder in the company, the values of the corporation are synonymous with mine or those of a small group of large shareholders. There is therefore no need for a board of trustees to oversee the corporation's values—the owners are perfectly capable of doing that themselves and an intermediary board would only serve to dilute their oversight. In contrast, as colinmayer plc and one of 10,000 shareholders, I have very little influence over the determination or implementation of the corporation's values. In particular, I cannot ensure that stakeholder as well as shareholder interests are protected. The board of trustees provides a means by which the values of the company can be both established and upheld.

The structure of the board of trustees can span anything from a conventional corporate board appointed by the shareholders with no security of tenure, to a self-appointed rotating membership with elections staggered over several years. It can be appointed by and be accountable to a membership that is restricted to shareholders as at present or extended to a wider body of stakeholders. New media and electronic voting systems offer substantial opportunities to broaden the group of participating stakeholders beyond what has been observed to date. The board can in other words be an inflexible, independent structure that provides a high degree of commitment to a wide variety of parties but be subject to no external control by any of them, or be the instrument of particular groups of individuals with little independence from them. The nature of the board will determine both the degree of trust that it instils in others and its exposure to them. Further details on the trust firm can be found in Appendix 1.

One particular form of the trust firm is the cooperative or mutual society in which there is no separation between ownership and stakeholder interests in the firm: the owners are its customers and employees. A successful example of such an organization is the John Lewis Partnership, owners of the highly respected chain of department stores in the UK. In response to concerns about the inequality of earnings and the condition of the employees in the firm he inherited, John Spedan Lewis, the son of the founder, created a staff council shortly after the First World War.

The council developed into a partnership in which all employees are partners of the company and elect representatives of a partnership council and board to set strategy and oversee the running of the firm, which is managed by the chairman and his executive directors. In signing away his rights to the firm, John Spedan Lewis created a constitution that laid down the structure of the partnership and the principles by which it should operate (its values), the first of which states 'the Partnership's ultimate purpose is the happiness of all its members, through their worthwhile and satisfying employment in a successful business. Because the Partnership is owned in trust for its members, they share the responsibilities of ownership as well as its rewards—profit, knowledge and power.'

The fact that there is no separation between owners and stakeholders is both a strength and weakness of the cooperative and mutual societies. Their strength is that they avoid conflicts between the two parties; their weakness is that they do not have access to external sources of equity capital. They are therefore a good model for activities (in, for example, the service sectors) that have little requirement for capital, but not for those (in, for example, manufacturing) which require a great deal.

Another example of trust firms is pension funds. They are run by boards of trustees that oversee the management of assets on behalf of long-term investors—current and future pensioners. They have suffered from two classes of problems. The first is a lack of competence on the part of the trustees to perform an effective 'stewardship' (oversight) role on behalf of their bene-ficiaries—the pensioners. The second is a failure to provide adequate protection for future generations of pensioners. The cause of the first problem is a lack of competence of some trustees and of the second is that their tenure is limited, thereby encour-aging them to promote investments which yield high short-term returns during their tenure at the risk of the long-term solvency of the fund beyond it.

These failures of pension funds demonstrate the importance of giving consideration to the composition and structure of boards of trustees. For example, by analogy with the contribution of experienced entrepreneurs and industrialists to the success of venture capital funds, the Industrial and Commercial Finance Corporation (ICFC) and active investor funds such as Hermes in the UK, boards of trustees of pension funds require the expertise of, amongst others, highly regarded individuals with previous asset management experience. Staggering their retirement and conferring more authority (for example chair and vice-chair of the board) on those with the longest remaining service diminishes the problems that the short-term horizons of imminently retiring trustees create.

A third example of the trust arrangement is the staggered board commonly found in US companies. The staggered board creates a degree of independence of the board from shareholders. Boards are appointed and accountable to their shareholders, but since only a fraction of the board can be replaced at any one time, several rounds of elections over several years are required to replace the board. As in the cooperative or mutual, boards could represent constituencies beyond their shareholders if the definition of the members of a firm included other stakeholders. It should be for firms to be able to define their membership as part of their articles of association or charter.

The nature of the governance of the firm will follow naturally from its defined purposes and membership. In fact, even if this is restricted to its shareholders and does not extend to any other stakeholder group, then there is still a need for its governance to take account of the shareholders' varying and potentially conflicting interests because, contrary to current impressions, shareholders are not all the same. The second instrument that is available to influence the degree of commitment and control of the firm is how control is allocated between different classes of shareholders.

Committed Shareholders

As a shareholder in the French industrial gases company Air Liquide or the cosmetics company L'Oreal, if you hold your shares for two years you may receive a loyalty bonus of 10 per cent more shares. Several other French companies have adopted similar arrangements to encourage longer-term shareholdings and the French Companies Act entitles every registered shareholder to double voting rights after having held their shares for two years.[9]

With growing concern about the declining holding period and increasing short-termism of shareholders, equivalent proposals are being considered elsewhere.[10]

The difficulty with the proposal is that, while it rewards shareholders financially for retaining their shareholdings, it does not allow them to commit to hold their shares for any particular period of time or signal their degree of commitment. Furthermore, it does not enhance the ability of long-term shareholders to exercise control.

The principle of one share one vote means that shareholders receive voting control in terms of the amount of capital they invest in a particular corporation (the number of shares that they hold) and the number of companies they invest in, but not in terms of the length of time for which they invest. They are therefore rewarded in control rights in regard to the depth of their commitment (the amount of capital they invest), the breadth of their commitment (the number of firms in which they invest), but not the length of their commitment (the time period for which they invest).

There is at present no means by which shareholders can indicate the length of time for which they wish to invest, so those who intend to hold their shares for a few days (or in the case of high frequency traders perhaps only milliseconds) have the same voting rights over the decisions of the corporation at the point in time at which they hold shares as those who intend to retain their shares for several years. The former category bear the consequences of their voting decisions for a negligible period, the latter for an extended period, but both have the same influence on the current decision of the corporation that may affect its performance for years to come.

This is nonsensical and gives rise to the fundamental deficiency of firms and markets, as has been previously described. For example, in relation to decisions about acquisitions and mergers, it implies that the power to determine outcomes rests with those who will dispose of their shares instantaneously and therefore have no interest whatsoever in the long-term performance of the corporation. It is as if we are conferring voting rights on members of the population who intend to renounce their citizenship tomorrow.[11]

Shareholders should be able to register the period for which they intend to hold shares and be rewarded (for example, pro-rata) in votes in relation to the length of time remaining before they are able to dispose of their shares. So a share with ten years to maturity might have ten times the votes of one with one year to maturity. Indeed, equality of treatment (a principle to which the law attaches considerable importance) would dictate that it is only fair to treat shareholders who in essence are holding ten times as much of the corporation's capital differently from the others. Appendix 1 provides further details on the shareholdings, board structure, and values of the trust firm.

Those shareholders who do not wish to make a commitment to retain their shareholdings would be free to hold and trade unregistered shares that carried no voting rights. The corporation would therefore be able to raise capital, as at present, from liquid stock markets that perform a vital price setting and information aggregation function, but would be controlled by committed shareholders.

Registration has two effects. First, it allocates voting control to shareholders in proportion to their prospective rather than retrospective period of holdings. In contrast, loyalty and double voting right shares reward shareholders for the past period of their holdings and therefore fail to make them more responsible for the future consequences of their actions. Indeed, to the extent that shareholders who have held shares for long periods in the past are more likely to sell them in the near future, they potentially reward an absence of commitment.

Second, registration restricts decisions on transfer of property in acquisitions to shareholders who are committed to the long-term prospects of the target and removes uncommitted shareholders from the decision process. The implications of this for the behaviour and performance of corporations would be profound. In the event of an acquisition, the decision on whether to accept an offer would primarily reside with the longest-term shareholders. There would therefore be an alignment of influence with interest, and control with commitment.

That is how it should be. We have accepted the principle of no taxation without representation. But we have not imposed the principle of no representation without commitment and the absence of such a principle has been extremely damaging. In particular, with the steady advancement of the privatization of public assets and the acceptance of market principles, we have progressively transferred control of the world's assets into the hands of those with no interest in their deployment. The increasing domination of short-term investors is no surprise in a system that confers as much influence on those seeking instantaneous gratification as those committed to enduring the rough with the smooth.

To illustrate how conflicts can arise between shareholders as well as between shareholders and other stakeholders, we will focus on an all-equity version of colinmayer plc. The equity capital of $300,000 is currently invested in an asset which will come to fruition and pay out cash to its shareholders in a few years' time.

The alternative risky investment is an acquisition that will pay out cash of $600,000 or nothing in the very near future, within a year. Long-term investors who do not need the cash soon are firmly opposed to the investment because of its highly risky nature. Short-term investors on the other hand view it very favourably. Notwithstanding its risky nature, they highly value the possibility of a quick cash payout which they desperately need to meet their personal liabilities—for them, the 'liquidity premium' outweighs the 'risk discount'.

Short-term shareholders therefore value the investment at more than the current value of the corporation of $300,000 and the corporation's share price rises. The management receives a positive signal from the stock market that shareholders value the investment and implements it. If it does not, then it can expect to be subject to the 'Cadbury treatment'—a predator sides with short-term investors to acquire the company—or the 'Hermes effect'—an activist fund builds up a position in the firm in conjunction with short-term investors, persuades management to change their mind, and generates a handsome profit for itself and other investors.

While liquidity is valuable and contributes to the share price setting process, it is one thing for it to be achieved through the trading of shares on the stock market ('secondary trading') and another for it to affect the primary funding of corporations. Far from contributing to the financing of corporations, as the above example illustrates, in satisfying the premium that short-term investors attach to liquidity, the stock market encourages corporations to contribute to that liquidity by paying out cash to their shareholders. That is why the stock market has been a net drain on, rather than contributor to the funding of corporations.

It negates the presumption that equity capital is permanent and thereby its association with committed capital.

According to a report for the British government in 2012, this has created a problem of 'short-termism' which 'occurs when companies invest too little, either in the physical assets of the business or in the intangibles which are generally the source of their competitive advantage'.[12] The report argues that short-termism is prevalent in the UK financial system and corporate sector, and urges asset holders (such as life insurance companies and pension funds), asset managers (who manage portfolios on behalf the asset holders), and directors of corporations to act as stewards of the long-term interests of their corporations according to fiduciary principles.[13] Not only is the feasibility of such widespread reform of behaviour in financial markets questionable, it could exacerbate the deficiencies of equity markets it seeks to correct by promoting long-term committed behaviour throughout the investment chain. Liquidity is an important component of financial markets and many investors do not wish to commit actively to oversight in the companies in which they invest.[14] While the report suggests that the problem of short-termism has become more acute, arguably there has never been a golden age of responsible equity trading on stock markets, as the South Sea Bubble of 1720 illustrates all too clearly. But what corporations did once and should again enjoy is a degree of insulation from excessive influence of short-term shareholders on their real activities by restricting external control to their long-term committed counterparts.

To avoid the hand of management being forced by short-term investors, colinmayer plc could choose to impose the requirement of 'no representation without commitment' by allocating the voting rights to its long-term shareholders. Short-term investors retain their access to liquidity on stock markets but relinquish their rights to determine the policies of the companies they trade. If, on the other hand, long-term investment is not integral to colinmayer plc's activities, then it will not need to relate control to commitment and it can allow all shareholders to retain their voting rights.[15]

There should be no presumption that it is always desirable for corporations to have long-term committed shareholders. In some cases, relatively short-term shareholdings are required to avoid exposure to other parties, including executive directors, who would exploit the inertia of committed shareholders. The rapid growth of private equity over the past two decades is a response to the inability of shareholders of publicly listed corporations to commit their investments for specified periods. That is what private equity funds achieve through a combination of modest amounts of equity and substantial volumes of debt raised through limited period vehicles for funding the formation of new companies and the restructuring of existing ones. They are well tailored to the particular functions that they are designed to perform, but also have significant weaknesses. The exclusion from stock markets restricts the access of the private companies to loss-absorbing equity finance available to publicly listed corporations and the limited purpose and relatively short periods of operation of the funds make them ill-suited to the longer-term development of major corporations. Private equity funds perform an important function, but can only provide a limited remedy for the deficiencies of public equity markets.

The solution in terms of the creation of registered shares with control rights corresponding to committed holding periods and unregistered shares ('free floats') with no such obligation is an example of a dual class share structure, which, as previously noted, is widely observed throughout the world, including the US, but not the UK. For firms to be able to choose their share structure there needs to be recognition that the equal treatment of shareholders is not synonymous with the equal treatment of a shareholding. In fact, equal treatment of shareholdings is discriminatory between shareholders because those who hold shares for long periods are fundamentally different from those who do not. It is discriminatory in exactly the same way as a principle that used to apply, namely one shareholder one vote, was discriminatory. That principle failed to recognize that shareholders who hold multiple shares in a company are different from those who hold one. Likewise, those who hold long-term shares are more committed than those with short-term shares. The treatment applies to the share, not to the shareholder, and it applies to the class of share, defined by amongst other things maturity, rather than to shares in general.

The reason why the dual class structure described here has not been widely observed to date is that the consequences of incremental developments that necessitate it have only just become evident for all to see. In the absence of an active market for corporate control and shareholder activism, shareholders exerted little influence on corporate conduct. There was therefore little need to restrain the control of short-term shareholders because none of them exerted much control. However, with the detrimental effects of the separation of ownership and control, as documented by Berle and Means, becoming progressively more evident, the degree of shareholder engagement intensified. As this occurred, shareholders steadily came to appreciate that their influence is as great and their rewards potentially greater from shortening their holding periods and so the problem of the misalignment of the interests of shareholders and companies became progressively more acute.

With the principles of governance and ownership described here in place, corporations will be able to tailor their commitment and control to their commercial needs—to commit to outside shareholders and other stakeholders, and to be assured of the commitment of long-term shareholders to the firm. They will thereby be fit for the purposes for which they were originally intended—to create new firms, to consolidate them as small and medium-sized enterprises (SMEs), and to promote their continuing growth and innovation as established corporations. They will be able to grant outside shareholders rights of control over private companies at their initial conceptual stage in return for commitment of their capital for the period required to demonstrate proof of concept. They will be able to encourage participation of creditors and employees in SMEs by assuring them that their interests are protected in the values of the organization through the board of trustees. They will be able to attract the committed risk capital required to promote innovation and investment in established corporations by restricting control rights to long-term shareholders while accessing liquid short-term stock markets. They will therefore achieve all of the functions that are sought of the corporation in delivering private values, and in addition to all of this they will be able to assume a public purpose as well.

Public Purpose

Before the Norman Conquest, guilds were established in Britain with the right 'to possess property now and hence-forth'.[16] After the Norman Conquest, they took on a trading function, which in turn developed into the craft guilds and companies of merchants in the 14th century, many of which are still in existence today. One in particular, the Staplers, became involved in overseas trade and, at the end of the 14th century, it received the first charter for foreign trade to countries bordering the North Sea and the Baltic.

These bodies developed a governance structure during the 14th century involving a governor, assistants, and deputies. The governor was given powers of executing justice amongst English merchants and, in 1404, the Staplers were granted rights to make statutes and ordinances for the discharge of the duties of the deputies and to punish English subjects who disobeyed their rules. Similar privileges were subsequently bestowed on the Merchant Adventurers and the Eastland Company.

So long as trade remained close at hand there was not much of a requirement to raise capital. While there might be rules requiring freemen to employ capital according to the rules of the fellowship, there was no central pooling of capital. However, the exploitation of further trading opportunities required more substantial investments to be made. The first form this took was the regulated companies that extended the guild principle into foreign activities. In the regulated company, each member traded with their own stock and on their own account subject to the rules of the company. Charters were acquired to confer a monopoly for the members of the company. Essentially, the regulated company was a restrictive practice that prevented competition occurring between members and allowing monopoly benefits to be exploited. The Merchant Adventurers were examples of this form.[17]

The distinguishing feature of the company was that members traded on a common rather than individual account—joint-stock. The first example of this was the Russia Company, which started its activities in 1553 under the governorship of Sebastian Cabot. The company raised £6,000 from £25 shares and was a primitive type of company formed for a single expedition, at the end of which it was wound up. The joint-stock corporation played an important role in the syndicates that were employed in the war against Spain in the second half of the 16th century. While both Portugal and Spain organized and financed exploration through the state, England chose the self-governing guilds. The state-run organizations had the advantage of access to financial resources, but suffered from their cumbersome central bureaucracy. Arguably the defeat of the Spanish Armada was a victory of the joint-stock corporation over the state.

Most famous of these corporations was the English East India Company, which operated on conventional trading company lines, liquidating capital at the end of each voyage. However, the requirement to keep its assets liquid when each stock was wound up put the English Company at a disadvantage in relation to its Dutch counterpart. From 1614 the joint-stock was subscribed for a period of a year, it adopted a perpetual existence in 1654, and in 1658 its capital became fixed and its shares transferable.

Throughout this period the corporation was viewed as a public agency.

> This idea that the object of a business corporation is the public one of managing and ordering the trade in which it is engaged, as well as the private one of profit for its members, may also be noticed in the charters granted to new corporations, especially in the recitals, and in the provisions usually found that the newly chartered company shall have the exclusive control of the trade intrusted to it.[18]

Some of the most famous subsequent stock corporations, such as the Bank of England and the South Sea Company, were actively involved in public financing, culminating in the disastrous attempt to convert the national debt into the stock of the South Sea Company. The Bubble Act of 1720, which made it illegal to act as a corporate body or to raise transferable stock without a royal charter, put an end to the growth of joint-stock companies. 'It was pertinently said of this statute that like all laws passed upon the exigency of an occasion, it had more of temporary malice and revenge than of permanent wisdom and policy.'[19] The major exceptions to the Act were the canal companies: between 1766 and 1800 more than a hundred canal acts were passed, eighty-one between 1791 and 1794. There were also a few scattered instances of new corporations in manufacturing, but basically the Act had the effect of arresting the development of the joint-stock corporation for the best part of a century.

The main impediment came not from the direct cost of the legislative process itself, but from the ability of vested interests and in particular of incumbent firms to oppose applications for incorporation.[20] The corporation was regarded as closely associated with monopoly: 'a number of merchants uniting and applying to the Government for an exclusive charter, to prevent others from engaging in the same commerce, and for a power to raise money by an open subscription in order to form their stock or capital are generally denominated companies'.[21]

Pressure for change came with an avalanche of applications for stock corporations for public works (gas, canal, dock, and bridge), insurance, and mining. Parliament was overwhelmed by applications and the law officers of the Crown could not deal with the demand. While in principle incorporation was possible after 1825, in practice it was difficult to enforce because judges treated firms as partnerships rather than as separate legal entities. This was rectified by the 1844 Act that required joint-stock companies with transferable shares and more than twenty-five partners to register with a government official. Remarkably, the control that the King and Parliament had exerted over the formation of corporations for several centuries was replaced by as simple an expedient as registration.

> Had Parliament not stepped into the fray in 1720, it seems plausible that courts would have continued to develop a common law of joint-stock companies that would have treated them as a separate legal person and permitted free transfer of shares, along with the right to vote for management. General incorporation, in other words, was Parliament's solution to a problem largely of Parliament's creation.[22]

The origins of the corporation were therefore in a public not private purpose. They were rights granted by King or Parliament to satisfy the requirements of monarch or state. It was only late in the day that the rights of individuals to incorporate were recognized. Eliminating the state's monopoly over rights of incorporation has been one of the most important contributions to the enhancement of economic well-being, but in the rush to liberate the corporation from the tyranny of the state, its potential to combine public with private purpose has been lost. In some circumstances it is entirely appropriate that the values and vision of the corporation should be those of particular individuals. In others they should reflect those of a broader group of stakeholders, including the citizens of local communities and nations.[23]

In essence the public enterprise merely lies at one end of the governance and ownership spectrum that has been described above. The membership of the corporation whose interests the board of trustees should uphold is that of communities and nations, and the breadth of ownership is extended to all their citizens in perpetuity. It is therefore at an extreme in terms of its breadth and length of commitment. Where it is applicable is in relation to activities for which these are the relevant constituencies—public goods conventionally defined or public interests.

There is no reason why a corporation has to be at one or other extreme—just public or private—it can be a combination of the two. Broadening the range of options through the introduction of the trust firm and shares of different maturities illustrates how this can be achieved. The values of companies can incorporate public and charitable as well as private purposes and the board of trustees can be responsible for upholding those purposes. This is best done not by having representatives of different constituencies on the board, but by making all members of the board responsible for all firm values. Likewise, some but not all of the shares in the corporation can be held in perpetuity to the benefit of the public at large. The fusion of public and private interests in one organization avoids the conflict that currently pervades relations between private corporations and regulators, and between state procurers of public services and private sector providers.

The tax system can be used to promote the adoption of public values by private corporations. The justification for levying taxes on the earnings of corporations as well as the income that investors derive from them is that corporations are legal entities distinct from their owners. Rather than paying corporation tax, those corporations that demonstrate a public purpose, and an effective governance mechanism for upholding it, could be supported by the tax system. They would be recipients of subsidies funded from corporation tax levied on corporations that have no public purpose. In other words, the rate of corporation tax should reflect the degree of public as well as private interest in the values and governance of corporations.

A primary difference between the private company with public purpose and the public enterprise is that the latter has access to tax revenues, which are not available to the former. This makes the depth of commitment of the corporation to other parties particularly great, but leaves taxpayers exposed to calls for further funding through the tax system. In essence, the taxpayer as shareholder in the corporation has unlimited liability. The advantage of the private corporation with public purpose is that it grants its shareholders the opportunity of limiting their liability in a way in which the shareholder of the public enterprise is unable to. This is the problem that corporations faced at the peak of public ownership in the 1970s and taxpayers encountered as the ultimate guarantors of the financial system in the late 2000s. They were over-committed to, and exploited by, management and unions of inefficient organizations in the first case, and bankers and asset managers of risk-taking financial institutions in the second. In both cases, it was natural for these groups to extract salaries, wages, and fees to the point that the governments that underwrote them were pushed towards bankruptcy.

UK plc is essentially a giant cooperative or mutual the membership of which extends to the nation as a whole. This solves the cooperatives' and mutuals' problem of not having access to adequate capital, but creates the opposite difficulty that no one can opt out of being a member. colinmayer plc also has values that incorporate a public purpose and a board of trustees whose function is to ensure that these values are upheld, but its shareholders are separate and commit a limited amount of capital.

The greater the powers conferred on the shareholders in co-linmayer plc in, for example, having rights of approval over major transactions, the less will be the authority of the board of trustees and the closer the firm will be to a pure private corporation. The less the authority of the shareholders, the more significance will be attached to the role of the trustees in upholding the purpose of the corporation and the more it will resemble a public enterprise. If, in the extreme, shareholders did not even have rights of refusal over new capital subscriptions, they would find themselves in a similar position to the unlimited liability of taxpayers in corporations. As well as establishing the values of the firm, its constitution will therefore also specify the relative powers and authorities of boards and owners.[24]

While the board of trustees uphold public interests, they are not regulators. Their role is to ensure that the interests of shareholders as well as stakeholders are respected. For example, in determining the reasonableness of charges to customers, the board of trustees will wish to be assured that they balance the interests of customers and shareholders. Regulators, in contrast, seek to impose limitations on the charges that regulated firms try to maximize. In overcoming the hurdles that conflicts between the regulator and firm inevitably create and embedding public values in the private organization, the unified approach of the trust firm is more practical, less expensive, and more effective than current regulatory arrangements.

We can illustrate this by demonstrating how the trust firm can resolve the conflict described in Chapter 2 between creditors and shareholders of corporations, and in particular banks. Where there are threats to countries' financial systems, the conflict is not just between banks' own investors but also between banks and society more generally, especially taxpayers, who are called upon to rescue failing banks. To avoid these conflicts, there has to be a volume of equity capital which is sufficient to cushion creditors and taxpayers against adverse events, and banks have to restrain themselves from engaging in risk-taking that threatens their solvency. In other words, they have to behave like trust firms in upholding values that reflect the interests of their creditors, in employing equity capital that is adequate to protect them against risks of failure, and in implementing governance arrangements which are sufficiently robust to deter the pursuit of detrimental risky activities.

In the presence of systemic risks, these values, capital, and governance have to include the public interest in the preservation of financial systems as well as the private interest of creditors. This can be encouraged through corporate tax rates which reward banks for incorporating public interests in their values, capital, and governance. Banks should take responsibility themselves for protection of the financial system as well as their investors and should be given incentives to do so. If they do not, then central banks and regulators face an inevitable dilemma between avoiding failures of financial systems and bailing out mismanaged banks (so-called 'moral hazard' problems). This dilemma results in the type of hesitant reaction to bank failures that was observed on both sides of the Atlantic in the initial stages of the recent financial crisis, and the adverse influence of public policy on bank lending to companies that, as described in Chapter 7, has occurred in the UK for more than a century.

Important though the protection of our financial system is, it pales into insignificance in relation to the most valuable public good of all—our survival—and here a remarkable feature of the trust firm emerges: it can reflect the values not just of current stakeholders, but even those who are yet to be born.

A Commons Tragedy

Suppose two persons have a common purpose, to which each may freely resort. The ordinary source of motives for economy is a foresight of the diminution in the means of future enjoyment depending on each act of present expenditure. If a man takes a guinea out of his own purse, the remainder, which he can spend afterwards, is diminished by a guinea. But not so, if he takes from a fund, to which he and another have an equal right of access. The loss falling upon both, he spends a guinea with as little consideration as he would use in spending half a guinea, were the fund divided. Each determines his expenditure as if the whole of the joint-stock were his own. Consequently, in a multitude of partners, where the diminution effected by each separate act of expenditure is insensible, the motive for economy entirely vanishes.

If a person puts more cattle into his own field, the amount of the subsistence which they consume is all deducted from that which was at the command of his original stock; and if, before there was no more than a sufficiency of pasture, he reaps no benefit from the additional cattle, what is gained in one way being lost in another. But if he puts more cattle on a common, the food which they consume forms a deduction which is shared between all the cattle, as well that of others as his own, in proportion to their number, and only a small part of it is taken from his own cattle.

So William Lloyd first described the 'tragedy of the commons' in two lectures at Oxford University in 1832.[25] The tragedy of the commons is not just an externality where an individual does not fully recognize the economic consequence of their actions (the effect on the partner of withdrawing money from the fund or on another farmer from the number of cows that are grazed), but an exploitation of a common asset to the detriment of the future (the depletion of the fund or the overgrazing of the commons). So the degradation of our environment and extinction of species are tragedies resulting from their commons characteristics.

Of course, we could take the commons into public ownership and allocate or auction slots on them to people to graze their cows like bays at airport terminals. This raises complex problems of who has rights to graze and on what terms. Hotly disputed though these are, they are not as complex as representing the rights of future unborn generations. What does preserving the commons for future generations mean? Does it literally imply leaving them undisturbed even if they are currently disease-infected swamps that could be turned into beautiful valleys? How should we determine whether future generations will welcome replacing the biodiversity that currently exists with the healthier environment that could be created?

These are decisions that governments have to take on behalf of their citizens all the time and we entrust them to do it for us. That is where the problem arises, because in fact we do not trust them. We do not trust them to resist a bribe to allocate more space to someone else's cows; to deliver the beautiful valley pictured in the brochures; or to reject a proposal to sell the whole thing off to a property developer for a substantial sum of money. We do not trust them with good reason because that is what they have always done in the past. The tragedy of the commons is a compendium of errors. It is not a problem of property as commonly conceived, but a failure of governance. Our objection to public ownership is not that it replaces common for individual values—in many areas of life we are perfectly willing to accept this—it is that we do not believe that the values will be delivered.

That this is so is illustrated by the fact that, where governance is reasonable and delivery effective, we are perfectly willing to accept and even welcome common values. One of the most successful public service organizations in the world is the British Broadcasting Corporation, the BBC, in the UK. There are debates about what the public purpose of the BBC should be, the level of the fee it charges its customers, its political neutrality, whether its commercial activities are compatible with its public obligations, and whether it is too large to manage efficiently. But broadly, the BBC is held in universally high respect and greatly valued for the functions it performs in one of the most controversial sectors of the economy.

The reason it works and has done so for ninety years is that it has both a governance and commercial structure that conforms to the trust firm described above. It is run according to a public charter overseen by a Trust whose role is to ensure that the Corporation abides by its public service obligations and is not subject to political interference. The BBC combines a commercial delivery of services through the Corporation with the maintenance of public values through the Trust. To the extent that this creates tensions, then the organization has to resolve them through its Trust and executive boards. It therefore protects the commons of public broadcasting from both private and political interests.

The problem of the commons is one of allocating control in companies. The trust firm solves the commons problem in a similar way to that in which pension funds solve the problem of providing for past generations of employees. Pension funds involve current generations of employees subscribing to a fund from which past generations of employees—the pensioners—derive benefits. The reason that current generations are willing to do this is that they know that they in turn will be beneficiaries of the pension fund when they retire and unless they fulfil their obligations to current generations of retirees, then the fund will cease to exist. This works so long as growing populations or increasing levels of productivity ensure that the amounts that current employees anticipate receiving when they retire exceed the sums that they have to contribute to support the past generation. However, as we are currently experiencing, this breaks down when growth stops and current employees anticipate being better off withdrawing from the fund.

Similarly, the long-term interests of stakeholders can be protected by creating overlapping generations of shareholders in trust firms. If currently half of the shareholders in colinmayer plc have shares that are due to mature in 5 years' time and half in ten years' time, and votes are proportional to the outstanding life of the shares, then two-thirds of the votes will reside with the latter group of shareholders. As we move closer to the maturity of the first category of shares in five years' time, then the fraction of the votes in the hands of the latter category increases towards 100 per cent. In five years' time, the company then issues new shares of ten years' maturity to replace the first category of shares that have matured. At that stage, two-thirds of the votes are again in the hands of shareholders, with shares of ten years to maturity.

So the control of the corporation is always in the hands of the shareholders with the longer horizon. This solves the commons problem as follows. First, controlling shareholders preserve the value of the commons in their first five years so that the subsequent controlling shareholders have the means to reward them in their second five years. If they fail to do so, then they confer an 'externality' (a benefit for which they are not compensated) on shareholders in their last five years who do not bear the subsequent consequences of the overgrazing. This therefore reverses the tragedy of the commons that current generations impose a negative externality on future generations; it does this by allocating control to future generations who seek to avoid conferring a positive externality on current generations.

Second, while controlling shareholders have the power to exploit non-controlling shareholders by restricting grazing over the next five years excessively, they will not do so because they want the next controlling shareholders to treat them equally fairly in their second five years. The trust firm therefore solves the commons problem by ensuring that their management resides with owners who have an interest in their preservation. Put simply, if there are overlapping generations of farmers who each graze on the commons for two years, always put the commons under the management of the farmers in their first year. They will ensure that the second-year farmers do not overgraze because they will be worried about what will be left for them in their second year, but they will not over-restrict the second-year farmers because they will want the first-year farmers to treat them equally fairly next year.

In effect, through a combination of overlapping shareholdings, weighting control to longer-term horizon shareholders, and requiring firms to uphold their values, companies can maintain consistently long shareholder horizons which reflect the interests of future as well as current generations of stakeholders. It is as if future generations of stakeholders have been granted votes over the current policies of the firm by conferring control on shareholders who have an interest in the long-term preservation of capital value. Far from abusing the interests of future generations of stakeholders, shareholders now become the vehicle by which they are granted a voice.

The corporation can determine the appropriate breadth, depth, and length of commitment to different stakeholders through choice of values, allocation of control rights between the board of trustees concerned with upholding those values, and shareholders concerned about capital value, i.e. allocation of control to shareholders with long-term interests. To date, we have failed to define with clarity what we value in our commons. We have not determined who is responsible for preserving them; and we have not ensured that those responsible for delivering what we value have ownership stakes that commit them to do so. We have therefore not put in place the means to avoid the erosion of the commons which, while not a natural state of the world or a consequence of our myopia or self-interest, is a reflection of our failure to establish the institutions required to protect them. And there are certain parts of the world that are particularly badly affected by this institutional failure.

Developing Nations

> Commit to those whose trust you need;
> Control those who treachery breed;
> Show firm commitment where there's firm control;
> And firm resistance to a funding hole.

A corporation is a two-faced organ. It has to justify the commitment of those who invest in it and exercise control over those who depend on it. That this is the predominant function of a bank is self-evident; that it is the core of all organizations is equally valid. For in every enterprise, be it large or small, financial or productive, there are those who seek to invest in others they do not trust, and those who cannot find support for the commitments they cannot make. Between them stands a corporation that has capital of sufficient breadth, depth, and length to command the respect of those it needs to attract and control over those who cannot reciprocate with the same degree of commitment to it. By virtue of its control, it grants capital to those who have none and access to those who are otherwise excluded from commercial activities. Without the dual and simultaneous provision of commitment and control, markets contract to the most rudimentary forms in which there are simultaneous transactions that demand neither commitment nor control. Nowhere is this more relevant than in those parts of the world where access is currently most deficient.

In the wake of the Asian financial crisis of 1997, there was a conventionally held view that many of the problems of the region stemmed from what was termed 'crony capitalism'—the diversion of public resources to powerful corporate interests.[26] Its cause was the structure of business in Asia based on large family, corporate, and financial groups that were able to exercise undue influence over their national governments. The solution was to move to the transparent, well-regulated, market-based systems of the Western economies with their more dispersed patterns of ownership.

Three years later, with the dot-com bubble burst and the subsequent collapse of Enron, Worldcom, and Arthur Andersen, the dispersed ownership and corporate governance systems of the US did not look too great either. A decade later, the financial crisis of 2008 suggested that the banking and regulatory systems of Europe and the US also had their problems. Fortunately, the Asian economies had not taken a blind bit of notice of the Western condemnation of their corporate systems and were therefore largely immune to the subsequent crises that hit the West. In fact, the only reason why the financial crisis was not a global one but essentially confined to Europe and the US is that many countries in the world did not adopt what was widely regarded as 'best practice' in banking and regulation—namely the UK and US models. Had the rest of the world followed the lead of the UK and US, then there would indeed have been a truly global crisis.

One explanation for why the advice emanating out of Washington was so inappropriate was that it did not actually reflect the underlying reason for the success of the US economy. The strength of the US is not its dispersed ownership, markets for corporate control, or stock market financing. As has been mentioned at various points, in many cases these are not present or relevant in the US. Equally important are the local banks, family firms, private equity, and takeover defences—namely all the features that were felt to be so abhorrent in the Asian economies. The real advantage of the US is that it has all of these plus the more conventional market features, namely it has an exceptional degree of diversity of its corporate and financial systems. In contrast, the UK, which has a much more thoroughbred dispersed ownership, market for corporate control system, has fared much less well. The main lesson to be learnt from the West is therefore one of diversity, not uniformity.

The reason why diversity is so important is that what is required to 'commit to those whose trust you need, and control those who treachery breed' is complex and diverse. In some cases a high degree of commitment to many parties is required; in others, being able to exercise external control with no commitments is essential. It is highly specific to the particular nature of the firm, what it does, where it is located, and the period in which it is operating. What is suitable for one firm is not for another, for one society is not for another, and for one technological age is not for another. Diversity is required across countries, industries, firms, and time.[27]

The failure of industrial and international policy around the world has been to try to prescribe solutions where none exist. That is not to say that there is nothing that should be done. There are many problems that need to be fixed. However, the identification of correct solutions requires a precise and deep understanding of the particular circumstances facing countries, societies, industries, and firms at particular points in time so that an appreciation of the right balance between commitment and control and the appropriate way of implementing them can be gained. There are no simple universal laws, such as the corporate governance codes which companies around the world have been urged to adopt by international agencies like the OECD. These can be damaging not only in advocating the adoption of inappropriate procedures, but also by imposing too much uniformity on corporate practices. They thereby threaten to create the global systemic failures that they seek to avoid.

There is evidence that in developed economies competition in product markets is a more significant influence on corporate performance than corporate governance.[28] The experience of some emerging markets is consistent with this. While there is little in common in the corporate governance of the state-dominated companies of China and the family owned businesses of India, there is a shared experience in the two countries of the beneficial effects of liberalization and deregulation of their product markets. An illustration of the importance of deregulation and competition relates to a financial revolution that is currently in progress. It is not happening under the skyscrapers of New York or in the boardrooms of London. It is not taking place in Beijing or Mumbai, but in the slums of Nairobi and in the markets of Kisumu in Kenya. It is not the micro-lending with which developing and emerging markets are closely associated, but something at the other end of the financial spectrum in the traditionally least exciting part of the financial system— payments.

The revolution is mobile money—the use of mobile phones to make financial transactions. Instead of going to a bank, people go to kiosks all over Kenya, to cash in money for credits on a SIM (subscriber identify module) card on their phones that they can then send to anyone anywhere in Kenya. Typically it is used for transmitting money from those working in Nairobi and other towns to those in rural communities who cash in the credits they receive on their phones at kiosks in their markets. It is cheap and safe because people can observe the credits that they receive for their cash instantaneously on their phones, and it bypasses the banking system.

Mobile money is transforming finance in developing countries. Just as mobile phones leapfrogged conventional landlines in terms of telephone usage in these countries, mobile money is leapfrogging traditional payments systems. In just six years since it started, M-Pesa—a mobile money service in Kenya provided by Safaricom, an affiliate of Vodafone—now undertakes more trans-actions than Western Union does globally. It has 13 million users (more than 50 per cent of the adult population), and at least one user in 70 per cent of Kenyan households.[29] Similar develop-ments are happening elsewhere—it is estimated that there were 140 mobile money ventures globally at the end of 2011.

What is determining the impact of mobile money in different countries is the response of the regulatory authorities to this development. In some countries, such as Kenya, the authorities believe that mobile money does not require much regulation. They are right because the main risks of mobile money are exactly the same as those of phone calls, namely an operating system's breakdown, not a financial system's failure. Oversight of operating systems is therefore required; prudential financial regulation is not. The holding of clients' monies can be regulated according to normal rules of custodianship.[30]

The position of the authorities in Kenya has come in the face of the inevitable strong opposition of banks that correctly regard this as a threat to their competitive position. In India, the central bank has taken the opposite view that mobile money is banking, should be regulated as such, and provided by banks. That in effect undermines the potential for other service providers to enter the market.

Transformational as it is for developing and emerging economies, mobile money has equally significant lessons for developed countries. It demonstrates that payments do not or need not have anything to do with banking. Payments are about safekeeping and transmission. The safekeeping of people's monies is fulfilled by such institutions as custodians; the transmission can be done by phone companies as well as banks. Banks do not have to be involved at all—unless the authorities force them to be.

What mobile money offers in developed economies is the potential for overcoming the fundamental impediment to the financing of industry that traditional banking has encountered. As providers of payments, central banks are legitimately concerned about the risks of bank failures, in particular economy-wide bank failures. As I have described for the UK, they have therefore sought to avoid bank failures by encouraging consolidations that reduce the exposure of banks to particular local markets and economies. This has come at the expense of local relationship banking and, in the case of the UK, of long-term small and medium-size company lending.

Part III: What We Should Do About It

The success of the corporation depends on its ability to balance its powers of commitment and control. The emphasis on the corporation to date has been on a vehicle that creates shareholder value by minimizing the costs of contracting its required inputs. But there is a large amount that unavoidably remains un-contracted and the willingness of the exposed parties to participate in the company as employees, customers, and purchasers depends on the trust that they have in the organization to uphold their interests.

In order to provide this, shareholders need to be able to demonstrate commitment to different individuals over time. It is difficult for both the dispersed shareholders that have emerged in the stock market oriented economies of the UK and the US, and the concentrated family owners of most other parts of the world to do this. In the first case, the problem is weak governance and consequential resort to takeover markets. In the second case, the private interests of dominant families frequently conflict with the commercial objectives of the corporation, particularly as ownership passes through different generations.

Credible commitments require firms to be able to establish clearly defined values to which they can convincingly demonstrate that they are bound. Capital is central to that and the form that it takes is a critical component of the ability of the firm to be able to demonstrate commitment. As the shareholder value view of the firm emphasizes, equity capital in principle provides a degree of commitment that other finance does not. However, this can be undermined by high dividend distribution policies or active markets for corporate control, both of which confer substantial external control on shareholders.

Debt capital does not provide the degree of commitment of equity in so far as creditors intervene when a firm is in default of its obligations. However, it allows firms to grow without dispersing their shareholdings and in that regard bank finance has been an important mechanism by which committed shareholders have been able to retain control in many parts of the world. The failure of the banking system to provide funding for growing corporations has contributed to the emergence of dispersed ownership in the UK.

Most significantly of all, the required balance between commitment and control varies appreciably across companies, industries, and time. Diversity in ownership, financing, and governance systems is needed to satisfy the requirements of firms. Attempts to protect parties through regulations are counterproductive in so far as they impose a degree of homogeneity that is in general not appropriate. Instead, corporations need to identify the forms in which they can provide credible commitments themselves. They do this through a combination of the structure of their governing boards and their ownership patterns.

Boards can vary from conventional executive dominated arrangements to boards of trustees. Shareholders can span the dispersed short-term investors that now dominate many companies to long-term committed participants. Different governance arrangements and structures can and should co-exist both within companies and countries. There are dual board structures and dual class shares; there are companies with and without takeover defences in particular countries; and there are companies that fundamentally alter their ownership and governance arrangements as they develop.

These properties of divergent and evolving companies are sources of their success and are explained by the function of firms as both commitment and control devices. They can contribute to rather than undermine the well-being of future generations through ownership structures that address the tragedy of the commons. They are particularly important in the context of developing and emerging economies. Furthermore, the social contribution of the corporation can be enhanced by recognizing the power of the tax system to align private interests with public welfare.

In all, to date we have made a right mess of our public policies in such a way as to create deficiencies of both commitment and control at the level of individual firms, the state, local banks, capital markets, and international agencies. The effects are devastating for our prosperity, our security, and our potential to survive. That we have mucked things up so badly may not be entirely surprising in the light of Mark Twain's contention that 'if man had created man then he would be ashamed of his performance'. Perhaps the problem is that he has and we are.

Chapter 10
Without End

'You are on earth; there is no cure for that.'
Hamm in Samuel Beckett's *Endgame*

In DeNile

The oldest surviving boat only made one trip in this world and that trip was to carry a dead body. It was the body of the Pharaoh Khufu (alias Cheops) who died in 2566 BC. The trip carried the body across the Nile to lay it to rest in the Great Pyramid of Giza. Not only was Khufu perfectly preserved, but so too was his boat and this was also laid to rest in a pit beside the Great Pyramid. In fact, it was so perfectly preserved that it could be completely reconstructed when it was discovered 4,500 years later in 1954.

The significance of the burial of the Pharaoh's boat alongside the Pharaoh was that although this was its last trip in this world, it was certainly not in the next. After its short voyage to the Pyramid, it was used to convey Khufu with the sun god Aten to the end of the world in the west. There they were joined by Osiris,

the god of the dead, and they travelled together into the underworld. Aten continued his journey in the boat to rise in the east
the next morning and every morning thereafter. The Pharaoh
meanwhile had done whatever he could to hasten his return to
this world—masks, mummification, storage of important
worldly goods, and clear sets of direction for the underworld—
so that his good soul in the other world could be reunited with his
well-preserved self in this at the earliest possible opportunity.
Since eternity was long in relation to his fragile existence, it
made eminent sense for the Pharaoh to devote a substantial
fraction of his present life to the one to come.

Religion was not only an important form of insurance for the
Pharaoh in his next life, but also a powerful means of control in
this. By restricting access to the gods through the priests he
appointed and temples he built, the Pharaoh ensured that the
people's dependence on the gods was a dependence on him both
in this life and the next. Even when Amenhotep IV broke with
polytheism and established the sun god Aten as the one and only
legitimate god, it strengthened rather than weakened his power
by undermining the priests whose livelihood depended on promoting a multiplicity of gods. So much so, that when they had
the first opportunity, they forced his successor, Tutankhamun, to
reinstate the previously discredited gods.

The emergence of subsequent religious movements was a
rebellion against this monolithic control structure and an attempt
to prize the spiritual if not the material destiny of the people away
from the kings. Covenants with one as opposed to many gods
allowed a coherent body of codes to be established which provided the ethical underpinnings of communities and concepts of
justice that were not solely determined by royal decree. 'Hold fast,

all of you together, to the Rope of Allah (i.e. this Qur'an), and be not divided among yourselves' says the Qur'an (3:103).

The corporation places us in the same position to our material well-being as the Egyptians were to their spiritual. We are not allowed to question the ethical principles underlying the corporation. We are required to accept shareholder supremacy as if it were given to us by divine authority. We are not able to go against the judgements of analysts, fund managers, and financial institutions as if they are priests with unique insights into our destinies. We are controlled by a structure over which we have no influence and from which we apparently have no escape.

At least you might think that, unlike the Pharaohs, the corporation does not have control over our afterlife—but even there you would be seriously wrong. The Egyptian Pharaohs knew that, try as they might, they could not bind their successors—the transition from Amenhotep IV (who changed his name to Akhenaten, meaning 'living spirit of Aten') to his son Tutankhamun, 'living image of Amun' (who changed his name back from Tutankhaten), is illustrative of that—so there was little irreversibility in the actions of one king for the next. In marked contrast, the activities of corporations can have substantial and enduring impacts, both positive and negative, for future generations. It is not the afterlife of the current generation that is at threat but the material life of all future generations. It is comparatively easy to encourage people to worry about their own afterlives, much harder to get them to focus on the life to come of their successors. We have not yet developed the intergenerational equivalent of the underworld to solve the impending destiny of our offspring.

The amoral nature of the corporation and the failure to internalize the well-being of future generations are intrinsically interrelated. The religious control structure of ancient Egypt concentrated power and wealth in the hands of the few. The Nile created a narrow strip of fertile agricultural land from which the Pharaohs could extract rents by taxing the farmers whose livelihood depended on it. The Pharaohs had a reliable system of preventing tax evasion by monitoring the height of the Nile using a Nilometer and determining how much tax they could therefore expect in any given year.

Likewise, the corporation is a rent extraction vehicle for the shortest-term shareholders. By threatening interventions such as takeovers and hedge fund activism, they can hold all other stakeholders, including longer-term shareholders, to ransom. Like the Pharaohs they have an infallible method of determining how much rent they can expect by auctioning control to the highest bidder. The power of the owners with the shortest horizon not only concentrates control and wealth amongst them and their agents, but is also the source of the failure to account for the interests of any generation other than their own. Competition may confer some of the benefits on their customers, but by focusing the horizon of the firm so closely on the near term, the well-being of all but the most immediate generation is disregarded. We should not therefore rely on competition to be the guardian of our offspring.

What have been progressively extinguished from the corporation are its values beyond its value to shareholders. Through the changing structure of the ownership and control of the corporation, we have developed organizations that are without principles. The principles can be derivative in the sense that they can be part of the process of creating shareholder value—the corporation will be good to its customers if it thereby improves its market position and performance, but it is not necessarily so because it does not fundamentally care about its consumers or employees.

It is a curious and depressing state of affairs. I have listened to chief executives of major telecommunication companies talking in frustration about their experiences of trying to call electricity or gas companies, knowing full well that that level of service is exactly what millions have to endure every day from their own corporations. As chief executives they extol the virtues of cost cutting and productivity improvements; as consumers they are vitriolic about bad customer service. If challenged, having initially denied that their own corporations suffer from any such problems, they will eventually imply that there is nothing else that they can do—they too are mere pawns of the divine forces of the corporation.

In Trust

The book is both a critique and a celebration of the corporation. It is a critique in terms of environmental, social, and economic disasters that the corporation has unleashed and will do so in increasing measure. More substantially, it is a critique in terms of the current conceptual nature of the corporation which was described in the first part of the book. It is a celebration in terms of its contribution to technological development, employment, prosperity. But more significantly, it is a celebration in terms of the yet unrealized potential of the corporation going forward, which is the subject of the third part of the book. Its conceptual failure and its future potential are linked by the process by which we got to where we are today, which is the subject of the second part.

The defect of existing economic models of the corporation is in not recognizing its distinguishing feature—the fact that it is a separate legal entity. The significance of this stems from the fact that it is thereby capable of sustaining arrangements that are distinct from those that its owners, its shareholders, are able to achieve. In viewing the corporation as the instrument of its shareholders, existing models that emphasize the role of the corporation in combining factors of production like capital and labour, reducing transaction costs, and being a nexus of contracts with different parties, fail to appreciate its more significant role in contributing to economic efficiency and prosperity. It can commit to others in a form in which its owners are not able to on their own.

Existing models also fail to account for the significance of some of the most important features of the corporation. The use of debt as against equity finance has limited relevance in the context of traditional models of the firm that do not acknowledge corporations as distinct legal entities, but it is highly pertinent where this is recognized. The degree of equity as against debt capital becomes an important component of the depth of commitment of the organization. Finance in the form of debt confers a degree of external control that more committed equity does not. The control does not come from the voting rights of shareholders but in decisions about financing, re-financing, and ultimately terminating the firm's operations. In the absence of adequate debt finance, because for example of deficiencies in bank lending to small and medium-sized enterprises, companies have inadequate access to capital and the depth of capital is insufficient. They become excessively reliant on shareholders whose commitment is critical but who seek to compensate for the inadequate engagement of banks by exercising control themselves.

For equity to be an effective form of commitment, shareholders have to relinquish some control over the running of the corporation. Dividend policy is important in that regard. The proportion of earnings distributed as dividends determines the external control of shareholders and therefore the limitations on the extent to which directors can themselves provide credible commitments to others. Likewise, the market for corporate control allows shareholders to impose changes in corporate policy without the approval of management, but in so doing it undermines the ability of management to be able to commit to other parties.

The corporation provides commitments in three ways—first, through determining the values of the organization. These relate to the value of inputs that it requires from different parties and for which it is unable formally to contract from them. So, for example, it needs the commitment and the dedication of certain types of skilled labour, some of which it can contract for but much it cannot. Second, it then has to be able to delegate to other people the ability to sustain those commitments which the owners of the corporation are unable themselves to provide. Third, it allows owners to align the period of their investments with those that the corporation has to undertake.

The corporation therefore requires three sets of principles. The first is that companies should have values. They should state unequivocally what their values are and there should be many of them. They should worship many gods, not one. Polytheism is needed in corporations because we wish to create many communities, not one. We want diversity to flourish and people to be able to choose between different sets of corporate values.

Values have to be both credible and consistent. They have to be believed and enduring. They have to stand the test of time and adversity—for better, for worse, for richer, for poorer, in sickness and in health. Corporate social responsibility was rightly dismissed as empty rhetoric and jettisoned when recession forced a return to more traditional shareholder value. Why should I trust an organization that is owned and controlled by anonymous, opportunistic, self-interested wealth seekers? Without commitment, there is no reason why there should be any trust in the corporation, however much its fine promotional material suggests otherwise. Values need value. They need to be valuable to those upholding them and costly to those who do not. They need to inflict pain on those who abuse them and gain on those who do not. Corporate social responsibility fails on all scores. There is no value associated with it or loss in value from not complying with it.

The value that is derived from values is the commitment that other parties make to the corporation. Without values that investors, employees, suppliers, and purchasers believe, they will not make investments that are beneficial to the corporation. The value of values is the value of these investments that the corporation, which is trusted, brings forth. To uphold these values, the corporation will have to abstain from engaging in activities that might diminish their investments. The owners and directors of the corporation who are in a position to abuse trust will have to tie themselves to the mast to restrain them from doing so. Odysseus had to turn to his sailors to tie the knots fast to bind him as he sailed past the Sirens.

The second principle, then, is that the corporation will have to turn to third parties to restrain it from defaulting in the future. These third parties are the custodians or trustees of the firm's values. They have no executive responsibility to administer the organization, but merely ensure that the stated values of the organization are respected at all times and for all relevant parties. They are fiduciaries of the different stakeholders of the corporation, similar to trustees acting for the beneficiaries of a trust. They are the priests and rabbis of the corporation, interpreting the values of the corporation and promoting their adherence at all times. Their presence changes the nature of the corporation from being a pure agency one, in which the directors act as the agents of the shareholders, to a mixed trust arrangement, in which the board of trustees acts on behalf of the designated stakeholders in the corporation. The executive directors therefore continue in a traditional agency relation with the investors, managing the assets on their behalf, subject to abiding by the values of the organization enforced by the trustees.

The difference from the conventional description of the corporation is that the actions of the corporation are constrained by its values. It provides the binding commitment that is required to lend credibility to the purpose of the organization and is missing from the vague aspirations of the corporate social responsibility movement. The pain that shareholders have to endure is that of forgoing attractive opportunities that might come their way but which are undertaken at the expense of others. Trust in the values of the organization is justified if a failure to uphold them costs more than they are worth.

The corporation is an island with its own constitution that remains intact as activities change and property is transferred. Employees, customers, and suppliers choose which island they want to be associated with and which corporate values they most respect. Their confidence in the persistence of corporate values encourages them in turn to commit to corporations and make investments that they would otherwise be reluctant to undertake. The infusion of trust in the corporation provides a fixed point, which is otherwise absent and around which investors and stake-holders can congregate.

The appointment of boards of trustees will not be suited to all companies at all times and will primarily be associated with public limited companies in which there is a sufficient breadth of participating investors to make the upholding of corporate values of significance. The dominant shareholder could set out the values of the corporation and appoint the first board of trustees to oversee the implementation of the values. So, far from diminishing incentives for entrepreneurship, the trust can allow the founding shareholder to ensure the preservation of the values that he or she has established and the longevity of the corporation that has been created.

Since it is a separate body from the executive, the board of trustees provides more effective governance than existing arrangements. At present, the roles of non-executive directors as both advisors and overseers of the executive are inevitably confused. In the trust firm the two functions are effectively separated, with the non-executives on the executive board acting in an advisory capacity to the executive, while the trustees provide oversight of the conformity of the executive with the values of the organization. In addition to enhancing trust and commitment, the trust firm therefore also addresses more conventional concerns about governance failures arising from the separation of ownership and control in dispersed ownership corporations.

There is one other key function that has to be performed and that is to determine the shareholding structure of the organization, since the third principle of the moral corporation is to allow enhanced control to be conferred on shareholders who commit to invest in the corporation for a long period. Minimum periods for which shares can be held before they are sold allow voting control to be concentrated on long-term investors. Controlling share-holders commit to remain with the corporation for the long periods of time it takes for certain investments to come to fruition. In addition to being able to uphold the values of multiple stakeholders, shareholders are then also able to promote long-term investments in a way in which it is currently difficult for them to do because of the easy exit routes that stock markets provide them.

The striking feature of time-dependent shareholdings is that they allow the interests of future generations to be upheld and 'the tragedy of the commons' to be addressed. By linking their control to the long-term performance of the corporation, share-holders act to promote the participation of other stakeholders now and in the future. This is the opposite of the normal problem that current shareholders impose on the corporation, of exploiting existing stakeholders at the expense of their future participation. They do this because they can derive the benefits today and extract them at the expense of future generations. If, on the contrary, returns only accrue at some time in the future, then shareholders will wish current actions to be of maximum future value and will reward their management accordingly—something which short-term shareholders will not do.

These three straightforward adaptations of current arrangements—establishing corporate values, permitting the creation of a board of trustees to act as their custodians, and allowing for time-dependent shares—together solve the fundamental problems of breaches of trust in relation to current and future generations. They can be achieved by recognizing that the membership of the corporation may extend beyond shareholders to other stakeholders and that equality of treatment of shareholders is not the same as equality of treatment of shares. The corporation should incorporate the interests of all parties that contribute to its development and reflect the length as well as the breadth and depth of their commitment.

Far from undermining our inheritances and legacies, the corporation becomes the guardian of our commercial conscience and permanent economic well-being. By establishing a vehicle in which stakeholders are willing to invest, it provides the means of access for the currently excluded. Knowing that their commitments will be respected and reflected in corresponding enduring commitments by the corporation, they make the sacrifices that the corporation will value. There is a mutual respect that creates a beneficial self-enforcing relationship which it is currently impossible to achieve because of the inability of the corporation to uphold long-term commitments.

The trust firm provides an appropriate balance between the forward-looking nature of the dispersed ownership corporation that is unburdened by past commitments and the pure trust that is constrained to uphold the original values of the founder in perpetuity. The former is the rational organization, calculating and ruthless, always seeking out the arrangement that serves it best for the future, irrespective of the consequences for others. The latter is the solid, reliable, trustworthy organization that sticks to its principles, even as the world around it changes. As we have systematically discarded faith in favour of rationality, we have discarded the latter for the former. Survival would suggest that only the pure rational forward-looking organization can survive in a competitive world where firm eats firm.

That this is not so is demonstrated by the continuing survival, indeed domination, of family over dispersed ownership firms around the world. If firms could operate without concern about the engagement and commitment of others, then indeed the most rational, calculating, forward-looking organizations would be the only ones to survive. But they are not, and they should not be, because the corporation has both a dependency on many other parties and the potential to assist them to flourish.

What the trust firm does is to address the problems of the ethical principles of firms, the interests of stakeholders other than shareholders and the promotion of long-term investment. It can also account for broader public interests beyond those of the investors and stakeholders in the corporation. The fiduciary responsibilities can extend to public as well as private interests and charitable as well as profitable. The fiduciary responsibility can be part public and part private. It can ensure that the corporation abides by certain publicly accepted criteria and the corporate tax system can be used to align the private incentives of the corporation with public values. This overcomes the problem of regulation imposing rules which corporations then seek to circumvent. The fiduciaries are knowledgeable and in a position to exercise discretion as well as rules, thereby eliminating the regulatory problems of homogeneity and inadequate information on the part of regulators.

As trust in corporations has collapsed, we have turned to governments to uphold social values instead. Trust in politically motivated, ambitious individuals who exercise monopoly control over a nation is no more attractive than placing it in profit-driven anonymous owners. Corporations that expound sound principles and demonstrate effective mechanisms for implementing them offer a more credible mechanism for upholding trust than government and provide the natural form in which the borders of the state can shift to the private sector. We can create real public–private partnerships in which the public and private interest are both represented by the values of the corporation, rather than the unworkable current attempts by governments to write contracts with corporations that are only interested in how much they can extract from the public sector at lowest effort.

The diversity of opportunity created by a combination of governance and ownership arrangements allows the boundaries of the corporation to be extended beyond that of the state. As our trust moves from centralized authoritarian governments to diverse corporations whose values create economic well-being, the need for public principles to be established at existing defined national levels diminishes. There will be some activities for which the physical immobility of individuals makes the determination of local public provision and principles important. But expanding interconnections and transportation make traditional national boundaries irrelevant. There is a need for public principles to be established at a global level, for, as Samuel Beckett has noted, there is no escape from being of this earth. As our national communities fade, we are increasingly part of a global community, which will be bound together by a common set of values.

These three functions of creating public and private values, a trust as well as an agency role on a board, and shares with time-dependent long-term control address the existing fundament failures of exploitation of current stakeholders and future generations. To illustrate, in contrast to the failings of corporations described at the start of the book, mobile phone and nanotechnology trust firms will promote independent research that tests not just the proposition that their products are safe, but the more stringent one that they are presumed unsafe unless proven to be otherwise with a high degree of confidence.

The pressure to engage in this type of research, which at first sight appears to be contrary to the corporations' own interests, comes from two directions. First, the boards of trustees will wish their corporations to undertake research that is consistent with their values and upholds the well-being of their stakeholders as well as shareholders. Second, the firms' controlling shareholders will press for research which can establish whether they are likely to have to bear the consequences of damaging revelations about the investments they have funded. They, too, will therefore promote the research necessary to establish the long-term safety of their corporations' investments. This will lower the cost of raising finance and encourage economic efficiency as well as ethical enterprise.

On the principle that there is nothing new under the sun, it is reasonable to ask why, if they are so desirable, have trust firms not been more widely observed to date? We have seen how we have got to where we are. Dispersed ownership emerged as a form of financing both internal growth and mergers. It was exacerbated by interference in the banking system that undermined long-term financing from banks and created an excessive reliance on equity finance. The effect of this was to establish a shareholding class for whom lack of commitment was fundamental. There is, as a consequence, currently no arrangement by which the owners of a corporation can fetter the discretion of their successors without relinquishing their control altogether. Shareholders can forgo voting rights, but at the expense of leaving the corporation at the mercy of unaccountable directors. The choice is an unattractive one and explains the reluctance of corporations to adopt it.

In contrast to the virtuous features of the trust firm, today's corporations are currently locked into 'a low trust' equilibrium in which neither investors nor stakeholders wish to invest for the long-term and firms duly respond by undertaking short-term investments. It is an equilibrium from which no one can individually deviate and only short-term investors can benefit. The trust firm offers a way of breaking out of this by aligning the control of corporations with the long-term interests of the relevant parties. It does this by addressing the fundamental defect of economies around the world—the threat of default—a failure to uphold and deliver what is promised, explicitly in contracts or implicitly in relations. It is this, not information problems or transaction costs or taxation, that has created a breakdown in trust and a reluctance to supply, purchase, or employ. By holding a sufficient breadth, depth, and length of capital, the trust firm is able to offer the commitment required to correct the failures of contracts and markets.

Firm Policy

The defects of the dispersed ownership Anglo-American systems are not unique. The family corporate groups that dominate Continental Europe and many other continents around the world are equally problematic. While they are not afflicted by short-termism to the same degree as their Anglo-American counterparts, they are infected with conflicts between the interests of the families and those of the firm, with internal rivalries between family members, and problems of succession between generations of family owners. Political processes are captured by financial institutions in the City of London and Wall Street, and by family dynasties elsewhere in the world.

Nor is the solution to the deficiencies of both dispersed and family owners to transfer power to the corporate executives of 'Main Street'. The last few years have been a testimony to the ability of boardrooms to promote their own well-being to the detriment of everyone else's. Neither legal nor political systems are capable of objectively restraining the powerful interest groups which prevail in different guises around the world. The mistaken belief that they are, has lulled us into a false sense of faith in the ability of our elected and appointed representatives to control the unelected and self-nominated owners and managers of the world's wealth on our behalf.

We should accept the futility of these arrangements and not continue to pretend that they can be remedied by applying them in ever-greater measure. We are witnessing a downward spiral of the pursuit of larger private benefits in the presence of progressively more restrictive and ineffective public policies. We should call a halt to this failed experiment in political economy and look elsewhere for alternative approaches to the management of 21st-century commercial affairs.

In particular, we should look to the corporation itself to take the lead in rectifying its own defects. Stop relying on government, the law, or regulators to provide the solutions and turn to corporations to start addressing them themselves. Begin from first principles as to what the purpose of the corporation is, what goals it is seeking to achieve, and what it needs to realize them. Establish what this means for the structure of the corporation— its ownership and its governance. Then consider how the interests of the corporation can be best aligned with those of society more generally and what incentives can be provided to encourage it to pursue ambitions that extend beyond its own.

There are four stages to the adoption of these proposals. Stage one is a paradigm shift. The ideas presented here need to be subject to careful scrutiny and, if they prove robust, they should then provide the basis for redefining the conventional view. Stage two is education. If correct, the new view should move from the pages of learned journals to the classrooms of the professional schools in business, government, and law in quick succession. We should recognize that the deficiencies of the tools which we teach our students and rethink them.

Stage three is to restructure the policy prescriptions of national governments and international organizations, such as the OECD and the World Bank. The final stage is the widespread adoption of new structures and systems in corporations around the world. Not only should they permeate existing firms, but they should be translated into the creation of new enterprises, in particular in developing and emerging economies.

What should practitioners and policymakers do in response? First, captains of industry should recognize the centrality of ownership and governance to the strategic positioning of their corporations. They should be bold in being willing to implement novel arrangements that fly in the face of convention. A single dispersed liquid shareholding class with a unitary board comprised of predominantly non-executive directors with short-term contracts may be appropriate for some firms, but not all. Others should consider very different arrangements with more than one class of shares, two- rather than one-tier boards with different proportions of non-executives on each, and rotating board membership. A third group of firms will require a combination of these structures. Owners and directors should not stick rigidly to particular arrangements. They should recognize the need for flexibility and adaptation of values, ownership, and boards over time. The purposes of firms should not be immutable and the means of achieving them should evolve.

Second, policymakers should examine whether there are features of their laws, regulations, or conventions that may discourage variety and experimentation. Are there impediments to issuing more than one class of shares with different voting rights deriving from corporate law, financial regulation, or the preferred practices of financial institutions and markets? Do rules or recommendations promote an unduly uniform approach to structuring boards and the exercise of corporate governance? Has government or central bank policy restricted the development of particular types of financial institutions and activities, for example bank lending to small and medium-sized companies? Is there adequate protection of minority investors in countries in which stock markets are relatively underdeveloped and access to stock market finance is limited? Do companies have sufficient latitude in determining their exposure to hostile acquisitions and the market for corporate control? Governance and ownership influence the competitive performance of firms; they also affect the competitive advantage of nations.

Over the ages we have come to appreciate that there is no natural order that requires us to be subservient to the authority of others, be they men, priests, kings, or gods. We can create concepts and institutions to assist rather than subjugate us. But in so doing we need to ensure that the resulting arrangements really are both practical and superior to what has gone before and the process by which we arrive at them does not impose serious costs along the way. We have endured plenty of inspiring visions of new orders that apparently justified violent means to establish them, only to discover that the supposed utopia is a hell on earth and the misery inflicted has destroyed countless millions in the process. What is being suggested here requires no riots, no violence, no fundamental changes in our capitalist system, just modest modifications to the most remarkable organ we have created to date which will give it an ethical, not an immoral heart—an Alice in Wonderland, not a Frankenstein.

As one sits on the deck of the steamship paddling down the Nile, one might be excused for believing that one is gently drifting through Ancient Egypt. After all, the hills beside the Valley of the Kings still glow a golden yellow as they must have done 3,000 years ago and the felucca gracefully glide across the waters in their time-honoured fashion. Occasionally one might catch a glimpse between the sand dunes and imagine a world beyond. Perhaps there really are forests in the Amazon and ice on the Poles. Perhaps there are cats with teeth so sharp they can tear a human apart and animals with necks so long their heads can reach to the trees. Perhaps there is a world eternal and a means by which we can create one.

Compendium

Concepts, Conclusions, and Consequences

'Anything that can be put in a nutshell deserves to remain there.'

Part 1: Concepts

➤ *Most relationships are based on trust, not contracts*
➤ *To establish trust it is necessary to demonstrate commitment*
➤ *Commitment requires the provision of dedicated capital that is irreversible or can only be withdrawn at a cost*
➤ *The volume of capital committed depends on its amount, scope, and duration (depth, breadth, and length)*
➤ *The focus of corporations should be on what they do and produce, not on what they are worth. They should be concerned with the quality of their products and the quality of life of their stakeholders*
➤ *Financial benefit is a product of quality and reliability, but quality and reliability are not a product of financial benefit*
➤ *The corporation can combine the traditional perspective on incentives, ownership, and control with the alternative view presented here of obligations, responsibilities, and commitment*

> ➤ *The corporation is a commitment device*
> ➤ *Its ability to do this derives from its independent legal form, and the separation between ownership and control*
> ➤ *In particular, the corporation can address the threat of default, which is the primary defect of contracts and markets*
> ➤ *By rectifying deficiencies of contracts and markets, the corporation can promote both economic efficiency and social welfare*
> ➤ *The moral corporation is an economically efficient corporation and a source of competitive advantage of nations*
> ➤ *Shareholders commit capital which is unprotected by contract. In return, they are granted certain control rights over the corporation and directors have a fiduciary responsibility to them*
> ➤ *Other stakeholders commit capital which is only partially or imperfectly protected by contract*
> ➤ *The interests of other parties are derivative of shareholder interests, not fundamental in their own right*
> ➤ *Protection through contracts is limited by their scope and effectiveness*
> ➤ *The exposure of other parties discourages their participation in the corporation and distorts the allocation of resources in an economy to activities that can engage in wealth transfers from them*
> ➤ *The participation of these stakeholders requires corporations to be able to demonstrate commitment to them*
> ➤ *Reputations only protect the interests of stakeholders to the extent that they enhance corporate earnings and shareholder value*
> ➤ *Regulation encourages instrumental behaviour that can be detrimental to other stakeholders by, for example, aligning the interests of directors closer with shareholders. It imposes uniformity where diversity is required*

➤ *The goals of the economically efficient provision of goods and services, technological innovation, and employment creation are not achieved by arrangements that confer property rights on one party and protect others inadequately through contracts and public law*

Part 2: Conclusions

➤ *Little attention has been given to date to the emergence of commitment and control across countries*
➤ *The nature of the corporation has evolved appreciably over the past 150 years from tightly controlled family organizations to widely held, institutionally owned entities*
➤ *Ownership became dispersed in the UK and US as a consequence of corporations issuing equity to finance their growth, in particular through acquisitions, and the payment of acquisitions for cash resulted in a withdrawal of equity capital from the corporate sector*
➤ *The failures of corporate governance in the presence of dispersed shareholders promoted markets in corporate control and shareholder activities*
➤ *Takeovers reflect disagreements over future strategy rather than poor performance, and are therefore less about disciplining bad management of poorly performing firms than changing the strategy of average performers*
➤ *Hostile takeovers have undermined the ability of directors as well as shareholders to commit to other parties. Problems of commitment have therefore become more acute in dispersed ownership systems*

➤ *Although they are frequently classified together, the UK and the US financial systems are fundamentally different. The US benefits from a diversity of forms of ownership, control, and financing which is a source of its competitive advantage and does not exist in the UK*

➤ *UK corporations are uniquely exposed to takeovers. They do not have the ownership protection that prevails in most countries in the world or the anti-takeover provisions in the US*

➤ *Whereas the UK is often upheld as a model of corporate governance standards, its exposure to takeovers has diminished stakeholder commitment*

➤ *In other countries, enterprises and larger corporations have relied more on banks for external finance. As a result, concentrated ownership, in particular in the hands of families, has prevailed elsewhere*

➤ *The provision of bank finance and venture capital to start-ups, and small and medium-sized enterprises, requires close and informed relations between investors and firms*

➤ *These were undermined in the UK by concerns about the fragility of banks which encouraged their consolidation in London to the detriment of enterprise lending*

➤ *The ownership of corporations differs markedly across countries*

➤ *There are merits and deficiencies of different forms of ownership*

➤ *Anonymity in dispersed ownership systems limits exposure of shareholders to others, but also deters provision of commitments by them*

➤ *On the other hand, there are conflicts between the interests of large shareholders and the corporation in concentrated ownership systems. The pursuit of private family interests can come at the expense of the commercial interests of the firm*

➤ *The purpose of corporations differs across countries. In the UK and the US, management is preoccupied with protecting dividends; in other countries there is a greater concern with preserving employment*

➤ *The evolving crisis of capitalism is a reflection of the erosion of the corporation as a commitment device through the exercise of excessive, not deficient shareholder control by dominant family shareholders in many countries and through dispersed ownership markets in others*

➤ *What is required is an approach that addresses the defects of dispersed ownership systems while recognizing their strengths, and working with rather than against them*

Part 3: Consequences

➤ *An appropriate balance needs to be struck between commitment and control*

➤ *The provision of commitment requires credible values, effective governance, and long-term shareholdings*

➤ *Market values are at best imprecise measures of the long-term prospects of the firm. The cost of employing capital in different uses is in general a more relevant consideration than market value*

➤ *Shareholder value is an outcome, not an objective. It should not drive corporate policy but be treated as a product of it*

➤ *In the trust firm, corporate values are upheld by the board of trustees and the voting power of shareholders is concentrated in registered shareholders in proportion to the time commitment of their investments*

➤ *The board of trustees and the maturity of shareholdings together determine the depth, breadth, and length of capital commitment*

➢ *Benefits of liquidity are retained by allowing a free market in unregistered shares*

➢ *The importance of liquidity and liquid markets should be recognized, but corporations should be able to insulate themselves from their effects on real productive activities*

➢ *Existing theories have failed to acknowledge adequately the role of corporate finance in balancing commitment and control in corporations. Theories that suggest that corporate finance does not matter or is merely a reflection of transaction costs, taxation, or information problems are incorrect—it is of first-order importance*

➢ *Dividend distributions reduce the amount of committed capital and increase shareholder control. High levels of leverage raise creditor control when corporate performance is poor. They may both discourage participation by other stakeholders*

➢ *The corporation can perform a public as well as a private function without creating the conflicts that currently exist between public contractors and private suppliers of public goods and services in public–private partnerships and regulated privatized corporations. The corporate tax system can be used to promote this*

➢ *The tragedy of the commons and environmental abuses can be addressed in the trust firm through establishing overlapping generations of shareholdings and conferring control on those with the longest remaining ownership period. Where governance is reasonable and delivery effective, we are perfectly willing to accept and even welcome common values*

➢ *Corporations can therefore become responsible themselves for upholding public and social interests without relying on governments and regulators to do this for them*

➤ *This allows governments and regulators to focus on relevant macro, systemic, and international issues rather than micro concerns about the functioning of individual organizations*

➤ *The commitment view of the firm provides a natural explanation for the varieties of capitalism that exist around the world and the changing nature of the firm. For example, it explains the prevalence of dual class structures and pyramids; the complex limited liability subsidiary structures that firms employ; why public listings in the UK are declining and private equity has increased; the use of poison pills and the prevalence of anti-takeover statutes in states in the US; and the persistence of staggered boards and limitations on the control of shareholders*

➤ *Diversity in corporate forms is required to meet the varying needs of countries, industries, and enterprises. In particular, the requirements of developing and emerging countries and enterprises are quite different from their developed and established counterparts*

➤ *Corporate values, ownership, and control should vary across firms, industries, countries, and time*

An Appendix

In Trust Firms

'The reader should feel no sense of loss from removal of an appendix.'

Adapted from the preface to George Bernard Shaw's *The Doctor's Dilemma*

While this appendix provides further details on the trust firm, it should not be a regarded as either a prescriptive or a definitive description of it. On the contrary, the book has argued that diversity of ownership and governance structures is a primary objective of the corporation. In that context, the trust firm should be regarded as an envelope within which corporations can choose their preferred ownership and governance arrangements, and this appendix as offering some preliminary and tentative suggestions as to the form it might take.

There are three components to the trust firm—its ownership, its board, and its values.

Share Ownership

The trust firm provides for shareholders to register their ownership for particular periods of time. During that period the shares will be inalienable (i.e. incapable of being transferred) from the individual in whose name they are registered. At the end of the period for which they are registered, alienability is restored and the shares are tradable on stock markets and elsewhere in the normal way.

During the registration period, shareholders are allocated voting rights which are proportional to the number of years (or part of a year) outstanding on registration. For example, if a shareholder purchased 1,000 shares in colinmayer plc on 12 May 2010 registered for ten years and it is now 4 August 2012, then at the time of purchase (and for one year thereafter) they will have had 10,000 votes and now they will have 8,000 votes. On 12 May 2019 their votes will have fallen to 1,000 and on 12 May 2020 the shares will become non-voting and tradable.

Companies may restrict choice of registration when they are issued to, for example, maturities of zero, one, three, five, or ten years. They can give shareholders the right to renew registration at the termination dates and they can provide for the conversion of existing unregistered into registered shares. Normal pre-emption rights may apply by which existing shareholders have first rights to subscribe to new issues and rights can be sold if they are not exercised.

The association of voting control with shareholder commitment could involve partial rather than complete inalienability of shareholder capital. Shares could be redeemable prior to maturity at a penalty and voting rights adjusted accordingly. For example, if shares could be redeemed by shareholders at any time prior to maturity at 50 per cent of the market price of the company's unregistered shares, then the voting rights associated with such shares could be 50 per cent of those of equivalent irredeemable shares.

Conversely, companies might have rights of repurchase of registered shares on pre-specified terms, for example at a premium above the market price of unregistered shares. This would allow acquirers to gain control of firms by purchasing the voting shares of registered shareholders, but restrict decisions on whether proposed offers are accepted to registered shareholders in proportion to the outstanding period of maturity of their shares. Unregistered shareholders would therefore not influence the outcomes of prospective acquisitions, but equal price rules would grant them rights to sell their shares on equivalent terms to registered shareholders. Furthermore, as at present 'squeeze out rules' would apply by which acquiring companies can compulsorily purchase outstanding (registered and unregistered) shares once a certain fraction of voting rights (e.g. 90 per cent) had been acquired.

A problem that normally afflicts proposals to distinguish between different types of financial assets is that they are prone to intermediation—an intermediary is established that undoes what they are designed to do by repackaging what they have on offer. This is another way of stating the Modigliani and Miller proposition on the irrelevance of finance. So, for example, governments frequently try to encourage longer-term high-risk investing by taxing capital gains (the appreciation in the value of an asset) more favourably than income (interest and dividend payments on debt and equity respectively). All this does is to encourage people to set up intermediaries that convert income into capital gains by, for example, 'rolling-up' (retaining) interest and dividends in an investment fund, converting them into capital gains, and allowing their investors to earn income at the lower capital gains tax rate by selling shares in the fund.

The loyalty shares discussed in Chapter 9 are potentially prone to this problem. If colinmayer plc offers a 10 per cent dividend bonus to its shareholders who hold shares for two years, then Colin Mayer Asset Management plc will be established to hold shares in colinmayer plc for two years and issue shares that its investors can trade as frequently as they like while still offering them a yield which includes the 10 per cent bonus.

The association of voting rights with holding periods in the trust firm is not subject to a similar problem. Colin Mayer Asset Management plc is established to try to exploit the fact that colinmayer plc allocates all the voting rights to its registered shares, which have to be held for ten years, by buying its registered shares and issuing the same number of registered shares that only have to be held for one year. It therefore effectively allows its investors to enjoy the voting rights in colinmayer plc, while only having to hold their shares for one year. It might therefore be expected to be encouraged by its investors to vote for policies in colinmayer plc that favour one- rather than ten-year horizon shareholdings, for example the high-risk investment which generates immediate payouts if it succeeds. But it can only create liquidity for its current shareholders in this way at the expense of its future investors and its overall long-term returns—the likelihood of it being able to repeat the high-risk investment trick repeatedly gets smaller and smaller as its chance of surviving over the ten years gets progressively less.

The difference between this and the previous example is that it is not a pure financial 'arbitrage' (exploitation of a price differential on what are in effect similar securities). It involves a change in a firm's investment policy and it is therefore not part of the Modigliani and Miller proposition that a change in financial policy for a given investment policy has no effect on firm value.

Another way of putting this is that, in the case of loyalty shares, it is possible to create 'derivative securities' which allow investors to earn the returns associated with the loyalty shares without holding the shares themselves and, where shareholders do hold the loyalty shares, to 'go short' (i.e. sell) securities that yield the same profile of returns as the loyalty shares, and therefore protect themselves against the risks associated with the long-term investments (so-called 'empty voting'). So investors do not have to bear the long-term investment risks associated with loyalty shares while still enjoying their bonus returns, thereby undermining the motive behind creating them in the first place. In contrast, this is not possible with controlling registered shares because by definition the holders of these shares exercise control over the activities of the corporation, which allows them to manipulate the value of any associated derivative securities to their advantage.

The reason that the allocation and holding of control shareholders is fundamentally different from pure financial securities is that the period of shareholding (its length), as well as the number of shareholders (the breadth) and the amount of capital committed per shareholder (their depth), are intimately related to the firm's real activities and in particular its investments. Whether the registered shareholders are active or passive depends on the balance between breadth and depth: a small number of shareholders holding a large amount of capital will be more active than a large number of shareholders holding the same amount of capital in total. The shorter the period for which the shareholders are committed, the less commitment will the firm be able to demonstrate to its other stakeholders. In some firms at some points in time, active shareholders holding shares for short periods will be optimal and, in others, passive shareholders with long-term shareholdings will be required. Investment and finance cannot be separated as they can with other financial instruments and as assumed in the Modigliani and Miller proposition. It is therefore not possible to engage in pure financial arbitrage or hedging.

Boards of Trustees and Directors

Other than in acquisitions, the primary function of shareholder voting is in regard to election of trustees and directors. Allocation of responsibility for appointment of trustees and directors can take a variety of forms. In a shareholder-oriented corporation, rights of appointment will fall to the registered shareholders. They can be responsible for the election of either trustees or directors or both. If the registered shareholders appoint the board of trustees, then the board can be responsible for appointment of the management board. Alternatively, the board of trustees can be self-appointing and the shareholders responsible for election of the directors. Voting rights can be extended to other parties such as employees but not necessarily with trustees or directors representing particular interest groups. Periods of appointment and the cycle of appointments of trustees and directors will vary between firms with, for example, overlapping periods of tenure in some firms and coincidental periods in others.

The chosen structure will determine the degree of commitment and control in the corporation. Self-elected boards of trustees with staggered periods of appointment electing the directors will have the greatest degree of independence from owners. In contrast, trustees and directors elected by shareholders for short periods with coincidental periods of appointment will be subject to the highest degree of accountability to shareholders. Other combinations will achieve different relations between commitment and control, and accountability can be extended to stakeholders by including them in the election process.

Corporate Values

The primary function of the board of trustees is to uphold the values of the corporation and ensure that the corporation abides by them. The values could initially be defined by the founders. They could be modified by the trustees on the basis of approval by different groups such as the registered shareholders and employees. The responsibilities of the trustees will vary across corporations, but could include oversight of the corporation's strategy, changes in policy, acquisitions, major transactions, and senior appointments. The directors will be responsible for keeping the trustees informed and consulting with them over such matters, and the trustees for ensuring that they are adequately informed and knowledgeable about the activities of the firm. The contribution of the trustees will be reflected in wise, informed, and balanced judgement about the conflicting values of the corporation. The performance of the directors will be measured by their preservation of the values as well as enhancement of the value of the corporation. It will be for the chairpersons of the respective boards to resolve disagreements, and the corporation's charter to determine where ultimate authority lies in the event of disputes being irresolvable.

The above features of the governance of the corporation—voting rights, appointment of trustees and directors, the corporate values, the authority of different parties in upholding those values—will be in the public domain so that all parties to the corporation are fully informed about the basis on which they are engaging with it.

Notes

Preface

1. Colin Mayer (1988), 'New Issues in Corporate Finance', *European Economic Review*, 32, 1167–83.

Introduction

1. Kenneth Libo, William Bernhard, John Loeb, and June Bingham (2007), *Lots of Lehmans: The Family of Mayer Lehman of Lehman Brothers: Remembered by His Descendants*, Center for Jewish History, Syracuse, NY: Syracuse University Press.
2. Margaret Ackrill and Leslie Hannah (2001), *Barclays: The Business of Banking, 1690–1996*, Cambridge: Cambridge University Press.

Chapter 1

1. John Mickelthwait and Adrian Wooldridge (2003), *The Company: A Short History of a Revolutionary Idea*, London: Weidenfeld & Nicolson.
2. The terms companies, corporations, enterprises, and firms are generally used quite interchangeably. Strictly, enterprises and firms include unincorporated businesses such as partnerships and sole proprietorships as well as corporations (or companies as they are more commonly described in the UK). This book is primarily about corporations, but where the broader concept is applicable, then the term firm is in general used.
3. This was recently reinforced by the US Supreme Court in *Citizens United v. Federal Election Commission*, No. 08-205 (21 January 2010), which ruled that corporations have the same political speech rights as individuals under the First Amendment.

4. In October 2006 the UK House of Lords upheld the rights of corporations to sue in defamation cases for damage to reputation even in the absence of specific evidence of financial loss, in *Jameel and Others (Respondents) v. Wall Street Journal Europe Sprl (Appellants)*, UKHL 44.
5. Source: United States Census Bureau, 2007 Census, *Statistics about Business Size*.
6. Sources: *Communiqué on Major Data of the Second National Economic Census*, National Bureau of Statistics of China, December 2009 and *Economic Census 2005 All India Report*, Government of India, Ministry of Statistics and Programme Implementation.
7. Average number of new limited liability companies registered per annum between 2004 and 2009. Source: The World Bank, *New Businesses Registered*.
8. IMF *Global Financial Stability Report*, April 2010.
9. IMF Staff Position Note, *Fiscal Implications of the Global Economic and Financial Crisis*, 9 June 2009.
10. Independent Commission on Banking (2011), *Final Report: Recommendations*, September.

Chapter 2

1. Theo Vermaelen (2009), 'Maximizing Shareholder Value: An Ethical Responsibility?' in Craig Smith and Gilbert Lenssen, *Mainstreaming Corporate Responsibility*, Chichester: Wiley.
2. Thomas Kochan, for example, regards the cause of corporate scandals as being 'the overemphasis American corporations have been forced to give in recent years to maximize shareholder value without regard for effect of their actions on other stakeholders', see Thomas Kochan (2002), 'Addressing the Crisis in Confidence in Corporations: Root Causes, Victims and Strategies for Reform', *Academy of Management Executive*, 17, 139–41.
3. Loizos Heracleous (2010), 'The Myth of Shareholder Capitalism', *Harvard Business Review*, April reporting on a study by Jacob Rose (2007), 'Corporate Directors and Social Responsibility: Ethics versus Shareholder Value', *Journal of Business Ethics*, 73, 319–31.
4. See Andrew Keay (2012), *The Enlightened Shareholder Value Principle and Corporate Governance*, London: Routledge.

5. Colin Mayer (1988), 'New Issues in Corporate Finance', *European Economic Review*, 32, 1167–83, and Jenny Corbett and Tim Jenkinson (1997), 'How is Investment Financed? A Study of Germany, Japan, UK and US', *Manchester School*, 65 supplement, 69–93.

6. Zephyr M&A report, http://www.bvd.co.uk/zephyrreport/Global%20FY 2009.pdf

7. McKinsey Global Institute (2011), *Mapping Global Capital Markets*.

8. World Federation of Stock Exchanges, http://www.world-exchanges.org/ files/file/stats%20and%20charts/2011%20WFE%20Market%20Highlights .pdf

9. Loans, non-equity, trade credit, account receivables. Source: World Bank Data.

10. Rounded up from $52.5 trillion for ease of calculations below. Bank for International Settlements, *Financial Statistics*.

11. World Bank Development Indicators.

12. Julian Franks, Colin Mayer, Paolo Volpin, and Hannes Wagner (2012), 'The Life Cycle of Family Ownership: International Evidence', *Review of Financial Studies*, 25, 1675–712.

13. International Labour Organization (2011), *Global Employment Trends*.

14. Anastasia Guscina (2006), 'Effects of Globalization on Labor's Share in National Income', IMF Working Paper WP/06/294 based on OECD statistics.

15. The International Labour Organization has recently estimated average global wages in 2009 at a higher figure of around $18,000 per annum on a purchasing power parity basis.

16. 'In principle it would be possible for the bondholders, by inclusion of various covenants in the indenture provisions, to limit the managerial behavior which results in reductions in the value of the bonds. Provisions which impose constraints on management's decisions regarding such things as dividends, future debt issues, maintenance of working capital are not uncommon in bond issues. To completely protect the bondholders from the incentive effects, these provisions would have to be incredibly detailed and cover most operating aspects of the enterprise including limitations on the riskiness of the projects undertaken. The costs involved in writing such provisions, the costs of enforcing them and the reduced profitability of the firm (induced because the covenants occasionally limit management's ability to take optimal actions on certain issues) would likely be nontrivial. In fact, since management is a continuous decision making process it will

be almost impossible to completely specify such conditions without having the bondholders actually perform the management function.' Pages 337–8, Michael Jensen and William Meckling (1976), 'Theory of the Firm: Managerial Behavior, Agency Costs and Ownership Structure', *Journal of Financial Economics*, 3, 305–60.

17. The terms directors, executives, and managers are generally used quite interchangeably. Strictly, directors are members of the board of a corporation and can be either executive or non-executive directors depending on whether they are responsible for the day-to-day running of the business. Managers are engaged in running the business, but not necessarily as members of the board.

18. In 'Adapting to the New Shareholder-Centric Reality: Creditor Protection' (mimeo 2012), Edward Rock discusses the power and limitations of legal concepts such as wrongful trading in the UK and fraudulent transfers in the US in protecting the interests of creditors when they conflict with those of shareholders.

19. O. Ferrell (2004), 'Business Ethics and Customer Stakeholders', *Academy o/ Management Executive*, 18, 126–9.

Chapter 3

1. For a discussion of the KarstadQuelle/Arcandor case, see 'Arcandor 2004–2009', The Oxford University Centre for Corporate Reputation.

2. This is illustrated by the reaction of Michael Fox, a founder of the Australian company Shoes of Prey, to a video on his company that was posted on the Web in March 2010: 'We're still in the process of picking ourselves up off the floor after witnessing first hand the fact that a 16 year-old YouTuber can deliver us 3 times the traffic in a couple of days that some excellent traditional media coverage has over 5 months' (Michael Fox blog, 26 March 2010).

3. Nicola Gennaioli, Andrei Shleifer, and Robert Vishny (2012), 'Money Doctors', Chicago Booth Paper, University of Chicago, No. 12–39, describe how trust can exacerbate deficiencies of financial markets by allowing investment managers to exploit their clients' trust. Managers 'help investors take risks and are entrusted to do so even when their advice is costly, generic and occasionally self-serving' (p. 3). The trust of investors encourages managers to pander to their clients' beliefs, even when they are biased, rather than to pursue contrarian strategies which could yield higher returns.

Consistent with this, Daniel Bergstresser, John Chalmers, and Peter Tufano (2009), 'Assessing the Costs and Benefits of Brokers in the Mutual Fund Industry', *Review of Financial Studies*, 22, 4129–56, report that mutual funds sold via brokers in the US earned their investors lower returns than directly purchased funds, even before accounting for fees charged.

4. Reported in Philip Inman, 'UK is Weak on Tackling White Collar Crime and Short Sellers, Says HBOS Boss', article in *The Guardian*, 27 June 2008.

5. John Coffee (2007), 'The Law and the Market: The Impact of Enforcement', *University of Pennsylvania Law Review*, 156, 229–311.

6. See John Armour, Colin Mayer, and Andrea Polo (2011), 'Regulatory Sanctions and Reputational Damage in Financial Markets', European Corporate Governance Institute, Finance Working Paper Series, No. 300.

7. Thomas Dowdell, Suresh Govindaraj, and Prem Jain (1992), 'The Tylenol Incident, Ensuing Regulation, and Stock Prices', *Journal of Financial and Quantitative Analysis*, 27, 283–301.

8. Jonathan Karpoff, John Lott, and Eric Wehrly (2005), 'The Reputational Penalties for Environmental Violations: Empirical Evidence', *Journal of Law and Economics*, 48, 653–75.

9. It comes with a warning that this is not investment advice, that the author takes no responsibility for anyone following this idea, that the past is no guide to the present let alone the future, that the author is not a registered member of the Financial Services Authority or any other certifying body, that he does not own an English estate, and that above all a more serious (and technical) discussion of this can be found in the article by Dean Foster and Peyton Young (2010), 'Gaming Performance Fees by Portfolio Managers', *Quarterly Journal of Economics*, 125, 1435–58.

10. A derivative is a financial contract between two or more parties whose value depends on that of an underlying asset, for example a share or a bond. An example of a derivative security is an option, which is a right to purchase or sell the underlying asset under pre-specified conditions at some time in the future.

11. Several studies record how financial service providers can profit from transforming simple financial products into more complex ones at little or no benefit to their investors. See, for example, Bruce Carlin (2009), 'Strategic Price Complexity in Retail Financial Markets', *Journal of Financial Economics*, 91, 278–87; John Chalmers and Jonathan Reuter (2012), 'What is the Impact of Financial Advisors on Retirement Portfolio Choices and

Outcomes?', National Bureau of Economic Research Working Paper No. 18158; and Xavier Gabaix and David Laibson (2006), 'Shrouded Attributes, Consumer Myopia, and Information Suppression in Competitive Markets', *Quarterly Journal of Economics*, 121, 505–40.

12. See Dean Foster and Peyton Young (2010), 'Gaming Performance Fees by Portfolio Managers', *Quarterly Journal of Economics*, 125, 1435–58.

13. Ponzi schemes are arrangements that pay investors from their own money or those of subsequent investors. They are named after Charles Ponzi who lured investors in the US in 1920 into a scheme which offered high returns funded in large part from cash received from other investors.

14. For a formal demonstration of this, see Volker Laux (2012), 'Stock Option Vesting Conditions, CEO Turnover, and Myopic Investment', *Journal of Financial Economics*, forthcoming.

15. See, for example, Andrei Shleifer and Robert Vishny (1990), 'Equilibrium Short Horizons of Investors and Firms', *American Economic Review*, 80, 148–53, for a description of how resources can be diverted towards short-term activities; and Patrick Bolton, Tano Santos, and José Sheinkman (2011), 'Cream Skimming in Financial Markets', National Bureau of Economic Research Working Paper No. 16804, for a model of how opaqueness in financial markets allows dealers in those markets to extract excessively high returns that attract too much talent from other sectors of the economy.

Chapter 4

1. See David Walker (2009), *A Review of Corporate Governance in UK Banks and Other Financial Industry Entities*, HM Treasury, UK; and Financial Reporting Council (2010), *The UK Corporate Governance Code*, London.

2. See European Commission (2010), *Corporate Governance in Financial Institutions and Remuneration Policies*, COM (2010) 284; and European Commission (2011), *The EU Corporate Governance Framework*, COM (2011) 164.

3. Charles Mackay (1848), *Memoirs of Extraordinary Popular Delusions and the Madness of Crowds*, London: Office of the National Illustrated Library.

4. In contrast, it has been suggested that laws may enshrine beneficial social norms: see, for example, Robert Cooter (1998), 'Expressive Law and Economics', *Journal of Legal Studies*, 27, 585–608, which draws on the extensive debate on law and morality referenced in the Further Reading appendix.

5. For example, Fahlenbrach and Stulz (2009) and Cheng, Hong, and Sheinkman (2010) report that banks which tied executive remuneration closely to their corporate earnings performed worse and took greater risks during the financial crisis than other banks. Rüdiger Fahlenbrach and Renee Stulz (2010), 'Bank CEO Incentives and the Credit Crisis', *Journal of Financial Economics*, 99, 11–26, and Ing-Haw Cheng, Harrison Hong, and Jose Scheinkman (2010), 'Yesterday's Heroes: Compensation and Creative Risk-Taking', ECGI—Finance Working Paper No. 285/2010. This does not diminish the significance of good corporate governance; for example, Andrew Ellul and Vijay Yerramilli (2011), 'Stronger Risk Controls, Lower Risk: Evidence from U.S. Bank Holding Companies', NBER Working Paper 6178, report that organizational risk controls in US bank holding companies were effective in restraining bank risk-taking.

6. See, for example, Mauro Bussani and Vernon Palmer (2003), *Pure Economic Loss in Europe*, Cambridge: Cambridge University Press.

7. *Ultramares v. Touche* 174 N.E 441, 444 (N.Y. 1931) (USA).

8. See, for example, *Caparo Industries plc (Respondents) v. Dickman and Others (Appellants)*, UKHL 2, February 1990 in which the UK House of Lords ruled that auditors do not owe a duty of care to potential investors who, in this case, bought a company that turned out to be less valuable than expected.

9. See *Caparo Industries plc (Respondents) v. Dickman and Other (Appellants)*, UKHL 2, February 1990, and *Moore Stephens (Respondents) v Stone Rolls Limited (Appellants)*, UKHL 39 in which it was determined that the auditors owed a duty of care to the company, not individual creditors. This was the last case to be argued before the UK House of Lords in July 2009 before its judicial functions were transferred to the Supreme Court.

Chapter 5

1. Charles Austin Beard (1933), 'Who Owns—and Who Runs—the Corporations', *New York Herald Tribune*.

2. Jerome Frank and Norman Meyers (1933), 'The Modern Corporation and Private Property: Adolf A. Berle, Jr., Gardiner C. Means', *Yale Law Review*, 42, 989–1000.

3. Robert Hessen (1983), 'The Modern Corporation and Private Property: A Reappraisal', *Journal of Law and Economics*, 26, p. 280.

4. Adolf Berle and Gardiner Means (1932), *The Modern Corporation and Private Property*, New York: Harcourt, Brace & World, pp. 2–3.

5. Adolf Berle and Gardiner Means (1932), *The Modern Corporation and Private Property*, New York: Harcourt, Brace & World, pp. 345–6.

6. Robert Hessen (1983), 'The Modern Corporation and Private Property: A Reappraisal', *Journal of Law and Economics*, 26, p. 275.

7. James Burnham (1941) subsequently developed the theme of the ascendancy of managerial power in his influential book *The Managerial Revolution: What is Happening in the World*, New York: John Day.

8. In fact, William Bratton and Michael Wachter (2008), 'Shareholder Primacy's Corporatist Origins: Adolf Berle and the Modern Corporation', *Journal of Corporation Law*, 34, 99–152, describe how *The Modern Corporation and Private Property* appeared in the middle of Berle's metamorphosis from being an advocate of shareholder supremacy and self-regulation in the 1920s to a corporatist and collectivist in the 1930s, and was hailed by *Time* magazine as being 'the economic Bible of the Roosevelt administration' (p. 120). The modern perception of Berle as an advocate of shareholder engagement derives from (somewhat misconceived interpretations of) the subsequent debate that ensued with Professor Merrick Dodd of the Harvard Law School.

9. For a more extensive discussion of this see Julian Franks, Colin Mayer, and Stefano Rossi (2009), 'Ownership, Evolution and Regulation', *Review of Financial Studies*, 22, 4009–56 and Julian Franks, Colin Mayer, and Stefano Rossi (2005), 'Spending Less Time with the Family: The Decline of Family Ownership in the United Kingdom', in Randall Morck (ed.), *A History of Corporate Governance Around the World: Family Business Groups to Professional Managers*, Chicago: Chicago University Press.

10. Frederick Lavington (1921), *The English Capital Market*, London: Methuen.

11. Cited in Frederick Lavington (1921), *The English Capital Market*, London: Methuen.

12. Conrad Matschoss (ed.), *Ein Kurzgefaßtes Lebensbild nebst einer Auswahl seiner Briefe*, Vol. 1, Berlin, p. 218, quoted in Jürgen Kocka (1999), 'The Entrepreneur, The Family and Capitalism: Some Examples from the Early Phases of Industrialization in Germany', in Jürgen Kocka (1999), *Industrial Culture and Bourgeois Society: Business, Labour and Bureaucracy in Modern Germany*, New York: Berghahn Books, p. 73.

13. On 13 December 2011, the US Securities and Exchange Commission (SEC) 'charged seven former Siemens executives with violating the Foreign Corrupt Practices Act (FCPA) for their involvement in the company's decade-long bribery scheme to retain a $1 billion government contract to produce national identity cards for Argentine citizens. Siemens was previously charged with FCPA violations and paid $1.6 billion to resolve the charges with the SEC, U.S. Department of Justice, and Office of the Prosecutor General in Munich'. SEC Press Release: 'SEC Charges Seven Former Siemens Executives with Bribing Leaders in Argentina', 13 December 2011, Washington DC.

14. Niall Ferguson (1998), *The World's Banker: The History of the House of Rothschild*, London: Weidenfeld & Nicolson, p. 79.

15. Friedrich von Gentz, quoted in Niall Ferguson (1998), *The World's Banker: The History of the House of Rothschild*, London: Weidenfeld & Nicolson, p. 84.

16. David Landes (1965), 'Technological change and development in Western Europe 1750–1914', in Hrothgar Habakkuk and Michael Postan (eds), *Cambridge Economic History of Europe*, Vol VI: *The Industrial Revolution and After*, Cambridge: Cambridge University Press, pp. 536–64.

17. Julian Franks, Colin Mayer, Paolo Volpin, and Hannes Wagner (2012), 'The Life Cycle of Family Ownership: International Evidence', *Review of Financial Studies*, 25, 1675–712.

18. Marco Becht and Colin Mayer (2001), 'Introduction', in Fabrizio Barca and Marco Becht, *The Control of Corporate Europe*, Oxford: Oxford University Press, and Julian Franks, Colin Mayer, Paolo Volpin, and Hannes Wagner (2012), 'The Life Cycle of Family Ownership: International Evidence', *Review of Financial Studies*, 25, 1675–712, for more recent data.

Chapter 6

1. Roger Carr speech at the Saïd Business School, University of Oxford, 9 February 2010, reproduced at http://www.sbs.ox.ac.uk/centres/reputation/Documents/Roger%20Carr%20Speech%209%20Feb%202010.pdf

2. 'Shorting' is borrowing shares and selling them on the promise of buying them back later. If the price of the shares falls you will make a profit and if it rises you make a loss. It is the opposite of borrowing money to invest in a stock (going 'long' in the stock) that you will then sell at a later date at a profit if the price rises and a loss if it falls.

3. House of Commons, Business, Innovation and Skills Committee (2010), 'Mergers, Acquisitions and Takeovers: The Takeover of Cadbury and Kraft', Ninth Report of Session 2009–10, 30 March, pp. 10 and 11.

4. Richard Roberts (1992), 'Regulatory Responses to the Rise of the Market for Corporate Control in Britain in the 1950s', *Business History*, 34, 183–200.

5. Leslie Hannah (1974), 'Takeover Bids in Britain Before 1950: An Exercise in Business "Pre-History"', *Business History*, 16, 65–77.

6. Richard Roberts (1992), 'Regulatory Responses to the Rise of the Market for Corporate Control in Britain in the 1950s', *Business History*, 34, p. 186.

7. Richard Roberts (1992), 'Regulatory Responses to the Rise of the Market for Corporate Control in Britain in the 1950s', *Business History*, 34, 183–200.

8. Source: Bureau van Dijk, Zephyr Annual M&A Report Global, 2011.

9. See the Kraft Foods Inc offer document for Cadbury Ltd., 9 November 2009.

10. *Financial Times*, 4 August 2011.

11. See Omesh Kini, William Kracaw, and Shehzad Mian (2004), 'The Nature of Discipline by Corporate Takeovers', *Journal of Finance*, 59, 1511–52, and Julian Franks and Colin Mayer (1996), 'Hostile Takeovers and the Correction of Managerial Failure', *Journal of Financial Economics*, 40, 163–81.

12. http://www.thisismoney.co.uk/money/news/article-2052217/Revealed-The-big-sums-paid-PR-advisers–shareholders-likely-shocked-fees.html

13. Martin Conyon, Sourafel Girma, Steve Thompson, and Peter Wright (2002), 'The Impact of Mergers and Acquisitions on Company Employment in the United Kingdom', *European Economic Review*, 46, 31–49.

14. Charles Brown and James Medoff (1988), 'The Impact of Firm Acquisition on Labor', in Alan Auerbach, *Corporate Take-Overs: Causes and Consequences*, London: University of Chicago Press, pp. 9–25.

15. There is a confusion in popular terminology between the public corporation as one that is in private ownership but listed on a public stock market (which is the meaning here), and one that is owned by the government or state. We refer to the former as publicly listed corporations and the latter as public enterprises.

16. Alfred Rappaport (1990), 'The Staying Power of the Public Corporation', *Harvard Business Review*, January–February, 96–104.

17. Tim Jenkinson and Colin Mayer (1994), *Hostile Takeovers: Defence, Attack and Corporate Governance*, London: McGraw-Hill.

18. Julian Franks and Colin Mayer (1996), 'Hostile Takeovers and the Correction of Managerial Failure', *Journal of Financial Economics*, 40, 163–81.
19. http://www.telegraph.co.uk/finance/newsbysector/retailandconsumer/76000 25/Stitzer-gets-40m-pay-off-after-Cadbury-sale.html
20. See Marco Becht, Julian Franks, Colin Mayer, and Stefano Rossi (2009), 'Returns to Shareholder Activism: Evidence from a Clinical Study of the Hermes UK Focus Fund', *Review of Financial Studies*, 22, 3093–129.
21. See Julian Franks and Colin Mayer (1998), 'Bank Control, Takeovers and Corporate Governance in Germany', *Journal of Banking and Finance*, 22, 1385–403.
22. Google Investor Relations (2004), 'Founders' IPO Letter'.
23. Steven Davidoff (2012), 'In Manchester United's IPO, a Preference for US Rules', Dealbook, *New York Times*, 10 July.
24. Porsche acquired a shareholding in the German car producer Volkswagen (VW) in 2005 to prevent a prospective takeover of VW. It subsequently entered into a joint venture with VW and is expected to be fully acquired by VW in the second half of 2012.
25. Explanations for limitations on the exercise of shareholder control and markets for corporate control are described in Margaret Blair and Lynn Stout (2001), 'Trust, Trustworthiness, and the Behavioral Foundations of Corporate Law', *University of Pennsylvania Law Review*, 149, 1735–810; Marcel Kahan and Edward Rock (2003), 'Corporate Constitutionalism: Anti-Takeover Provisions as Precommitment', *University of Pennsylvania Law Review*, 152, 473–522; and Lynn Stout (2007), 'The Mythical Benefits of Shareholder Control', *Virginia Law Review*, 93, 789–809.
26. *Air Products & Chemicals, Inc. v. Airgas, Inc.*, 16 A.3d 48 (Del. Ch. 2011), p. 152.
27. *Air Products & Chemicals, Inc. v. Airgas, Inc.*, 16 A.3d 48 (Del. Ch. 2011), pp. 117–18.
28. *Air Products & Chemicals, Inc. v. Airgas, Inc.*, 16 A.3d 48 (Del. Ch. 2011), p. 120. The fact that the three nominees of Air Products on Airgas's board supported management's contention that the bid from Air Products undervalued the firm was an important factor in convincing the court that the management of Airgas had indeed acted in good faith.
29. The influence of investor horizons on acquisitions is described in a paper by Jose-Miguel Gaspar, Massimo Massa, and Pedro Matos (2005), 'Shareholder Investment Horizons and the Market for Corporate Control', *Journal of Financial Economics*, 76, 135–65. They report that firms with

short-term shareholders, who hold their shares for short periods of time, are more likely to be taken over and display worse share price performance during and after acquisitions than those with longer-term shareholders.

30. For example, Johnson, Karpoff, and Yi (2011) find that firms which have takeover defences when they 'go public' (issue their shares on a stock market for the first time) in an initial public offering (IPO) have 'customers, suppliers or strategic partners who are vulnerable to changes in the firm's operating strategy'. They find that 'an IPO firm's valuation and subsequent operating performance both are positively related to the use of takeover defenses, particularly when it has dependent customers, suppliers, or strategic partners' and 'that use of takeover defenses is positively related to the longevity of its business relationships'. William Johnson, Jonathan Karpoff, and Sangho Yi (2011), 'Why Do Firms Have Takeover Defenses?', Social Science Research Network Working Paper No. 1923667.

31. Dennis Robertson described corporations as 'islands of conscious power in this ocean of unconscious co-operation like lumps of butter coagulating in a pail of buttermilk', referring to them as internal organization structures operating in the invisible hand of the market—Dennis Robertson (1923), *Control of Industry*, London: Nisbet.

32. For example, Klein and Zur (2011) report that 'hedge fund activism significantly reduces bondholders' wealth' and involves 'an expropriation of wealth from the bondholder to the shareholder'. April Klein and Emanuel Zur (2011), 'The Impact of Hedge Fund Activism on the Target Firm's Existing Bondholders', *Review of Financial Studies*, 24, 1735–71.

Chapter 7

1. The reference to 'man' here or elsewhere in the book is not intended to have any connotations of gender.

2. Adam Smith (1759), *The Theory of Moral Sentiments*, ed. David Raphael and Alec Macfie, Indianapolis, IN: Liberty Fund, 1981, Book IV, Chapter 2, pp. 271–2.

3. Adam Smith (1776), *An Inquiry Into the Nature and Causes of the Wealth of Nations,* Vol. I ed. Roy Campbell and Andrew Skinner, vol. II of the Glasgow Edition of the Works and Correspondence of Adam Smith, Indianapolis, IN: Liberty Fund, 1981, Book IV, Chapter II.

4. See, for example, Amartya Sen (1977), 'Rational Fools: A Critique of the Behavioural Foundations of Economic Theory', *Philosophy and Public*

Affairs, 6, 317–44 and Fabienne Peter and Hans Bernhard Schmid (2007), *Rationality and Commitment*, Oxford: Oxford University Press.

5. For details on these arrangements see Randall Morck and Fan Yang (2010), 'The Shanxi Banks', NBER Working Paper 15884, April.

6. Phyllis Deane (1965), *The First Industrial Revolution*, Cambridge: Cambridge University Press.

7. Philip Cottrell (1980), *Industrial Finance 1830–1914: The Finance and Organization of English Manufacturing Industry*, London: Methuen.

8. Sydney Checkland (1975), *Scottish Banking: A History, 1695–1973*, Glasgow and London: Collins.

9. Dieter Ziegler (1992), 'The Crisis of 1878: Some Remarks', *Economic History Review*, 45, p. 142.

10. Thomas Bullion (1850), *The Internal Management of a Country Bank*, quoted in Philip Cottrell (1980), *Industrial Finance 1830–1914: The Finance and Organization of English Manufacturing Industry*, London: Methuen, p. 211.

11. See, for example, William Kennedy (1987), *Industrial Structure, Capital Markets and the Origins of British Economic Decline*, Cambridge: Cambridge University Press.

12. Richard Tilly (1989), 'Banking Institutions in Historical Perspective: Germany, Great Britain and the United States in the Nineteenth and Early Twentieth Century', *Journal of Institutional and Theoretical Economics*, 145, 189–209.

13. See, for example, Michael Collins (1998), 'English Bank Development within a European Context', *Economic History Review*, 51, 1–24. Jeremy Edwards and Klaus Fischer (1994), *Banks, Finance and Investment in Germany*, Cambridge: Cambridge University Press, question some common assertions about German bank finance, and Jeremy Edwards and Sheilagh Ogilvie (1996), 'Universal Banks and German Industrialization: A Re-Appraisal', *Economic History Review*, 49, 427–46, cast doubt on the conventional interpretation of German banking history.

14. Peter Mathias (1969), *The First Industrial Nation: An Economic History of Britain 1700–1914*, London: Methuen, pp. 352–3.

15. Peter Mathias (1969), *The First Industrial Nation: An Economic History of Britain 1700–1914*, London: Methuen, pp. 419–20.

16. Mark Roe (1994), *Strong Managers, Weak Owners*, Princeton: Princeton University Press.

17. Alfred Chandler (1990), *Scale and Scope: The Dynamics of Industrial Capitalism*, Cambridge: Harvard University Press.
18. *The Report of the Committee on Finance and Industry*, June 1931, Cmd 3897, para. 404.
19. For a history of ICFC and its associated companies see Richard Coopey and Donald Clarke (1995), *3i: Fifty Years Investing in Industry*, Oxford: Oxford University Press.
20. See Ralf Becker and Thomas Hellmann (2003), 'The Genesis of Venture Capital—Lessons from the German Experience', CESifo Working Paper Series, No. 833.
21. See Ann Soderblom and Johan Wiklund (2006), *Factors Determining the Performance of Early Stage High-Technology Venture Capital Funds*, UK Department of Trade and Industry (DTI), March.
22. Josh Lerner, Yannis Pierrakis, Liam Collins, and Albert Bravo Biosca (2011), 'Atlantic Drift: Venture Capital Performance in the UK and US', Nesta Research Report, June, report that while historically there has been a significant difference in venture capital returns between the UK and the US, these have declined over the last decade due to falling returns in the US.
23. For information on the comparative performance of venture capital and private equity in the US, see Robert Harris, Tim Jenkinson, and Steven Kaplan (2012), 'Private Equity Performance: What Do We Know?', Fama-Miller Working Paper, Chicago Booth Research Paper, No. 11–44.
24. Bonnie Buchanan and Tina Yang (2005), 'The Benefits and Costs of Controlling Shareholders: The Rise and Fall of Parmalat', *Research in International Business and Finance*, 19, 27–52; Paolo Campana (2012), 'Failures of Rationality and the Perverse Effect of Trust and Reputation in Corporate Frauds: Evidence from the Parmalat Bankruptcy', Working Paper, University of Oxford; and Guido Ferrarini and Paolo Guidici (2005), 'Financial Scandals and the Role of Private Enforcement: The Parmalat Case', European Corporate Governance Institute Law Working Paper No. 40.
25. A joint report of the Italian Senate Finance and Treasury, and Industry, Trade and Tourism Commissions, cited in Stefania Chiaruttini (2010), 'Parmalat, un caso di trasferimento di rischio industriale e di credito sui risparmiatori: cause e rimedi', *Analisi Guiridica dell' Economia, Studi e Discussioni sul Diritto dell'Impresa*, 2, 367–82.

26. Bonnie Buchanan and Tina Yang (2005), 'The Benefits and Costs of Controlling Shareholders: The Rise and Fall of Parmalat', *Research in International Business and Finance*, 19, 27–52.

Chapter 8

1. Jeremy Edwards, John Kay, and Colin Mayer (1987), *The Economic Analysis of Accounting Profitability*, Oxford: Oxford University Press.

2. The seminal paper on this is Bruce Johnson, Robert Magee, Nandu Nagarajan, and Harry Newman (1985), 'An Analysis of the Stock Price Reaction to Sudden Executive Deaths: Implications for the Managerial Labor Market', *Journal of Accounting and Economics*, 7, 151–74, which reports positive share price reactions to the announcements of deaths of founder CEOs and negative reactions to those of professional CEOs. Rachel Hayes and Scott Schaefer (1999), 'How Much are Differences in Managerial Remuneration Worth?', *Journal of Accounting and Economics*, 27, 125–48, report a positive share price reaction of managers who die suddenly on the job as against a negative one for those who resign for alternative employment.

3. Although this quote is frequently attributed to Keynes, it in fact originated as 'it is better to be vaguely right than exactly wrong' in chapter 22 of Carveth Read (1914), *Logic: Deductive and Inductive*, London: Simpkin, Marshall, Hamilton, Kent & Co. Ltd., in the context of the impossibility of the absolute precision of language.

4. See Paul Hawken, Amory Lovins, and L. Hunter Lovins (1999), *Natural Capitalism: Creating the Next Industrial Revolution*, Boston, MA: Little, Brown and Company.

5. Obituary of Lord Weinstock, *Daily Telegraph*, 24 July 2002.

6. Mary O'Sullivan (2006), 'Living with the U.S. Financial System: the Experiences of GE and Westinghouse in the Last Century', *Business History Review*, 80, 621–55.

7. Masaru Yoshimori (1995), 'Whose Company Is It? The Concept of the Corporation in Japan and the West,' *Long Range Planning*, 28, 33–44.

8. In another indication of the relative importance attached to financial and real considerations, a survey by Graham, Harvey, and Rajgopal (2005) reports that 80 per cent of US managers would 'decrease spending on R&D, advertising and maintenance to meet an earnings target. More than

half (55.3%) state that they would delay starting a new project to meet an earnings target, even if such a delay entailed a small sacrifice in value' (pp. 32 and 35). John Graham, Campbell Harvey, and Shiva Rajgopal (2005), 'The Economic Implications of Corporate Financial Reporting', *Journal of Accounting and Economics*, 40, 3–73.

9. Paul Samuelson (1969), 'The Way of an Economist,' in Paul Samuelson (ed.), *International Economic Relations: Proceedings of the Third Congress of the International Economic Association*, London: Macmillan, 1–11.

10. See Frank Easterbrook (1984), 'Two-Agency Cost Explanation of Dividends', *American Economic Review*, 74, 650–9, for a description of how dividends affect external monitoring and control.

11. See Julian Franks, Colin Mayer, and Luc Renneboog (2001), 'Who Disciplines Management in Poorly Performing Companies?', *Journal of Financial Intermediation*, 10, 209–48.

12. Independent Commission on Banking (2010), *Final Report: Recommendations*, September.

13. See Sheridan Titman (1984), 'The Effect of Capital Structure on a Firm's Liquidation Decision', *Journal of Financial Economics*, 13, 137–51, and Sheridan Titman and Roberto Wessels (1988), 'The Determinants of Capital Structure Choice', *Journal of Finance*, 43, 1–19.

14. There is accumulating evidence of the relation between capital structure and commitment to employees. Firms that treat their employees fairly as measured by high employee-friendly ratings maintain low debt ratios—Kee-Hong Bae, Jun-Koo Kang, and Jin Wang (2011), 'Employee Treatment and Firm Leverage: A Test of the Stakeholder Theory of Capital Structure', *Journal of Financial Economics*, 100, 130–53.

15. Firms' leverage is also related to investment by other stakeholders. For example, it is negatively related to the R&D expense intensity of suppliers and customers—Jayant Kale and Husayn Shahrur (2007), 'Corporate Capital Structure and the Characteristics of Suppliers and Customers', *Journal of Financial Economics*, 83, 321–65.

16. For example, union bargaining is found to have a substantial impact on corporate financing decisions—David Matsa (2010), 'Capital structure as a Strategic Variable: Evidence from Collective Bargaining', *Journal of Finance*, 65, 1197–232—and strong union laws are less effective in preventing lay-offs when financial leverage is high—Julian Atanassov and Han Kim (2009), 'Labor and Corporate Governance: International Evidence from Restructuring Decisions', *Journal of Finance*, 64, 341–74.

17. For example, leverage is found to increase with unionization rates and to decrease with the use of human capital—Christopher Hennessy and Dmitry Livdan (2009), 'Debt, Bargaining and Credibility in Firm–Supplier Relationships', *Journal of Financial Economics*, 93, 382–99.

18. For evidence of changes in leverage in commercial and investment banking prior to the financial crisis see Sebnem Kalemli-Ozcan, Bent Sorensen, and Sevcan Yesiltas (2011), 'Leverage across Firms, Banks and Countries', National Bureau of Economic Research Working Paper No. 17354.

19. Prasanna Gai, Andrew Haldane, and Sujit Kapadiaz (2011), 'Complexity, Concentration and Contagion', *Journal of Monetary Economics*, 58, 453–70.

20. Hansard Commons Debate, 26 July 1855, vol. 139, cc1378–1397, 1378.

21. In re Sea, Fire and Life Assurance Co. (1854) quoted in Bishop Hunt (1936), *The Development of the Business Corporation in England, 1800–1867*, Cambridge, MA: Harvard University Press, p. 99.

22. Quoted in J. Saville (1956), 'Sleeping Partnerships and Limited Liability, 1850–1856', *Economic History Review*, 8, 418–33, p. 429.

23. *Economist*, 18 December 1926, p. 1053.

24. See Kenneth Ayotte and Henry Hansmann (2012), 'Legal Assets as Transferable Bundles of Contracts', *Michigan Law Review*, forthcoming for a discussion of this.

25. Independent Commission on Banking (2011), *Final Report: Recommendations*, September.

26. William Scott (1912), *The Constitution and Finance of English, Scottish and Irish Joint-Stock Companies to 1720*, Vol. 1: *The General Development of the Joint-Stock System to 1720*, Cambridge: Cambridge University Press.

27. Ron Harris (2004), 'Institutional Innovations, Theories of the Firm and the Formation of the East India Company', Berkeley Program in Law and Economics, Working Paper Series.

28. Henry Hansmann and Reinier Kraakman (2000), 'The Essential Role of Organisational Law', *Yale Law Journal*, 110, 387–440.

29. Wendy Carlin and Colin Mayer (2003), 'Finance, Investment and Growth', *Journal of Financial Economics*, 69, 191–226. Innovative firms in Europe choose corporate forms which are most conducive to R&D—Sharon Belenzon, Tomer Berkovitz, and Patrick Bolton (2009), 'Intracompany Governance and Innovation', National Bureau of Economic Research Working Paper No. 15304.

30. See Jeff Gordon and Colin Mayer (2012), 'The Micro, Macro and International Design of Financial Regulation', Oxford University, mimeo.

31. See The Institute for Family Business (2011), 'The UK's Oldest Family Businesses—Stability in Troubled Economic Times', 20 October.

32. Geoffrey Jones (2000), *Merchants to Multinationals: British Trading Companies in the Nineteenth and Twentieth Centuries*, Oxford: Oxford University Press, p. 341.

Chapter 9

1. They resemble Gandhi's concept of trusteeship: 'those who own money now, are asked to behave like trustees holding their riches on behalf of the poor' (Mohandas Gandhi, *Trusteeship*, Ahmedabad: Navjivan Publishing House), albeit in the context of corporations rather than individuals.

2. Harold James (2012), *Krupp: A History of the Legendary German Firm*, Princeton: Princeton University Press, p. 261.

3. Julian Franks and Colin Mayer (1998), 'Bank Control, Takeovers and Corporate Governance in Germany', *Journal of Banking and Finance*, 22, 1385–403.

4. Vikas Mehrotra, Randall Morck, Jungwook Shim, and Yupana Wiwattanakantang (2011), 'Adoptive Expectations: Rising Sons in Japanese Family Firms', National Bureau of Economic Research Working Paper No. 16874.

5. For evidence of a negative impact of succession on the performance of family owned firms, see Nicholas Bloom and John Van Reenen (2007), 'Measuring and Explaining Management Practices Across Firms and Countries', *Quarterly Journal of Economics*, 122, 1351–408, and Belen Villalonga and Raphael Amit (2006), 'How Do Family Ownership, Control and Management Affect Firm Value?' *Journal of Finance*, 80, 385–417. Sraer and Thesmar report that family firms listed on the French stock market outperform widely held firms, even where the firms are run by the descendants of the founder—David Sraer and David Thesmar (2007), 'Performance and Behavior of Family Firms: Evidence from the French Stock Market', *Journal of the European Economic Association*, 5, 709–51.

6. For evidence of the significance of equity markets in the dilution of family ownership in some European countries see Julian Franks, Colin Mayer, Paolo Volpin, and Hannes Wagner (2012), 'The Life Cycle of Family

Ownership: International Evidence', *Review of Financial Studies*, 25, 1675–712.

7. This should not be confused with what is currently known as a trust company, which is an organization, frequently owned by a bank, which performs fiduciary functions of agency and trusts.

8. For evidence that industrial foundations contribute to the financial performance of firms as well as enhancing non-financial, social measures of performance, see Henry Hansmann and Steen Thomsen (2012), 'Virtual Ownership and Managerial Distance: The Governance of Industrial Foundations', mimeo.

9. See the paper of the European Corporate Governance Forum Working Group on *Proportionality*, June 2007.

10. See Patrick Bolton and Frederic Samama (2012), 'L-Shares: Rewarding Long-Term Investors', mimeo. On the importance of the longevity of corporations and its implications for corporate governance, see Margaret Blair (2004), 'Reforming Corporate Governance: What History Can Teach Us', *Berkeley Business Law Journal*, 1, 1–44, and Andrew Schwartz (2012), 'The Perpetual Corporation', *George Washington Law Review*, 80, forthcoming.

11. The consequences of conflicts between current and future shareholders for corporate behaviour are described in Patrick Bolton, José Sheinkman, and Wei Xiong (2006), 'Executive Compensation and Short-Termist Behavior in Speculative Markets', *Review of Economic Studies*, 73, 577–610, and Patrick Bolton, José Sheinkman, and Wei Xiong (2006), 'Pay for Short-Term Performance: Executive Compensation in Speculative Markets', *Journal of Corporation Law*, 30, 721–48. They show how during speculative bubbles, current shareholders encourage executives to pursue short-term investments and activities such as earnings manipulations that allow them to trade to their benefit at the expense of future shareholders.

12. *The Kay Review of UK Equity Markets and Long-Term Decision Making, Final Report*, Department for Business, Innovation and Skills, London, July 2012.

13. There is some emerging evidence of a relation between the horizons of managers and investors and the performance of their firms. See, for example, Murad Antia, Christos Pantzalis, and Jung Chul (2010), 'CEO Decision Horizon and Firm Performance: An Empirical Investigation', *Journal of Corporate Finance*, 16, 288–301; Francois Brochet, Maria Loumioti, and George Serafeim (2012), 'Short-Termism, Investor Clientele,

and Firm Risk', Harvard Business School Working Paper No. 12-072; and John Asker, Joan Farre-Mensa, and Alexander Ljungqvist (2012), 'Comparing the Investment Behavior of Public and Private Firms', European Corporate Governance Institute Finance Working Paper.

14. The role of liquidity in promoting corporate governance is described in Ernst Maug (1998), 'Large Shareholders as Monitors: Is There a Trade-Off between Liquidity and Control?', *Journal of Finance*, 53, 65–98, who argues that liquidity facilitates the formation of share blocks, and in Alex Edmans (2009), 'Blockholder Trading, Market Efficiency, and Managerial Myopia', *Journal of Finance*, 64, 2481–513, who suggests that liquidity promotes the alignment of share prices with underlying fundamentals of corporate performance and avoidance of short-termism by facilitating sales of shares by blockholders in companies in which they have uncovered detrimental information.

15. Francois Brochet, Maria Loumioti, and George Serafeim (2012), 'Short-Termism, Investor Clientele and Firm Risk', Harvard Business School Working Paper No. 12-072, report that there is an association between the short-term orientation of companies and the short-term nature of their investor base.

16. William Scott (1912), *The Constitution and Finance of English, Scottish and Irish Joint-Stock Companies to 1720*, Vol. 1: *The General Development of the Joint-Stock System to 1720*, Cambridge: Cambridge University Press, p. 3.

17. Clive Schmitthoff (1939), 'The Origins of the Joint-Stock Company', *University of Toronto Law Journal*, 3, 74–96.

18. Samuel Willison (1909), *The History of the Law of Business Corporations Before 1800*, Committee of the Association of American Law Schools, Select Essays in Anglo-American Legal History, vol. 3.

19. Bishop Hunt (1936), *The Development of the Business Corporation in England, 1800–1867*, Cambridge, MA: Harvard University Press, p. 8.

20. Ron Harris (2000), *Industrializing English Law*, Cambridge: Cambridge University Press.

21. Thomas Mortimer (1801), 'Every Man His Own Broker or a Guide to the Stock Exchange', 13th edition, quoted in Bishop Hunt, *The Development of the Business Corporation in England, 1800–1867*, Cambridge, MA: Harvard University Press.

22. Paul Mahoney (2000), 'Contract or Concession? An Essay on the History of Corporate Law', *Georgia Law Review*, 34, 873–93.

23. Einer Elhauge (2005), 'Sacrificing Corporate Profits in the Public Interest', *New York University Law Review*, 80, 101–209, argues that corporations may legitimately pursue public interest goals that conflict with shareholder value.

24. The role of constitutions in upholding commitments is widely discussed in legal and political theory. See, for example, Douglass North and Barry Weingast (1989), 'Constitutions and Commitment: The Evolution of Institutional Governing Public Choice in Seventeenth-Century England', *Journal of Economic History*, 49, 803–32. Richard Eells, who it is believed coined the phrase 'corporate governance' in Richard Eells (1960), *The Meaning of Modern Business*, New York: Columbia University Press, discusses constitutions in a corporate context in Richard Eells (1962), *The Government of Corporations*, New York: The Free Press of Glencoe.

25. William Lloyd (1832), 'Two Lectures on the Checks to Population Delivered Before the University of Oxford', Oxford: Oxford University Press.

26. Alan Greenspan (1998), 'The Current Asia Crisis and the Dynamics of International Finance', Testimony of the Chairman Before the Committee on Banking and Financial Services, U.S. House of Representatives, 30 January; Michel Camdessus (1998), 'Good Governance Has Become Essential in Promoting Growth and Stability', *IMF Survey*, 27: 3, 9 February.

27. For contrasting evidence on the role of relationships and informal financial arrangements in Chinese growth, see Franklin Allen, Jun Qian, and Meijun Qian (2005), 'Law, Finance and Economic Growth in China', *Journal of Financial Economics*, 77, 57–116, and Meghana Ayyagari, Asli Demirgüç-Kunt, and Vojislav Maksimovic (2010), 'Formal Versus Informal Finance: Evidence from China', *Review of Financial Studies*, 23, 3048–97.

28. See, for example, Franklin Allen and Douglas Gale (2000), 'Corporate Governance and Competition', in Xavier Vives (ed.), *Corporate Governance: Theoretical and Empirical Perspectives*, Cambridge: Cambridge University Press, and Stephen Nickell (1996), 'Competition and Corporate Performance', *Journal of Political Economy*, 104, 724–46.

29. Ignacio Mas and Daniel Radcliffe (2011), 'Scaling Mobile Money', *Journal of Payments Strategy and Systems*, 5.

30. See Michael Klein and Colin Mayer (2011), 'Mobile Banking and Financial Inclusion: The Regulatory Lessons', Policy Research Working Paper Series 5664, The World Bank.

Further Reading

Chapter 1 In the Beginning

There is a large literature on the impact of predation and island isolation on the behaviour of species, in the context of the Galapagos and other locations. See, for example:

Silke Berger, Martin Wikelski, Michael Romero, Elisabeth Kalko, and Thomas Rödl (2007), 'Behavioral and Physiological Adjustments to New Predators in an Endemic Island Species, the Galápagos Marine Iguana', *Hormones and Behavior*, 52, 653–63;

Richard Coss (1999), 'Effects of Relaxed Natural Selection on the Evolution of Behaviour', in Susan Foster and John Endler (eds), *Geographic Variation in Behaviour: Perspectives on Evolutionary Mechanisms*, Oxford: Oxford University Press; and

John Kricher (2006), *Galápagos: A Natural History*, Princeton: Princeton University Press.

On evolutionary economics, see:

Richard Nelson and Sidney Winter (1982), *An Evolutionary Theory of Economic Change*, Cambridge, MA: Harvard University Press.

For excellent introductions to firms, institutions, and markets, see:

Douglass North (1990), *Institutions, Institutional Change and Economic Performance*, Cambridge: Cambridge University Press;

John Roberts (2004), *The Modern Firm: Organizational Design for Performance and Growth*, Oxford: Oxford University Press;

Jean Tirole (1988), *The Theory of Industrial Organization*, Cambridge, MA: MIT Press; and

Oliver Williamson (1998), *The Economic Institutions of Capitalism: Firms, Markets and Relational Contracting*, New York: Free Press.

Chapter 2   Morals and Markets

The modern concept of the firm was first discussed in:

Armen Alchian and Harold Demsetz (1972), 'Production, Information Costs, and Economic Organization', *American Economic Review*, 62, 777–95;

Ronald Coase (1937), 'The Nature of the Firm', *Economica*, 4, 386–405; and

Michael Jensen and William Meckling (1976), 'Theory of the Firm: Managerial Behavior, Agency Costs and Ownership Structure', *Journal of Financial Economics*, 3, 305–60.

For alternative views of capitalism, see:

Franklin Allen and Douglas Gale (2000), *Comparing Financial Systems*, Cambridge MA: MIT Press;

Ronald Dore (2000), *Stock Market Capitalism: Welfare Capitalism Japan and Germany versus the Anglo-Saxons*, Oxford: Oxford University Press; and

Peter Hall and David Soskice (2000), *Varieties of Capitalism: The Institutional Foundations of Comparative Advantage*, Oxford: Oxford University Press.

On long-tailed risks, see:

Nassim Taleb (2007), *The Black Swan: The Impact of the Highly Improbable*, London: Allen Lane.

For a classic account of the early history of property and contract, see:

Henry Maine (1861), *Ancient Law: Its Connection With the Early History of Society, and Its Relation to Modern Ideas*, London: John Murray.

For a good account of comparative corporate law, see:

Reinier Kraakman, Paul Davies, Henry Hansmann, Gerard Hertig, Klaus Hopt, Hideki Kanda, and Edward Rock (2009), *The Anatomy of Corporate Law: A Comparative and Functional Approach*, Oxford: Oxford University Press.

On the law of corporate crime, see:

James Gobert and Maurice Punch (2003), *Rethinking Corporate Crime*, Cambridge: Cambridge University Press.

Chapter 3   Reputation

The classic article in economics on reputation is:

David Kreps and Robert Wilson (1982), 'Reputation and Imperfect Information', *Journal of Economic Theory*, 27, 253–79.

Some important references on trust relationships are:

George Akerlof (1984), An *Economic Theorist's Book of Tales*, Cambridge: Cambridge University Press;

Kenneth Arrow (1972), 'Gift and Exchanges', *Philosophy and Public Affairs*, 1, 343–62;

Francis Fukuyama (1995), *Trust: The Social Virtues and the Creation of Prosperity*, New York: Free Press; and

Diego Gambetta (2000), 'Can We Trust Trust?', in Diego Gambetta (ed.), *Trust: Making and Breaking Cooperative Relations*, Department of Sociology, University of Oxford, 213–37.

For discussions about incentives and relational contracts, see:

Robert Gibbons and Rebecca Henderson (2012), 'Relational Contracts and Organizational Capabilities', *Organization Science*, forthcoming; and

Denise Rousseau, Sim Sitkin, Ronald Burt, and Colin Camerer (1998), 'Not So Different After All: A Cross-Discipline View of Trust', *Academy of Management Review*, 23, 393–404.

Chapter 4   Regulation

For debates on law and morality, see:

Ronald Dworkin (1977), *Taking Rights Seriously*, Cambridge, MA: Harvard University Press; and

Herbert Hart (1961), *The Concept of Law*, Oxford: Oxford University Press.

On regulation, see:

Jean-Jacques Laffont and Jean Tirole (1993), *A Theory of Incentives in Procurement and Regulation*, Cambridge, MA: MIT.

The importance of law and regulation in promoting economic development is discussed in:

Rafael La Porta, Florencio Lopez-de-Silanes, and Andrei Shleifer (1998), 'Law and finance', *Journal of Political Economy*, 106, 1113–55; and

Rafael La Porta, Florencio Lopez-de-Silanes, Andrei Shleifer, and Robert Vishny (1997), 'Legal determinants of external finance', *Journal of Finance*, 52, 1131–50.

On financial crises, see:

Franklin Allen and Douglas Gale (2007), *Understanding Financial Crises*, Oxford: Oxford University Press;

Douglas Diamond and Philip Dybvig (1983), 'Bank Runs, Deposit Insurance and Liquidity', *Journal of Political Economy*, 91, 401–19;

John Kenneth Galbraith (1955), *The Great Crash, 1929*, Boston: Houghton Mifflin; and

Charles Kindleberger (1978), *Manias, Panics and Crashes*, New York: Basic Books.

Chapter 5 Evolving Enterprises

Different patterns of ownership around the world are discussed in:

Fabrizio Barca and Marco Becht (2001), *The Control of Corporate Europe*, Oxford: Oxford University Press;

Rafael La Porta, Florencio Lopez-de-Silanes, and Andrei Shleifer (1999), 'Corporate ownership around the world', *Journal of Finance*, 54, 471–517; and

Mark Roe (2003), *Political Determinants of Corporate Governance: Political Context, Corporate Impact*, Oxford: Oxford University Press.

The implications of dispersed ownership for corporate governance are described in:

Albert Hirschman (1970), *Exit, Voice, and Loyalty: Responses to Decline in Firms, Organizations, and States*, Cambridge, MA: Harvard University Press;

and the evolving structure of companies in:

Alfred Chandler (1990), *Scale and Scope: The Dynamics of Industrial Capitalism*, Cambridge, MA: Harvard University Press; and

Michael Jensen (1989), 'The eclipse of the public corporation', *Harvard Business Review*, 67, 61–74.

Chapter 6 Bought and Closed

The market for corporate control was first discussed in:

Henry Manne (1965), 'Mergers and the Market for Corporate Control', *Journal of Political Economy*, 73, 110–20;

and evidence on the performance of takeovers in:

Michael Jensen and Richard Ruback (1983), 'The Market for Corporate Control: The scientific evidence', *Journal of Financial Economics*, 11, 5–50.

Some of the problems with acquisitions are described in:

Sanford Grossman and Oliver Hart (1980), 'Takeover Bids, the Free-Rider Problem and the Theory of the Corporation', *Bell Journal of Economics*, 11, 42–64; and

Andrei Shleifer and Lawrence Summers (1988), 'Breach of Trust in Hostile Takeovers', in Alan Auerbach (ed.), *Corporate Takeovers: Causes and Consequences*, Chicago: Chicago University Press.

The benefits of competition in corporate law are discussed in:

Roberta Romano (1993), *The Genius of American Corporate Law*, Washington DC: American Enterprise Institute Press.

Chapter 7   Capital and Commitment

The classic work on bounded rationality is:
Daniel Kahneman, Paul Slovic, and Amos Tversky (1982), *Judgment Under Uncertainty: Heuristics and Biases*, Cambridge: Cambridge University Press.

The origins of behavioural theories of the firm were in:
Richard Cyert and James March (1963), *Behavioral Theory of the Firm*, Oxford: Blackwell.

Good discussions of the history of the financing of British industry can be found in:
Philip Cottrell (1980), *Industrial Finance 1830–1914: The Finance and Organization of English Manufacturing Industry*, London: Methuen;
Phyllis Deane (1965), *The First Industrial Revolution*, Cambridge: Cambridge University Press; and
William Kennedy (1987), *Industrial Structure, Capital Markets and the Origins of British Economic Decline*, Cambridge: Cambridge University Press.

The role of banks in German corporate activity is described in:
Jeremy Edwards and Klaus Fischer (1994), *Banks, Finance and Investment in Germany*, Cambridge: Cambridge University Press; and
Alexander Gerschenkron (1962), *Economic Backwardness in Historical Perspective: A Book of Essays*, Cambridge, MA: Harvard University Press.

For a history of the emergence of banking in China, see:
Linsun Cheng (1897), *Banking in Modern China, Entrepreneurs, Professional Managers and the Development of Chinese Banks, 1897–1937*, Cambridge: Cambridge University Press.

For a history of state banking in the United States, see:
Howard Bodenhorn (2002), *State Banking in Early America*, Oxford: Oxford University Press.

On the theory of banking, see:
Douglas Diamond (1984), 'Financial Intermediation and Delegated Monitoring', *Review of Economic Studies*, 51, 393–414;
Xavier Freixas and Jean Charles Rochet (2008), *Microeconomics of Banking*, Cambridge, MA: MIT Press; and

Alan Morrison and William Wilhelm (2007), *Investment Banking: Institutions, Politics, and Law*, Oxford: Oxford University Press.

For the role of commitment, see for example:
Jon Elster (2000), *Ulysses Unbound*, Cambridge: Cambridge University Press.

Chapter 8   Value and Values

On the measurement of capital and profit, see:
John Hicks (1939), *Value and Capital*, Oxford: Oxford University Press.

A good introduction to corporate finance is:
Richard Brealey, Stewart Myers, and Franklin Allen (2010), *Principles of Corporate Finance*, New York: McGraw-Hill.

Other important references on corporate finance are:
Oliver Hart (1995), *Firms, Contracts, and Financial Structure*, Oxford: Oxford University Press;
Michael Jensen and William Meckling (1976), 'Theory of the Firm: Managerial Behavior, Agency Costs and Ownership Structure', *Journal of Financial Economics*, 3, 305–60; and
Oliver Williamson (1988), 'Corporate Finance and Corporate Governance', *Journal of Finance*, 43, 567–92.

For a history of corporate finance, see:
Jonathan Baskin and Paul Miranti (1997), A *History of Corporate Finance*, Cambridge: Cambridge University Press.

Chapter 9   Governance and Government

For an analysis of alternative forms of ownership and control, see:
Margaret Blair (1995), *Ownership and Control: Rethinking Corporate Governance for the Twenty-First Century*, Washington DC: Brookings;
Henry Hansmann (1996), *The Ownership of Enterprise*, Cambridge, MA: Harvard University Press; and
Mark Roe (1994), *Strong Managers, Weak Owners: The Political Roots of American Corporate Finance*, Princeton, NJ: Princeton University Press.

On the tragedy of the commons, see:
Elinor Ostrom (1990), *Governing the Commons: The Evolution of Institutions for Collective Action*, Cambridge: Cambridge University Press.

Chapter 10   Without End

For a discussion of the afterlife in Ancient Egypt, see:

Jan Assmann (2005), *Death and Salvation in Ancient Egypt*, New York: Cornell University Press; and

John Casey (2009), *After Lives*, Oxford: Oxford University Press.

Index

About the Author

Colin Mayer is the Peter Moores Professor of Management Studies at the Saïd Business School at the University of Oxford. He is an Honorary Fellow of Oriel College, Oxford and of St Anne's College, Oxford, and a Professorial Fellow of Wadham College, Oxford. He is an Ordinary Member of the Competition Appeal Tribunal and a Fellow of the European Corporate Governance Institute.

Colin Mayer was the first professor at the Saïd Business School in 1994, the Peter Moores Dean of the Business School between 2006 and 2011, and the first Director of the Oxford Financial Research Centre between 1998 and 2005. He has served on the editorial boards of several leading academic journals and assisted in establishing prestigious networks of economics, law, and finance academics in Europe at the Centre for Economic Policy Research and the European Corporate Governance Institute. He was a Harkness Fellow at Harvard University, a Houblon–Norman Fellow at the Bank of England, the first Leo Goldschmidt Visiting Professor of Corporate Governance at the Solvay Business School, Université de Bruxelles, and has had visiting positions at Columbia, MIT, and Stanford universities.

Colin Mayer was chairman of Oxera Ltd. between 1986 and 2010, and was instrumental in building the company into what is now one of the largest independent economics consultancies in Europe. He has consulted for numerous large corporations and for governments, regulators, and international agencies around the world.

SAIT Library

10244477

	DATE DUE	